Instructional Design

A Systematic Approach for Reflective Practice

Neal Shambaugh
WEST VIRGINIA UNIVERSITY

Susan G. Magliaro
VIRGINIA TECH

PEARSON

Boston   New York   San Francisco

Mexico City   Montreal   Toronto   London   Madrid   Munich   Paris

Hong Kong   Singapore   Tokyo   Cape Town   Sydney

Senior Editor:	Arnis E. Burvikovs
Series Editorial Assistant:	Kelly Hopkins
Marketing Manager:	Tara Kelly
Senior Production Editor:	Karen Mason
Editorial Production Service:	Stratford Publishing Services
Composition and Manufacturing Buyer:	Andrew Turso
Electronic Composition:	Stratford Publishing Services
Interior Design:	Stratford Publishing Services
Cover Administrator:	Kristina Mose-Libon

For related titles and support materials, visit our online catalog at www.ablongman.com.

Between the time website information is gathered and then published, it is not unusual for some sites to have closed. Also, the transcription of URLs can result in typographical errors. The publisher would appreciate notification where these errors occur so that they may be corrected in subsequent editions.

Library of Congress Cataloging-in-Publication Data
Unavailable at press time.

ISBN 0-205-38966-X

Printed in the United States of America

10 9 8 7 6 5 4 3 2 1   09 08 07 06 05

Brief Contents

Contents

Contents

Preface

NOTE TO READERS

This book was written for teachers at all levels of experience. Each of the chapters is matched with one or more of the Interstate New Teacher Assessment and Support Consortium (INTASC) core standards. The INTASC standards were designed to apply to all teachers, regardless of content area or expertise. For new teachers, this book guides you to construct instruction; for experienced teachers, it prompts you to deconstruct or unpack some of your assumptions about teaching and to rethink student learning outcomes, assessment tools, teaching strategies, and technology possibilities. For those of you who are not teachers, this book can help you understand the complexity of teaching. The types of decisions that teachers make apply to all learning settings.

Instructional design (ID) is a systematic process to help you think through important educational issues and make informed decisions in your teaching. This book uses instructional design to help you systematically develop instruction at two levels: first at the lesson level and then at the unit level. Lessons are examined first, because it is at the lesson level that issues of learning outcomes, assessment, teaching, and technology come into play and where a teacher makes decisions for daily and weekly instruction.

These decisions are organized in an ongoing cycle of decision making called the Teacher Decision Cycle. The chapters on lesson and unit development are organized around this cycle of five questions:

1. What will students learn? LEARNING OUTCOMES
2. How will you know if students learned? ASSESSMENT
3. How will you assist students to learn? TEACHING
4. How will media and technology help students to learn? TECHNOLOGY
5. How will technology decisions help you to rethink decisions for questions 1 through 4?

We believe technology is a teaching decision, and the choice to use technology should be primarily guided by its potential to help students learn. We have provided a separate chapter on technology, as we believe that the technology question can also be used as an opportunity to reconsider learning outcomes, assessment, and teaching.

To guide you through the experience of making these decisions, we provide Design Activities. We believe the best way to learn to design anything is *to* design. The Design Activities were developed to provide opportunities for thinking and reflecting on your teaching decisions as you design lessons and units.

NOTE TO INSTRUCTORS

This book is written for both new and experienced teachers and also for those students who are or who might become educators in some setting. This text is not a second edition of our previous book, *Mastering the Possibilities: A Process Approach to Instructional Design*, which was written for graduate courses in instructional design (ID). Both are similar in that they use a "process approach," in which Design Activities guide the reader through experiencing the ID process. The instructor's guide describes the conceptual basis for the book and provides guidance on implementing the Design Activities.

These books were not designed to provide deep coverage of instructional design but rather to assist newcomers in understanding and using instructional design. Mastery of instructional design, like mastery of any other intellectual process, takes a wide variety of experiences over time. We have made the design decisions for this book based on our ID teaching experiences in assisting the learning of undergraduate and graduate students.

"Why should teachers learn instructional design?" In the following section, we make a case of ID for teachers by connecting ID to the INTASC core standards. In Section I, we ask: "How are learning and teaching connected?" and "What's the difference between planning and instructional designing?"

The ID process begins in Section II. Rather than calling this section Needs Assessment or Analysis, as you would find in most ID texts, we title it "Understanding Your Classroom," which we feel characterizes the value of needs assessment for teachers. Learning more about the content to be taught, who one's students are, and the reality of the learning context provides the scope of Section II.

Section III addresses lesson development, and Section IV addresses unit development. We frame instructional development for teachers as a set of teacher questions regarding learning outcomes, assessment, teaching, and technology. We represent this decision making as the Teacher Decision Cycle, which helps teachers systematically think about and make decisions in lessons and units.

Section V discusses the issues that influence curriculum development, as many of these issues comprise the "context" for lessons and units. The final chapter prompts readers to reflect and evaluate their learning by using this text, as well as looking to the future in terms of National Board Certification®.

HOW CAN INSTRUCTIONAL DESIGN IMPROVE MY TEACHING?

National Board for Professional Teaching Standards

The National Board for Professional Teaching Standards® was created in 1987 to acknowledge professional teachers. All of its certifications are based on five core principles. These principles state that all teachers should be advocates for their students and that they should know their content areas and know how to teach these subjects. Teachers are also responsible for student learning, and they systematically think about their classroom practice and learn from experience. Finally, teachers are not alone but are members of a learning community. One of the principles worth highlighting is Principle 4: "Teachers systematically think about their classroom practice and learn from experience." This core principle provides an important foundation for this text. We advocate that instructional design helps teachers become better teachers through systematic development, teaching, reflection, and revision.

INTASC STANDARDS

Another means to connect teaching to instructional design is through the Interstate New Teacher Assessment and Support Consortium (INTASC) model core standards for licensing new teachers. The Council of Chief State School Officers (CCSSO) and member states developed the INTASC standards. INTASC is primarily made up of state education agencies, which are responsible in their states for teacher licensing and professional development. The INTASC model core standards apply to all teachers regardless of content area or expertise. The INTASC task force that developed these standards determined that it would be inappropriate to develop different standards for beginning and advanced teachers and that "distinctions . . . are in the degree of sophistication teachers exhibit in the application of knowledge rather than in the kind of knowledge needed" (Council of Chief State School Officers. 1992. *Model standards for beginning teacher licensing, assessment and development: A resource for state dialogue.* Washington, DC: Author. www.ccsso.org/content/pdfs/corestrd.pdf).

On the next page, we list the INTASC core standards. Column two provides descriptive titles to distill the essence of the standards. In column three, we list the text chapters that address each of the standards. We use *pedagogical content knowledge* to characterize Principle 1, that teachers should understand their content areas and be able to teach the content. We label Principle 2 as *developmentally appropriate teaching.* Understanding the developmental needs of all learners informs good teaching decisions. We characterize Principle 3 with the term *learner differences.* We will discuss in Chapter 3 learner differences in terms of learner characteristics, diversity, multiculturalism, and special needs.

INTASC Core Standard®	Descriptive Label	ID Connections in This Text
Principle 1: The teacher understands the central concepts, tools of inquiry, and structures of the discipline(s) he or she teaches and can create learning experiences that make these aspects of subject matter meaningful for students.	1. Pedagogical content knowledge	Throughout text: Teacher inquiry Chapter 1. Connecting Learning and Teaching
Principle 2: The teacher understands how children learn and develop, and can provide learning opportunities that support their intellectual, social and personal development.	2. Developmentally appropriate teaching	Chapter 1. Connecting Learning and Teaching
Principle 3: The teacher understands how students differ in their approaches to learning and creates instructional opportunities that are adapted to diverse learners.	3. Learner differences	Chapter 3. Context Content, Learners, and Context Chapter 4. Determining Learning Outcomes Chapter 8. Designing and Teaching Units
Principle 4: The teacher understands and uses a variety of instructional strategies to encourage students' development of critical thinking, problem solving, and performance skills.	4. Teaching repertoire	Chapter 4. Determining Learning Outcomes Chapter 5. Exploring Assessment Options Chapter 6. Exploring Teaching Options Chapter 7. Exploring Technology Options Chapter 8. Designing and Teaching Units
Principle 5: The teacher uses an understanding of individual and group motivation and behavior to create a learning environment that encourages positive social interaction, active engagement in learning, and self-motivation.	5. Learning environments	Chapter 1. Connecting Learning and Teaching Section III, Developing Lessons

We characterize Principle 4 as *teaching repertoire*. Increasing one's teaching skills in terms of multiple teaching strategies is one possible goal for all teachers' professional development.

We characterize Principle 5 as *learning environments*, which can be designed by teachers to help students learn. Learning environments do not automatically exist but are jointly developed by teacher and students.

Principle 6 deals with the teacher's use of *communication* strategies to foster active learning between teacher and student. This principle suggests

INTASC Core Standard®	Descriptive Label	ID Connections in This Text
Principle 6: The teacher uses knowledge of effective verbal, nonverbal, and media communication techniques to foster active inquiry, collaboration, and supportive instruction in the classroom.	6. Communication	Chapter 7. Exploring Technology Options
Principle 7: The teacher plans instruction based upon knowledge of subject matter, students, the community, and curriculum goals.	7. Pre-unit thinking	Chapter 2. Connecting Planning and Designing Chapter 3. Content, Learners, and Context Chapter 7. Exploring Technology Options Chapter 8. Designing and Teaching Units
Principle 8: The teacher understands and uses formal and informal assessment strategies to evaluate and ensure the continuous intellectual, social, and physical development of the learner.	8. Assessment	Chapter 5. Exploring Assessment Options Chapter 7. Exploring Technology Options
Principle 9: The teacher is a reflective practitioner who continually evaluates the effects of his/her choices and actions on others and who actively seeks out opportunities to grow professionally.	9. Reflective professional	Chapter 1. Connecting Learning and Teaching Chapter 8. Designing and Teaching Units Reflective Questions End of Design Activities and End of Chapters Chapter 10. Reflecting on Your Learning
Principle 10: The teacher fosters relationships with school colleagues, parents, and agencies in the larger community to support students' learning and well-being.	10. Relationship-building	Chapter 8. Designing and Teaching Units Chapter 9. Developing Curriculum

INTASC Core Standards (CCSSO, 1992) and Matching Text Chapters, from Council of Chief State School Officers. 1992. *Model Standards for beginning teacher licensing, assessment and development: A resource for state dialogue.* Washington, DC: Author. www.ccsso.org/content/pdfs/corestrd.pdf. Used with permission of the Council of Chief State School Officers.

the need for teachers to attend to their own literacy development, which includes writing, speaking, listening, and verbal literacy, as well as to what it means to be literate in different content areas. Principle 7 evaluates one's knowledge of subject matter, students, community, and curriculum goals, collectively organized in this book around the ID process needs assessment. We label this activity as *pre-unit thinking* (and labeled it as pre-lesson thinking in Section III of this text), where we prompt you to think about content, learners, and the context of learning.

Principle 8 addresses formal and informal *assessment*. Teachers come to understand that assessment can take many forms, not just formal tests and grading, and that assessment can also be an ongoing teaching activity where individual student needs and progress can be documented. Principle 9 acknowledges the *reflective professional* category and to what extent thinking about teaching translates into action. Finally, we label Principle 10 as *relationship building*. Teaching benefits from tapping assistance in and out of the classroom, including other education professionals, parents, community leaders, and those from outside agencies.

Using This Text

HOW THIS TEXT IS ORGANIZED

This text is organized to guide you through the ID process and to use the Design Activities in each chapter to build lessons and a unit of instruction. Here is a visual organizer for the five sections of this text.

I. Making Connections
Learning ↔ Teaching
Planning ↔ Designing

Section I explains how learning ID can help you become a better teacher.

II. Understanding Your Classroom
Content
Learners
Context of School and Classroom

Section II prompts you to learn more about what is to be taught by your students, who your students are, and a better understanding of the school and classroom context in which students are learning.

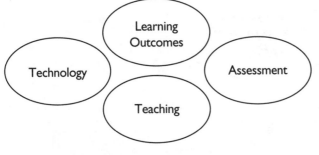

Learning Outcomes

Technology

Assessment

Teaching

ID is presented as a set of teacher decisions: learning outcomes, assessment, teaching, and technology.

III. Developing Lessons
Learning Outcomes
Assessment
Teaching
Technology

IV. Developing Units
Learning Outcomes
Assessment
Teaching
Technology

Section III addresses teacher decisions at developing lessons.

Section IV addresses teacher decisions at developing units.

V. Growing as a Teacher
Developing Curriculum
Reflecting on Your Learning

Section V concludes the text with a chapter on developing curriculum and a chapter on reflecting on your teaching.

TEACHER DECISION CYCLE

The Teacher Decision Cycle in this book is used as a questioning framework to develop lessons and units. The first question to be asked is: *"What will your students learn?"* As a teacher, you are responsible for translating state standards into learning outcomes. Knowing these learning outcomes, you can proceed along the cycle to answer questions regarding assessment, teaching, and technology. The cycle of teacher decisions and the chapters devoted to each question are visualized as follows.

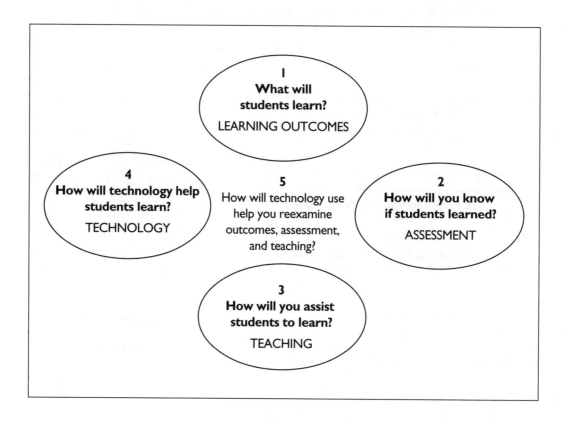

Teacher Decision Cycle	Section III Chapters
1. What will students learn?	Chapter 4: Determining Learning Outcomes
2. How will you know if students learned?	Chapter 5: Exploring Assessment Options
3. How will you assist students to learn?	Chapter 6: Exploring Teaching Options
4. How will media and technology help students learn?	Chapter 7: Exploring Technology Options
5. How will technology decisions help you rethink previous decisions?	Wrapup: Completing Your Lessons

CHAPTER FEATURES

Each chapter includes the following features:

Beginning of chapter

Main idea of this chapter. The major focus for each chapter is identified.

INTASC standards. The major INTASC core standards addressed by the chapter are listed, along with our descriptive titles to alert you to their significance.

Focus questions. Focus questions identify the scope of the chapter.

Listing of design activities.

Visual organizer. A visual identifies the major sections in the chapter.

Body of chapter

Text. The text of the chapters was written to support your actual thinking and decision making within the Design Activities. Throughout the text, we periodically summarize what has been written by using bulleted text or summary tables.

Design Activities. The purpose of these hands-on exercises is to guide you through lesson and unit development by using the instructional design process. Thus, you directly experience what it means to systematically design instruction. Some Design Activities may precede the text to activate your thinking. Other Design Activities record your decisions in the development of lessons or units.

Reflective questions. Within each Design Activity, we ask you to reflect on the implications in your teaching.

Key words. Definitions of key words are italicized and can be found in the Glossary at the end of the text.

End of chapter

An idea worth thinking about. The chapter concludes with a quotation that prompts you to think beyond the chapter in a new way.

Reflective teaching. A practicing teacher contributes a vignette on the dilemmas of teaching for new and experienced teachers.

Teacher inquiry. This section suggests topics for studying your teaching.

References and resources. References cited in the text are listed, as are helpful resources, articles, books, and websites.

Acknowledgments

We would like to thank the students in our graduate and undergraduate instructional design courses, who over the years taught us a great deal of what it means to teach and learn instructional design. ID courses frequently include all types of educators, including new and experienced teachers.

We would like to thank Whitney Hatcher, who supplied the secondary science unit, and Abigail McCarty and Annie Ripley, who collaborated on the elementary health unit. Cara Cashdollar, Andrea Hidock, and Cathy Statler, teacher education students, provided feedback on all of the chapters. Justin Moore, Jessica Shimp, and Pamela Deering, students in a graduate ID course, suggested improvements to the Teaching Decision Cycle. Stephanie Runion provided the Reflective Teaching vignettes at the end of the chapters and the reteaching example. Her five years of teaching experience provided an ideal perspective and voice for new and experienced teachers. We should also like to thank a cohort of educators from Rockbridge County, Virginia, who prompted much of our thinking about ID for teachers.

Thanks to Van Dempsey, Sarah Steele, and Jaci Webb-Dempsey, colleagues in the Benedum Collaborative Model of Teacher Education at West Virginia University. Van, as director of the Collaborative, provides tireless leadership and a vision and belief in school change. Sarah orchestrates practica for several hundred students and keeps smiling through all of it. Jaci manages the action research requirement in the five-year WVU teacher education program but, more than that, is a person to talk to and a pleasure to work with. Thanks, of course, to the teachers in the collaborative's twenty-eight professional development schools. Numerous suggestions from these teachers who supervised new teachers probably found their way into this text in one way or another.

We would like to thank the reviewers of this text, who improved it with their suggestions: Don Ely, Syracuse University; Sara McNeil, University of Houston; Martin Ryder, University of Colorado at Denver; and Brent Wilson, University of Colorado. Thanks to Arnis Burvikovs, Senior Editor of Educational Psychology, Leadership, and Technology at Allyn & Bacon, who kept this project in front of us. We also give our grateful thanks to Nancy Forsythe, who believed in our process approach.

We would like to thank our respective spouses for putting up with our schedules. Writing requires a discipline that takes you away from life. We thank them once again for being close by and for being our greatest fans.

This work marks more than ten years that we have been promoting the use of instructional design for better learning and better teaching. To promote instructional design, a person must also practice and live it, and we have learned much about the teaching of ID from our students and from each other. Our sustained work during this period demonstrates that students deserve teachers who love what they do.

Neal Shambaugh & Susan Magliaro

SECTION

I

Making Connections

1 Connecting Learning and Teaching

Main Idea of This Chapter
Establishing a foundation for your teaching helps you understand your teaching decisions.

INTASC Standards Addressed in This Chapter

Principle 1 PEDAGOGICAL CONTENT KNOWLEDGE: The teacher understands the central concepts, tools of inquiry, and structures of the discipline(s) he or she teaches and can create learning experiences that make these aspects of subject matter meaningful for students.

Principle 2 DEVELOPMENTALLY APPROPRIATE TEACHING: The teacher understands how children learn and develop and can provide learning opportunities that support their intellectual, social, and personal development.

Principle 3 LEARNER DIFFERENCES: The teacher uses an understanding of individual and group motivation and behavior to create a learning environment that encourages positive social interaction, active engagement in learning, and self-motivation.

Focus Questions

- What are your beliefs about teaching and learning, and how have they changed over time?
- What makes an effective teacher?
- What kind of educator do you want to be?

Design Activities

DA 1: What Is Learning? What Is Instruction?
DA 2: Learning Principles List
DA 3: What Is Effective Teaching?
DA 4: Your Mission Statement

CONNECTIONS

Before we work through the instructional design (ID) process, we need to establish connections between learning and teaching and between planning and instructional design. Figure 1.1 visualizes these connections and the sequence of the sections in Chapter 1 and Chapter 2.

FIGURE 1.1.
Making Connections in Chapters 1 and 2.

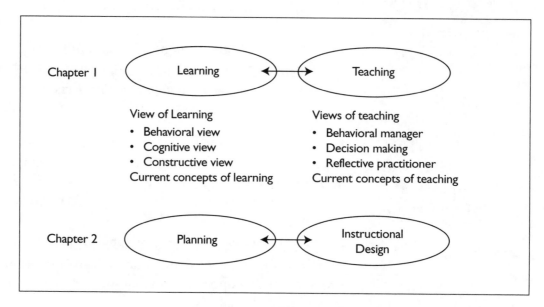

Chapter 1 examines different views on learning by describing three learning theories and a current conceptualization of what we know about learning from research. We then describe three historical views of teaching and describe the features of learning environments that promote the transfer of learning from the classroom to the students' world.

The four Design Activities in this chapter are particularly important, because they record on paper your views on teaching and learning. You will revisit these drafts in Chapter 10, Reflecting on Your Learning. Collectively, these Design Activities describe the kind of educator you want to be. Before we look in more detail at how people learn, record your perceptions of learning and instruction.

What Is Learning?
What Is Instruction?

Task Rationale   The purpose for this first activity is to define these two important terms.

Task Guidelines   1. What is learning?
2. What is instruction?

Reflectivity   • Cite some examples from your student or teaching experiences that led to what you wrote.
• How do you feel about what you wrote?

Without some reflection, these can be daunting questions. What you write probably represents the basis for your teaching decisions. Now that you have written about your views, let us proceed to the next section, which summarizes the development of different views of learning.

VIEWS OF LEARNING

Historical development of learning theories

Over the past century, three theoretical approaches have provided the primary guidance for instructional practice: *behaviorism, cognitive psychology*, and *constructivism*. Mayer (1992) suggested three metaphors that parallel each of these approaches and provide ways of thinking about these theories. These metaphors are learning as response acquisition, learning as knowledge acquisition, and learning as knowledge construction. Next, we briefly discuss each learning theory and its corresponding implications for the design of instruction (Wildman, 1996).

Behavioral learning theory

Behavioral psychology dominated the study of human learning during the first half of the twentieth century. From a behavioral perspective, learning is the *acquisition of responses* to features in our environment. Learning is achieved through frequent responding and immediate reinforcement of appropriate behaviors. Humans learn over time through the gradual shaping of these desired responses.

Adopting the behavioral theory provides an organized and systematic set of guidelines for instructional design. First, given that the value of the reinforcement is based on the individual learner's needs and interests, the teacher-designer must allow for individual pacing and progress. Subject matter has an inherent organization that must be programmed so that one learns in the appropriate sequence. Consequently, design decisions must follow the caveat "Teach first things first." The sequence of this book follows a logic of first establishing important connections (Chapters 1–2) and then learning about content, learners, and context (Chapter 3), lesson development (Chapters 4–7), and unit development (Chapter 8).

Specific learning objectives specify the performance of the actual task to be mastered. A task analysis (see Chapter 3) breaks down the behavior needed to complete the task into the correct sequence of behaviors. Learning is demonstrated by objective measures in which behavior is defined and measured according to some behavioral indicator.

Cognitive learning theory

Mayer's second metaphor, learning as *knowledge acquisition*, reflects the cognitive theory, which has been dominated by the information-processing model of human memory. Beginning in the 1960s and continuing today, learning theorists turned to studying mental models and mental processes, such as thinking, remembering, and problem solving. Key memory structures and processes were identified, with the computer as the metaphor for the human memory system. Memory and recall depend on the quality of processing. New information is built onto existing knowledge structures. Internal executive control is required to enable the entire system to function efficiently.

ID considerations expanded, adopting the cognitive theory. Instruction is designed to promote thinking activity that approximates an expert. The lesson and unit development of expert teachers are discussed in Chapter 2, and we provide learning aids in the form of lesson and unit plan outlines. These tools structure your thinking and teaching decisions. Such task structure is a feature of cognitive learning theory.

Using a cognitive learning theory in one's teaching means that appropriate activities are designed for students to help them "process" new information. In addition, specific learning strategies are taught to ensure that the learner efficiently acquires information or solves a problem. This book's Teacher Decision Cycle uses a set of questions to unpack the decision making of expert teachers. Another cognitive strategy is the use of organizers as instructional aids to help teachers structure conceptual knowledge. The organizers at the beginning of each chapter in this book visually represent the scope of the chapter, and tables throughout the text summarize important ideas.

Social constructivist learning theory

Since the 1980s, learning has been depicted as *knowledge construction*. In what is most frequently termed a constructivist framework, unique understandings are assumed to be natural, and responsibility for learning resides primarily with the learner. Of particular importance is the assumption that all thinking is embedded in particular settings, and these, along with learning tools and tasks, must be taken into account in designing instruction.

There are many different kinds of constructivism (Phillips, 1995). *Radical constructivism* views understanding as totally individual (e.g., von Glaserfeld, 1984). A Piagetian approach is predominantly individual, and social interaction is seen as a catalyst (Greeno, Collins, & Resnick, 1996). *Social constructivism* (e.g., Vygotsky, 1978) emphasizes the social world to define reality and knowledge.

Learning goals and activity are the focus within teacher–learner interactions. The idea of *communities of learners* (Brown, 1994) is that both teachers and students are learners. Learning involves problems that are relevant to the learner and frequently emerge during learning activity. Teachers, other adults, or peers do not disseminate information but assist learners (Tharp & Gallimore, 1988). Assessment practices have students solve real-life problems and promote self-reflection and learner responsibility. This theory provides the basis for the Design Activities in this book. The best way to learn how to develop lessons and units is to design, teach, reflect, and improve them.

Figure 1.2 visualizes the metaphoric differences of learning according to these three theories and their implications for instructional design.

Summary of Learning Theories, Metaphors, and ID Use		
Learning Theory	**Metaphor of Learning Theory**	**Implications for ID**
Behavioral theory	Learning as response acquisition	• Individual progress • Content sequencing • Analysis of learning task • Assessment keyed to behavior
Cognitive theory	Learning as knowledge acquisition	• Structure activity • Support expert development • Learning strategies • Organizers • Assessment keyed to performance on activity
Constructivist theory	Learning as knowledge construction	• Share control with students • Emergent understandings • Authentic activity • Peers and adults assist learner • Assessment includes self-reflection and learner responsibility

FIGURE 1.2. Learning Theories, Metaphors, and ID Use.

Current concepts of learning

The following sections describe the five major themes of learning that have emerged from the last thirty years of research. This summary is based on work from the National Research Council (NRC) documented in *How People Learn* (Bransford, Brown, & Cocking, 2000). The sixteen experts who wrote this report consulted many other experts in their fields.

Organizing knowledge in memory

Research in cognition has identified two types of conceptual mechanisms to explain how humans store learning as short-term or working memory and as long-term memory. If we had only short-term memory, our behavior and thinking would be limited to the amount of information we could remember and recall quickly. Without a means for storing this learning, we would have to start all over again. Research has demonstrated that there are limits to what information people can hold in their short-term memory without repeating the learning.

Researchers have also studied how people learn the meaning and understanding of information by developing and retaining personally meaningful structures in their minds. If you knew how each of your students made sense of and used new information, then you could present this information more effectively. Teachers must also attend to the ways in which they structure and present new information or learning activities. Assessment requires ongoing review of student learning as students make sense of new knowledge in unique ways. Teachers encourage students to consider more correct representations of new knowledge, skills, or procedures.

Solving problems

Research on expert–novice differences has contributed directly to the purpose of school as envisioned by the National Commission on Teaching and America's Future (1986)—namely, to prepare students for the global economy. Attributes valued in this global economy are abilities to learn more than one job, adjust and adapt to changing conditions, communicate with others, and solve problems. Solving any problem requires exposure to strategies that help the learner determine relevant information and the problem type, formulate a technique to solve the problem, and evaluate the result. The research into how experts solve problems has given us an understanding of what information they acquire and how they organize, represent, and interpret this knowledge for particular problem types and situations.

Developing learners

Taking a developmental view of students provides teachers with insights on learner differences and different conceptions of how humans generally learn in stages over their lifespan. Piaget's stage theory of cognitive development (i.e., sensorimotor, preoperational, concrete operational, and formal operational stages) gives teachers typical characteristics of cognitive abilities at each stage (Driscoll, 2000). Family, friends, role models, the community, and one's ideological and social culture provide additional influences. Other views of child development may take a more holistic or systems view of children in their environment (Bronfenbrenner, 1979) and address different influences of biology, psychology, and social factors.

Another aspect of a developmental perspective is the differences between children and adult learners in terms of *learner characteristics*. Examples of learner characteristics are age, gender, educational level, achievement level, prerequisite knowledge and skills, socioeconomic background, learning preferences, motivation, beliefs and attitudes, and expectations. Understanding students' learning characteristics can enable you to adjust your teaching to meet the needs of individual students.

A third aspect of the developmental view is an individual's different ways of interacting with the world and of learning from the world. The field of special education contributes understanding of the vast differences in children's physical, cognitive, and social capabilities. Special education teachers and specialists can be critical collaborators in helping general education teachers respond appropriately to the success of these individuals.

Learning how to learn

Cognitive research has also provided insights on how humans understand how they learn and make judgments on changing the way they learn, sometimes referred to as *metacognition*, or thinking about one's thinking. This topic raises teachers' awareness to the differences in how individuals learn and provides ways of responding to these differences. Study strategies, which help individual students become aware of how they learn, can be incorporated into learning activities. Different reading and studying strategies are useful here, such as different techniques for note taking that help students recall and use information.

Living and learning in the world

Researchers have acknowledged the influence of the social and cultural context of learning. Learning to cope in a global economy requires, then, that teaching takes into account the social environment in which children live and that these influences can be included in learning activities. Involving parents and the community in school decisions acknowledges the social and cultural heritage of children within the school. One of the characteristics of an effective teacher, discussed later in this chapter, is helping students apply what they are learning in school to participating in unique forms of activity in the global community.

Learning principles

Many teachers use *learning principles* from one or more learning theories in their teaching. A learning principle is a statement about ways people learn that is based on a learning theory that is backed by research (Ormrod, 2000). For example, shaping is a behavioral principle that involves reinforcing a gradual change in behavior until the desired behavior is reached. An example of applying this learning principle is when a teacher helps students experience success in small writing tasks and then progressively increases the scope of the writing.

The next Design Activity asks you to identify the learning principles that match your view of teaching and the theory (or theories) that support them. This activity requires that you read outside sources to learn more about the educational application of these learning principles.

Learning Principles List

Task Rationale Identifying learning principles that are important to you can help you document a theoretical foundation for your teaching, a foundation that may tap principles from more than one learning theory.

Task Guidelines
1. Identify one article or book chapter that addresses each of the three learning theories: behavioral, cognitive, and constructivist.
2. Read each article or chapter and record the learning principles that are important in your teaching.
3. On a separate piece of paper, identify and record ten learning principles and label each with the appropriate learning theory or theories. For each, provide an example of how this learning principle is used or could be used in your teaching.

Learning Principle	Learning Theory	Example

Reflectivity
- Which learning theory was predominant?
- Why did you favor or not favor a particular learning theory?

VIEWS OF TEACHING

Historical views of teaching

Different views of teaching have evolved in a way somewhat parallel to the shifting views on how humans learn. Three views are presented here in terms of their predominant metaphor.

Teacher as behavioral manager

The first view of the teacher, as conceptualized by the research community, was the skilled manager of student behavior and a master of technique (Clark & Yinger, 1987). In this view, which is still valued today, a competent teacher possesses a set of skills or competencies, usually evaluated by standardized achievement measures (Good & Brophy, 1987). So, what could be wrong with this view? Isn't this what we are paying teachers for? Is this not what is known as a master teacher?

Taken literally, the implication of this view is that good teaching involves mastery of technique and that teachers react rather than act as professionals. Professionals in any field call upon their expertise, as well as on the expertise and codes of conduct developed by others. Master teachers call on years of experience in appraising "where" their students are, both developmentally and academically. The agenda that teachers are responsible for is much too complex to be addressed by a technical approach. No bag of tricks is large enough to account for the endless contingencies facing a teacher. There is no index comprehensive enough for the new teacher to consult.

Teacher as decision maker

The image of the teacher as behavioral manager came to be complemented by a view of the teacher as a skilled decision maker. This second wave of researchers examined aspects of teacher thinking, which was based on the conceptualization of the teacher as a human who acts and thinks. Teaching was viewed as a trio of thoughts: a teacher's theories and beliefs, the planning of what one does before teaching, and the thinking during the actual implementation of the planning. This view acknowledged the reciprocal effect that teacher thinking had on student behavior, teacher actions, and student achievement (Clark & Peterson, 1986) and that student achievement, for example, had on changes in teacher thinking and actions.

The goals for the teacher thinking research program were to (a) describe the mental lives of teachers, (b) understand how the behavior of teachers takes on numerous forms and functions, and (c) understand how humans manage the complexity of classroom teaching. This second view of teaching corresponds to a cognitive portrayal of teaching (Clark, 1983).

Teacher as reflective practitioner

A new view of the teacher then emerged that acknowledged teacher thinking and actions, but within a rich context of influences, activities, interactions, and change. In addition to the unpredictability of the classroom, other constraints and opportunities entered the picture, including the influences of parents, schools, and state and national governments (Borko & Shavelson, 1990). Teaching that acknowledges this complexity and uncertainty requires teachers who can experiment, reframe, and reflect during and after teaching. Thus, teachers came to be viewed as *reflective practitioners* (Schön, 1983, 1987) who are continually engaged in their own learning as well as the learning of their students. This view of the teacher operating within a changing context resonates with the third theory of learning—namely, the social constructivist view.

Figure 1.3 summarizes how the different learning theories align with different views of teaching.

FIGURE 1.3.
Matching Learning Theories with Views of Teaching.

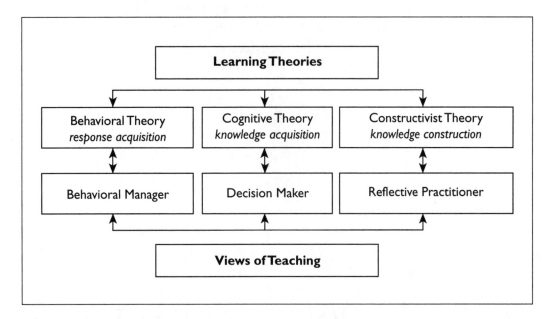

This short summary of how researchers have conceptualized human learning and teaching suggests a number of caveats to the academic view:

- Each of the three learning theories and views of teaching has merits.
- A teacher must master many skills, but this development takes time and desire, resources, and administrative support.
- New teachers tend to value competency in technique and management of student behavior more than reflective thinking.
- Instructors in public schools and higher education, other educators, parents, and politicians look at educational issues in different ways.
- Just because the research community views teaching as a reflective activity does not mean that teachers believe this or that they choose to be reflective.

This text is based on our view that teachers are skilled decision makers but that teachers must continually reflect and adjust their teaching in response to changing classroom conditions and an ongoing awareness of student needs.

How do you view teaching?

It is sometimes difficult to know how to proceed when reading conceptual views of teaching, as described by the foregoing discussion of learning environments. The next Design Activity asks you to identify words or short phrases that describe your view of effective teaching.

DESIGN ACTIVITY 3

What Is Effective Teaching?

Task Rationale This task provides another means of examining your views on teaching.

Task Guidelines
1. List the top three features that characterize effective teaching.
2. List three qualities of effective teaching that you would like to develop as a teacher.
3. List three habits or behaviors you would like to change.

Reflectivity
- Elaborate briefly on the reasons why you chose your three features of effective teaching.

Your views of learning and teaching

The following Design Activity taps what you wrote in earlier Design Activities, including (a) your initial definitions of learning and instruction, (b) your list of learning principles, and (c) your beliefs about effective teaching.

DESIGN ACTIVITY 4

Your Mission Statement

Task Rationale The purpose of this task is to crystallize your learning principles into a draft statement that guides your instructional development efforts.

Task Guidelines This activity may require multiple drafts over time, so trust yourself to make an initial mission statement and then revise one or more times, until you are satisfied with the results.
1. Prioritize your list of Learning Principles to a top-five list.
2. In a paragraph, pull together your ideas about learning and instruction, using some of your learning principles.

Reflectivity • Write about the thinking and strategies that went into completing your mission statement paragraph. This question is a metacognitive question.
• What were your reactions to this activity and to what you wrote?

Current concepts of teaching

The degree to which a teacher is able to support the *transfer* of learning from the classroom to applications outside the school is directly related to the learning environment "created" by the teacher. The four interconnected features of learning environments discussed next were developed from research conducted by the Cognition and Technology Group at Vanderbilt University (Bransford, Brown, & Cocking, 2000). Although discussed separately, these features overlap and support each other.

Learner-centered

The principal characteristic of a learner-centered learning environment is the degree to which a teacher values what students know and the source for their understanding. This means continually learning about students' backgrounds, interests, and concerns and adapting instruction to take advantage of students' interests. In addition, learner-centeredness values students' representations of their understanding. Although younger students' conceptual understandings may be faulty, the teacher addresses these difficulties by first seeing the types and ranges of misrepresentations. A third feature of a learner-centered environment is the teacher-as-learner, or the degree to which teachers see themselves as learners, actively integral to student inquiry, rather than as always knowing the answer. In a global society, no one is privileged to have all the answers, and teachers can model this ongoing learning attitude by engaging in learning activity with students. A fourth characteristic of a learner-centered environment is student responsiveness or the degree to which a teacher supports student learning by an ongoing process of "where students are" and where they as teachers "need to be." Responsiveness can take other forms, including personal concern for students, responsive feedback, strong expectations, and the modeling of moral and responsible behavior.

Knowledge-centered

A major characteristic of knowledge-centered learning environments is the degree to which they foster student understanding of knowledge and how students use this knowledge in a variety of applications. Success depends directly on the teachers' awareness of this goal; the design for understanding in lessons, units, and curricula; and its implementation. This design for understanding is discussed in later chapters. Instructional design provides the structure to improve the likelihood of success in this area. Coming to understand the developmental differences of children helps the teacher design appropriate instruction.

Assessment-centered

The major characteristic of an assessment-centered learning environment is the degree to which assessment is used to monitor student learning and give constructive feedback to students as they learn. Assessment in this context contributes to student learning rather than merely being an evaluative judgment. Many of the skills we urge children to learn for survival in the global economy require teacher feedback—feedback that is consistent, constructive, and prompt. Peer assessment or feedback is underused as an assessment tool. Another important criterion to an assessment-centered learning environment is alignment of teaching and assessment decisions. If problem solving is the goal for the future citizenry of a global economy, then assessing student understanding, competence, and mastery must be conducted by using problem-solving activities in a variety of applications.

Community-centered

Manning, Curtis, and McMillen (1996) identify several characteristics of community. The first characteristic is having a community vision. What are our values? Where do we want to go, and how do we get there? Having a vision for your teaching and a collective vision shared with students creates a shared learning environment where students could become less passive and more invested. A second characteristic of community is having interpersonal skills. Can we get along and have true dialogue over differences? Do we truly value relationships? Interpersonal skills become an important item in content learning and require instructional time. A third characteristic for community is the value of human diversity. Can we come to understand others outside our perspective? Can we suspend judgment and learn from others? Diversity becomes another component to what is taught and learned. Finally, a fourth characteristic of community is the empowerment of people. Can we help ourselves by using our abilities and sensibilities to help others? In short, if we can build community in schools, the "learning transfer" is significant, and students can model community for others in their neighborhoods.

Figure 1.4 summarizes the features of the four interconnected aspects of today's learning environments, all of which can be designed by the teacher.

FIGURE 1.4.
Feature Summary of Learning Environments.

	Features of Learning Environments
Learner-centered	• Student backgrounds, interests, concerns • Student representations • Teacher as learner • Responsiveness to student needs
Knowledge-centered	• Student use of knowledge • Design for understanding • Students' individual differences
Assessment-centered	• Monitoring of student learning • Alignment of teaching with assessment
Community-centered	• Community vision • Interpersonal skills • Human diversity • Empowerment of people

Used with permission of the National Academy of Sciences.

New teachers frequently write about their desire to create student-centered environments. The previous discussion suggests several items to consider in the design of instruction. These features provide an experienced teacher with a checklist if learner-centered environments are the goal. Other features suggested here, such as knowledge, assessment, and community, contribute to the transfer of school learning to the learner's wider world.

Recapping Chapter 1: Making Connections

- We connected teaching with instructional design by identifying how different chapters of the text matched one or more of the INTASC principles for new and experienced teachers.
- Chapter 1 connected teaching and learning by viewing the historical evolution of learning theories and views of teaching. You can still find educators, parents, and politicians who subscribe to each of the views discussed in this chapter.
- Chapter 2 will contrast the differences between planning and instruction. We will examine four different ID models that have been designed to help teachers think more systematically about their teaching.

An Idea Worth Thinking About	"Learning is a human enterprise. With this understanding, we cannot dismiss or ignore the value of our beliefs about learning in the design of learning opportunities. Such a stance complicates designing, but it also opens the doors for many possibilities." *(Shambaugh & Magliaro, 1997, p. 4)*

By continually reexamining your views and beliefs on learning and teaching, you remain cognizant that your intentions as a teacher appropriately address student learning.

Reflective Teaching

"A Note to All Readers" . . . from Stephanie Runion

At the end of each chapter, you will find a section entitled "Reflective Teaching." I am the author of these reflective teaching scenarios. I am a public school teacher and have taught Title I for the past four years in public schools. I have received a bachelor's degree in elementary education, a master's degree in reading, and, most recently, my second master's, in technology education.

As I read through this text, I tried to think of a teaching experience that I have either had personally or encountered that would tie into the main theme of each chapter. I hope that you, as a teacher, find my reflectivity beneficial as you design and develop lessons and units to use in your classroom settings.

As I began to write for each of the chapters, one central theme kept running through my head. Teaching is an extremely complex profession! What do you do when you spend forty-five minutes a day, five days a week, trying to help a child learn basic sight words but the child just doesn't seem to be making any progress? What do you do when you *know* a child could make leaps and bounds when it comes to reading if only the child practiced with guidance at home, but you can't get the parent to commit to your suggestions? What do you do when you want more than anything to teach reading but the students in your class are too hungry, too tired, or too worried about "grown-up" issues like custody to care much about reading?

No matter what stage of teaching you are in—just beginning or just about ready to retire—your job as a teacher will change each and every day. As a teacher, you have many issues and concerns running through your head simultaneously on a daily basis. It's a constant juggling act! It truly takes a teacher who is knowledgeable, prepared, and dedicated to be able to keep all of the balls in the air.

Best of luck to you in your education and as you begin your career as a teacher. I truly believe that you have chosen one of the most challenging and rewarding professions in the world. Best wishes!

Teacher Inquiry

- Describe any investigation you have conducted about your teaching. What do you believe teacher inquiry is about?
- What learning principles form the core basis for your teaching? Which new learning principles interest you, and how will you apply them in your teaching? Which of these might form the basis for teacher research?
- Consider joint research with one or more peers. Your focus might be on use of a particular teaching strategy. Your inquiry might involve teachers in your school or one or more teachers from a neighboring school.

REFERENCES

Borko, H., & Shavelson, R. J. (1990). Teacher decision making. In B. F. Jones & L. Idol (Eds.), *Dimensions of thinking and cognitive instruction* (pp. 311–345). Hillsdale, NJ: Erlbaum.

Bransford, J. D., Brown, A. L., & Cocking, R. R. (Eds.). (2000). *How people learn: Brain, mind, experience, and school* (expanded ed.). Washington, DC: National Academy Press.

Bronfenbrenner, U. (1979). *The ecology of human development: Experiments by nature and design.* Cambridge, MA: Harvard University Press.

Brown, A. L. (1994). The advancement of learning. *Educational Researcher, 23*(8), 4–12.

Clark, C. M. (1983). Research on teacher planning: An inventory of the knowledge base. In D. C. Smith (Ed.), *Essential knowledge for beginning educators.* Washington, DC: American Association of Colleges for Teacher Education.

Clark, C. M., & Peterson, P. L. (1986). Teachers' thought process. In M. C. Wittrock (Ed.), *Handbook of research on teaching* (3rd ed.). (pp. 255–296). New York: Macmillan.

Clark, C. M., & Yinger R. J. (1987). Teacher planning. In J. Calderhead (Ed.), *Exploring teachers' thinking.* London: Cassell.

Driscoll, M. P. (2000). *Psychology of learning for instruction* (2nd ed.). Boston: Allyn and Bacon.

Good, T. L., & Brophy, J. E. (1987). *Looking in classrooms* (4th ed.). New York: Harper & Row.

Greeno, J., Collins, A., & Resnick, L. (1996). Cognition and learning. In D. Berliner & R. Calfee (Eds.), *Handbook of educational psychology* (pp. 15–46). New York: Macmillan.

Manning, G., Curtis, K., & McMillen, S. (1996). *Building community: The human side of work.* Cincinnati, OH: Thomson Executive Press.

Mayer, R. E. (1992). Cognition and instruction: Their historic meeting within educational psychology. *Journal of Educational Psychology, 84*(4), 405–412.

National Commission on Teaching and America's Future. (1986). *What matters most: Teaching for America's future.* New York: National Commission on Teaching and America's Future.

Ormrod, J. E. (2000). *Educational psychology: Developing learners*, 3rd ed. Upper Saddle River, NJ: Merrill.

Phillips, D. C. (1995). The good, the bad, and the ugly: The many faces of constructivism. *Educational Researcher, 24*(7), 5–12.

Schön, D. A. (1983). *The reflective practitioner: How professionals think and act.* New York: Basic Books.

Schön, D. A. (1987). *Educating the reflective practitioner: Toward a new design for teaching and learning in the professions.* San Francisco: Jossey-Bass.

Shambaugh, R. N., & Magliaro, S. G. (1997). *Mastering the possibilities: A process approach to instructional design.* Boston: Allyn and Bacon.

Tharp, R. G., & Gallimore, R. (1988). *Rousing minds to life: Teaching, learning, and schooling in social context.* Cambridge, U.K.: Cambridge University Press.

von Glaserfeld, E. (1984). An introduction to radical constructivism. In P. Watzlawick (Ed.), *The invented reality* (pp. 17–40). New York: W. W. Norton.

Vygotsky, L. S. (1978). *Mind in society: The development of higher psychological processes.* Cambridge, MA: Harvard University Press.

Wildman, T. M. (1996). *Learning: New understandings and imperatives* (white paper). Blacksburg, VA: Virginia Polytechnic Institute & State University, Center for Excellence in Undergraduate Teaching.

RESOURCES

Print Resources

Reflectivity

Brookfield, S. D. (1995). *Becoming a critically reflective teacher.* San Francisco: Jossey-Bass.

Teaching is viewed through four critical lenses: teacher autobiographies, students, peer perceptions, and theoretical literature. Tools suggested include teaching diaries, role model profiles, participant learning portfolios, structured critical conversation, the Critical Incident Classroom Questionnaire, and the Good Practices Audit.

Posner, G. (2000). *Field experience: A guide to reflective teaching* (5th ed.). Boston: Allyn and Bacon.

Guides students through field experiences.

Schön, D. A. (1983). *The reflective practitioner: How professionals think in action.* New York: Basic Books.

This title is one of the most cited books on professional reflectivity. The author writes in the context of the architectural design studio, but his thoughts on the "reflective practitioner" also apply to teaching.

Schön, D. A. (1987). *Educating the reflective practitioner: Toward a new design for teaching and learning in the professions.* San Francisco: Jossey-Bass.

Discusses the "paradoxes and predicaments" of reflecting within professional activity. Includes three examples of reflectivity.

Taggart, G. L., & Wilson, A. P. (1998). *Promoting reflective thinking in teachers: 44 action strategies.* Thousand Oaks, CA: Corwin Press.

Makes a case for three types of reflective thinking: technical, contextual, and dialectical. Describes activities to introduce reflective thinking to teachers. Describes observations, journals, teaching evaluation rubrics, narrative, mental models, and action research as tools to develop reflectivity.

Tertell, E. A., Klein, S. M., & Jewett, J. L. (Eds.). (1998). *When teachers reflect: Journeys toward effective, inclusive practice.* Washington, DC: National Association for the Education of Young Children.

Reflective stories from eighteen teachers discussing inclusion and developmentally appropriate practice. Each teacher discusses and provides reflective comments and resources.

Text may be helpful for teachers looking to use reflectivity in their teacher inquiry.

Zeichner, K., & Liston, D. P. (1996). *Reflective teaching: An introduction*. Mahwah, NJ: Erlbaum.

Designed for the new and student teacher, this ninety-two-page handbook is organized into four categories: Before the Teaching Experience, Methods of Observation, During the Teaching Experience, and After the Teaching Experience.

http://www.iloveteaching.com/mentor/

An online guide to using this text.

Learning Theory

Bransford, J. D., Brown, A. L., & Cocking, R. R. (Eds.). (2000). *How people learn: Brain, mind, experience, and school* (expanded ed.). Washington, DC: National Academy Press.

This book summarizes a science of learning and concentrates on a cognitive psychology and the important concerns of social and cultural contexts to learning. This text is also available online: www.nap.edu

Driscoll, M. P. (2000). *Psychology of learning for instruction*, 2nd ed. Boston: Allyn and Bacon.

Well-organized, compact, and readable treatment of learning theories and learning applications.

Duckworth, E. (1987). *The having of wonderful ideas and other essays on teaching and learning*. New York: Teachers College Press.

Implementing a Piagetian view of constructivist principles. See "A Child's-Eye View of Knowing," "Learning with Breadth and Depth," "The Virtues of Not Knowing," and "Teaching as Research."

Fosnot, C. T. (Ed.). (1996). *Constructivism: Theory, perspectives, and practice*. New York: Teachers College Press.

Implementing constructivist principles in learning settings.

Gagné, R. M. (1985). *The conditions of learning and theory of instruction* (4th ed.). New York: Harcourt Brace.

How one designs specific conditions for learning, depending on the type of learning. A classic worth reading and rereading.

Gruber, H. E., & Voneche, J. J. (1995). *The essential Piaget*. New York: Basic Books.

Skinner, B. F. (1968). *Technology of learning*. Englewood Cliffs, NJ: Prentice-Hall.

Translates behaviorist principles for instructional settings.

Tharp, R. G., & Gallimore, R. (1988). *Rousing minds to life: Teaching, learning, and schooling in social context*. Cambridge, U.K.: Cambridge University Press.

Implementing a Vygotskian view of constructivist principles.

Views of Teaching and the Teacher

Council of Chief State School Officers. (1992). *Model standards for beginning teacher licensing, assessment and development: A resource for state dialogue*. Washington, DC: Author. www.ccsso.org/content/pdfs/corestrd.pdf

Goodlad, J. (1984). *A place called school*. New York: Prentice-Hall.

Study of American schools and teaching.

Holmes Group. (1986). *Tomorrow's teachers*. East Lansing, MI: Author.

Report on views of effective teaching.

Holmes Group. (1990). *Tomorrow's schools*. East Lansing, MI: Author.

Report on the principles for design of professional development schools.

Holmes Group. (1995). *Tomorrow's schools of education*. East Lansing, MI: Author.

Report on how teacher education programs need to change to fully implement the "partnership" idea of professional development schools.

Manning, G., Curtis, K., & McMillen, S. (1996). *Building community: The human side of work*. Cincinnati, OH: Thomson Executive Press.

Teachers may spend some time in schools addressing parental involvement in their students' education. Parental involvement is a special form of community building. This is a business book, but it combines concepts and tools with a human view of work.

Shulman, L. S. (2004). *The wisdom of practice: Essays on teaching, learning, and learning to teach.* San Francisco: Jossey-Bass.

A convenient resource of twenty-three essays from Shulman, a leading advocate of teaching and teachers in public schools and higher education. Visionary ideas coupled with pragmatic suggestions for implementation.

Task Force on Teaching as a Profession. (1986). *A nation prepared: Teachers for the 21st century.* New York: Carnegie Corporation of New York.

Recommended establishment of a national certification board.

Web-Based Resources

INTASC Model Core Standards for Licensing Teachers
www.ccsso.org/content/pdfs/corestrd.pdf

The Interstate New Teacher Assessment and Support Consortium (INTASC) standards were developed by the Council of Chief State School Officers and member states. Copies of the INTASC standards can be downloaded from the council's website. CCSSO is a nonpartisan, nationwide, nonprofit organization of public officials who head departments of elementary and secondary education in the states, the District of Columbia, the Department of Defense Education Activity, and five U.S. extrastate jurisdictions.

Learning Theories

Theory into Practice Database
http://tip.psychology.org/

Web-based links with brief summaries of fifty major theories of learning and instruction.

Reflectivity

Reflect: How can I reflect upon my teaching practice? Active Learning Practices for Schools. http://learnweb.harvard.edu/alps/reflect/index.cfm

Views of teaching and the teacher

American Association of Colleges of Teacher Education
www.aacte.org

Holmes Scholars Program
www.holmes-scholars.org

A program of the Holmes Partnership (formerly the Holmes Group) to support minority graduate students in education.

National Council for Accreditation of Teacher Education
www.ncate.org

2 Connecting Planning and Designing

Main Idea of This Chapter
*Instructional design is a comprehensive way
to think about teaching.*

INTASC
Standards
Addressed in
This Chapter

Principle 7 PRE-UNIT THINKING: The teacher plans instruction based on knowledge of subject matter, students, the community, and curriculum goals.

Principle 9 REFLECTIVE PROFESSIONAL: The teacher is a reflective practitioner who continually evaluates the effects of his or her choices and actions on others and who actively seeks opportunities to grow professionally.

Focus Questions

- What are the qualities of a good lesson plan and a good instructional design?
- In what different ways do teachers plan?
- What are the qualities of a good ID model for teachers?

Design Activities

DA 5: Design a Lesson
DA 6: How Teachers Plan
DA 7: Critique an ID Model

LESSON PLANS AND INSTRUCTIONAL DESIGNS

Teacher education programs use lesson plans to help new teachers develop habits of lesson planning and reflectivity. Meanwhile, the planning habits and routines of practicing teachers vary considerably. Whatever the differences in planning, an effective lesson plan identifies a focus for student learning and provides sufficient details to implement instruction. This chapter examines differences in planning between experienced and new teachers and summarizes the benefits and downsides of lesson plans, and the qualities of a good lesson plan (see Figure 2.1).

FIGURE 2.1.
Visual Organizer for Chapter 2.

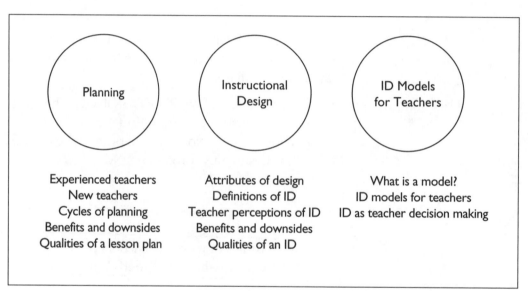

Experienced teachers
New teachers
Cycles of planning
Benefits and downsides
Qualities of a lesson plan

Attributes of design
Definitions of ID
Teacher perceptions of ID
Benefits and downsides
Qualities of an ID

What is a model?
ID models for teachers
ID as teacher decision making

Instructional design, meanwhile, is a more comprehensive process that guides one in identifying learning outcomes, assessment tools, and teaching strategies and in evaluating one's teaching. This chapter next looks at the attributes of design in general and provides several definitions of instructional design. As with planning, we summarize the benefits, downsides, and qualities of a good instructional design. Four examples of ID models for teachers are provided, one of which depicts instructional design as teacher decision making. We use this view of ID to organize the text.

Lesson planning exercise

To help you appreciate the thinking that goes into lesson planning, work through the following Design Activity. This activity is best done before coming to class, so that you have some time to identify a short lesson or activity, one that you could teach in ten minutes or less. Another variation, subject to the instructor's decision, is to meet in groups and plan a lesson to address a specific instructional problem the instructor gives you. Then each group could implement the lesson and see the different ways that the lesson could be taught and the different ways that groups viewed the content, students, and choice of teaching strategy.

DESIGN ACTIVITY 5

Design a Lesson

Task Rationale

The purpose of this Design Activity is to reveal what you know about instructional design by using a task familiar to teachers. This activity is designed to prompt you to think about the issues in designing instructional activities, as well as see the influence your beliefs play in these features.

Task Guidelines

1. Identify a *short activity or lesson* that you are familiar with.
2. Describe the *learners* for this lesson and the goal of the instruction.
3. Outline or sketch the major *features* of this instructional activity in whatever format or detail you need to actually teach the lesson.
4. Teach the lesson. Brief your peers on who they are as students and then take ten minutes to implement the lesson.

Reflectivity

- What experience have you had in teaching this lesson?
- What did you learn from teaching this lesson to your peers and hearing their feedback?
- What categories of information made up your lesson plan?
- Did your lesson plan decisions match your views of teaching, as examined in Chapter 1?

PLANNING

Planning by experienced teachers

Planning is an important activity for teachers that serves many functions. The predominant function of planning is to transform school curriculum to classroom instruction. School curriculum can be based on school district traditions or on new initiatives determined by teachers or school district administration or mandated by the state. More recently, school curriculums are expected to demonstrate that students know particular knowledge or skills, as outlined by state and national standards. Curriculum design influences are addressed in Chapter 9.

The scope of teacher planning depends on several factors. Lesson plans are usually devoted to daily activities, although a lesson plan may span several days. Lesson plans may include teacher- or student-led activities as well as learning objectives, procedures, materials and technology needed, time requirements, areas for enrichment or reteaching, and assessment. Unit plans, meanwhile, connect related lesson plans and feature a broader scope of learning outcomes.

Experienced teachers tend to concentrate on units and decisions related to activities (Clark & Yinger, 1979). Planning appears to work best for experienced teachers when it serves as a flexible framework for their teaching rather than as a rigid script (Clark, 1983). Lesson planning remains the predominant concern of student teachers (Griffin, Hughes, Barnes, Defino, Edwards, Hukill, & O'Neal, 1982).

Teachers' lesson plans can be detailed and written out because of a teacher's desire to be organized or to reduce anxiety and uncertainty. In some schools, written lesson plans are required. Schools may emphasize curriculum materials, such as a newly adopted commercially designed system, activity sheets, textbooks and supporting materials, and physical manipulatives. Plans can take the form of written details, lists, or outlines. For many teachers, nothing is written out at all. Instead, experienced teachers possess a visual or mental sense of the flow of lessons (Morine-Dershimer, 1979). The activity flow or sequence of instruction in a unit will be discussed in Chapter 8.

Cycles of planning

Teacher planning is conducted at different cycles (Yinger, 1980) (Figure 2.2). The first cycle involves the *school year*. Developing lessons and units will be easier if they reflect goals for the school year. The school calendar can be used to identify time for teaching units within the school year. Holidays, teacher working days, grading deadlines, and other dates should be considered. Increasingly, planning for the school year involves matching the content of textbooks to state standards.

A second cycle involves a school's *grading cycle*. Decisions may include a reasonable set of lessons and student activities to provide sufficient information for grading decisions. Time management and a process for recording grades become significant decisions for a new teacher. For teacher candidates, the teacher who will be supervising their teaching, known as the cooperating teacher, can suggest an initial strategy.

A third cycle involves *unit plan development*, the topic of Chapter 8. Units support overall learning goals for the school year, which were addressed in the first cycle of planning. The exact number of lessons for a unit depends on how teaching activity is organized over time to address the goals of lessons and units.

FIGURE 2.2.
Cycles of
Teacher Planning.

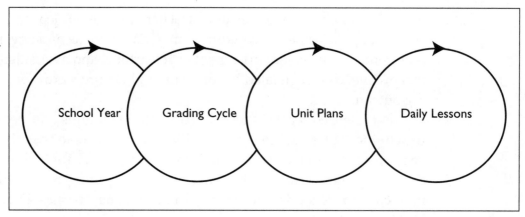

The fourth cycle of planning involves *lessons*, which are covered in Chapters 4 through 7. Working through the next Design Activity, you are likely to discover that daily planning for some teachers consists of filling in a small box in a planning booklet. Beginning teachers spend a lot of time writing lesson plans until they learn more about students and activity management and develop confidence in their teaching.

To see the individual ways teachers plan, complete the following Design Activity and share the results with others.

How Teachers Plan

Task Rationale   Discover the different ways that new and experienced teachers plan.

Task Guidelines for Teacher Candidates

1. Observe your cooperating teacher and take notes of what your teacher does.
2. Schedule a time to talk with your teacher about the lesson that was taught.
3. Write about how your cooperating teacher plans for the school year and across the grading cycle.
4. To what extent does your cooperating teacher use units?
5. With the teacher's permission, make copies of whatever lesson planning materials your teacher uses.
6. Discuss lesson planning procedures the cooperating teacher uses and what you might adopt for your planning habits.

Task Guidelines for Teachers

1. Summarize how you plan for the school year and for daily teaching.
2. Describe the different ways that fellow teachers plan.
3. Are there unique planning strategies that work for you?

Task Guidelines for In-Class Discussion

1. Share examples of teacher planning documents and summarize the differences.
2. What experiences have you had with lesson planning, and what formats have you used?

Reflectivity
- What did you learn about your planning approach?
- How different is your planning from that of your cooperating teacher or your peers?
- What planning habits would you like to develop?

Planning by new teachers

New teachers plan differently from expert teachers. Generally, new teachers spend more time thinking and writing down their lesson plans. The details help new teachers cope with the demands of daily teaching. Once a sense of control develops, new teachers begin to reflect on teaching and what they learned in their teacher education programs, such as having a classroom management plan, transitions between lessons, and pacing activities (Bullough, 1989). Initially, new teachers are more concerned with student behavior than with learning outcomes. The focus for learning in new teachers' lessons is generally recorded as student activity, without a clear statement of what students will learn. New teachers also search for existing activities and strategies to hold students' attention. Their initial view of what constitutes a learning outcome, a teaching strategy, and an assessment tool is unclear.

Benefits of planning

Planning brings numerous benefits, despite the differences in how this planning is written down. Whether it's detailed plans or mental notes, planning provides some of the following benefits for teachers:

- *Provides* reference for activity procedures, materials needed, and alternative activities.
- *Off-loads* teaching decisions to a written plan, allowing concentration on implementation and student performance.
- *Documents* your teaching in terms of state standards, school policies, and national certification.
- *Stores* details for future teaching.
- *Shares* details with other teachers.
- *Gives* you confidence during your teaching day.

Downsides of planning

The benefits of planning far outweigh the downsides, as summarized in Figure 2.3.

Responses to Criticisms of Planning	
Downside of planning	Response to criticism
Planning habits need to be learned and take time	Develop organizing skills and confidence Takes time to become a skilled teacher
Plans cannot always be used	Identify options Develop teacher thinking while teaching Develop improvisational skills
Written plans require time	Documents teaching Shares lessons with others Demonstrates that student learning results from one's teaching
Other teachers do not plan	Planning should be based on individual needs Planning contributes to being prepared

FIGURE 2.3. Criticisms of Teacher Planning and Responses.

Qualities of a good lesson plan

The qualities of a good lesson plan include the following:

- *Reflects* goals for the school year.
- *Records* daily detail for teaching.
- *Indicates* a focus for learning, rather than a statement of student activity.
- *Specifies* learning objectives, or what students will learn.
- *Clarifies* how student learning will be assessed.
- *Identifies* teaching strategies used and the rationale for key materials (e.g., books).
- *Organizes* teaching and student activity in terms of introduction, review, new material, activity-practice, closure, or assignments.
- *Lists* procedures to follow.
- *Estimates* time for each instructional and student activity.
- *Suggests* implementation and alternative procedures.
- *Reflects* on implementation and adjustments for future teaching.

INSTRUCTIONAL DESIGN

What is design?

Herbert Simon (1996), a Nobel Prize winner in economics and one of the founders of cognitive science, regarded design as a problem-solving process, which is "aimed at changing existing solutions into preferred ones" (p. 111). The goal of design, according to Simon, is to achieve the best possible solution with the information available. Design, then, is a human activity, which develops responses to changing human needs.

Gordon Rowland, who has written about creative possibilities as an instructional designer, shares this pragmatic view. A design process, according to Rowland (1993), helps to create a solution but also helps to better understand the problem itself, so that a proposed solution is more informed than a first impression. A design process guides us to rethink or reframe the problem (see Schön, 1987). This reframing helps us see the problem in a new light, view the different perspectives of others, and better understand the complex nature of what appears to be a simple problem (Figure 2.4).

Because design is about addressing human needs, any design activity benefits from social interaction (Rowland, 1993). A possible design solution may result from solo thinking, but inviting other people to consider, propose, feed back, and evaluate may improve on the "existing situation." Although the solo designer may reflect on the options, essentially having a dialogue or conversation with oneself, this reflection is carried out within a context of human wants and needs.

FIGURE 2.4.
Purposes for
Design.

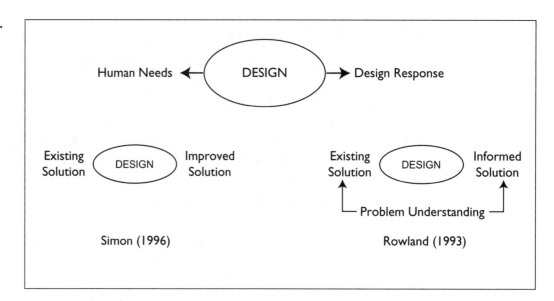

Design is also a professional activity and can be taught; otherwise, this would be a short book. Like any other professional activity, design knowledge and experience require time to develop. Any form of design work can quickly become complicated, thus the need for a process to guide us.

Christopher Clark (1995) makes the case that teachers *are* designers. Clark describes the professional teacher "as a complex individual doing very complicated work in a sometimes stressful, sometimes rewarding, always uncertain and dynamic variety of settings" (p. 124). Teachers are active, ready to learn, wise and knowledgeable, diverse and unique. Thus, the professional development of teachers, according to Clark, should be a matter for teachers themselves to design. "To carry off the concept of self-directed professional development, we, as teachers, must begin to think of ourselves as designers. We must design ourselves, and continue to revise, redesign and learn from experience" (p. 125).

So far, we have built up the following attributes for design as a human endeavor, as summarized in Figure 2.5.

Given these attributes, what exactly is instructional design? How is an instructional design process different from a planning process? These topics are addressed next.

FIGURE 2.5.
Attributes of
Design.

Attributes of Design
• Design is a pragmatic (and enjoyable) activity.
• Design processes aid us in reaching a solution through a better understanding of the problem.
• Design processes invite human involvement.
• Design processes are teachable.
• Teachers are designers.

What is our definition of instructional design?

As with teaching, there is no one agreed-on definition of instructional design. How you view ID can be seen in what you design, so all instructional designers have an internal, tacit, perhaps "fuzzy" view of ID that guides them. Nevertheless, definitions provide us with a starting point to clarify what we mean by instructional design. Here is our definition of instructional design.

Instructional Design	"An intellectual process to help teachers systematically analyze learner needs and construct structured 'possibilities' to responsively address those needs." *(Shambaugh & Magliaro, 1997)*

Several important ideas comprise our definition. Next, we unpack this definition to suggest how our view of ID might assist your teaching.

Intellectual process

The use of "intellectual process" in our definition acknowledges the skills and experiences of teachers. ID can be regarded as a form of intellectual problem solving that uses the same forms of critical thinking, decision making, flexibility, intuition, and access to tools found in other fields (Nelson, Magliaro, & Sherman, 1988). We have learned from teachers that instructional problems are better characterized as instructional challenges associated with student needs. The types of instructional challenges found in classrooms are inherently complex; they involve interconnected issues of school culture, societal expectations, and local views of what should be taught and how this content should be taught. Reflectivity is a unique aspect of teachers' intellectual thinking that requires them to continually appraise and adjust their teaching decisions.

Systematic

The word *systematic* is a characterizing feature of instructional design and the source for much of its power. What we mean by *systematic* is an orderly, regular, and uniform activity. Systematicity is provided in two ways. First, the development of instruction is broken down into distinct phases of activity so that we can look at the educational issues addressed in each phase. Although we will look at four variations of the ID process later in this chapter, the major phases of ID activity are "determining what is needed," "developing a designed response," "trying out the response," and "evaluating the results" (Figure 2.6). Being systematic also helps teachers document their practice with structure and regularity.

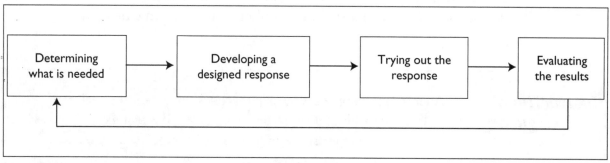

FIGURE 2.6. Instructional Design as a Linear Systematic Process.

A second feature of systematicity is to interconnect these activity phases, so that what we learn in one phase informs decisions to be made in the next phase. Although overly simplistic, this linear sequence between components can become a cycle if one repeats the process. Many ID processes are represented in models similar to Figure 2.6 but vary in their details. For example, some ID models identify some interconnections that occur simultaneously, and a change in one connection may require a change in another location on the model.

Analyze learner needs

The word *analyze* suggests breaking down, classifying, and dissecting. Instructional design provides a set of tools to determine the needs of the learner. These needs are not as simple as "what students do not know." Learning needs may involve developmental issues, which include physical, psychological, and social needs. In addition, understanding the needs of your students requires a sense of the school culture, as well as the specific classroom environment and dynamics.

Construct structured possibilities

The analysis component of instructional design prompts us to look at new teaching strategies, assessment approaches, or instructional technology opportunities. "Structured possibilities" means making informed decisions based on this new knowledge and understanding, but in ways that keep learning in the forefront of teaching decisions.

Responsively address student needs

Responsiveness to student needs is an important criterion for successful instructional design. Instructional design, with its systematic features, prompts the designer or teacher to be clear and specific about student needs and learning outcomes. With this clarity of purpose, we can make more informed choices as to how these needs and outcomes can be met, tried out, and evaluated.

What are other definitions of instructional design?

Other textbook writers have defined instructional design. Here is a definition by Smith and Ragan (1993) in their first edition of *Instructional Design*.

Instructional Design	"The systematic process of translating principles of learning and instruction into plans for instructional materials and activities." *(Smith & Ragan, 1993, p. 2)*

Note the use again of "systematic process." The major attribute of this definition is the use of learning principles as the basis for learning activities. Learning principles are derived from educational psychologists' research over many years. Learning principles provide an informed foundation for the design of instruction, rather than relying on folk theory alone. Now see how Smith and Ragan's definition changed in their second edition of *Instructional Design*.

Instructional Design	"The systematic and reflective process of translating principles of learning and instruction into plans for instructional materials and activities, information resources, and evaluation." *(Smith & Ragan, 1999, p. 2)*

Note the use of "systematic and reflective process." Reflectivity is not usually addressed in ID models. We believe that instructional design is a deliberate form of reflectivity and can incorporate personalized forms of teacher reflection as ongoing information to the instructional development process. The "reflective" nature of instructional design, as suggested by Smith and Ragan (1999), is an overarching concern of ours in this text, as teacher reflection is a major aspect of teacher education programs (Valli, 1992). The notion that "teachers should be reflective practitioners" is one of the Interstate New Teacher Assessment and Support Consortium (INTASC) core standards for licensing teachers (CCSSO, 1992). "If change is to occur, reflective thinking must become a taken-for-granted lens through which preservice teachers conceptualize their practice" (Ross & Hannay, 1986). Here is another definition of ID:

Instructional Design	"A systematic thinking process to help learners learn." *(Zook, 2001, p. 20)*

The thinking behind this definition will help us understand what ID is about. Zook (2001), who also believes that teachers are designers (calling them design-teachers), uses three familiar questions (Mager, 1984) associated with taking a vacation to characterize the ID process: Where are we going? What will we do when we get there? How will we get there? Relating these questions to instructional design, we can see that the concerns for trips match the concerns of teachers.

Trip Concerns	Teacher Concerns
Where are we going?	Learning outcomes
What will we do when we get there?	Learning assessment
How will we get there?	Learning activities

Planning for a trip can be a complicated undertaking, depending on the complexity of the trip. There are many decisions to make, and one decision is likely to affect the others. If you have not planned a trip before, then the task is doubly hard. This book was written to help you sort out the important issues of making decisions on lesson and unit development.

Teachers' perceptions of instructional design

Compared with individualistic approaches to planning lessons and units, instructional design supports teacher decisions organized around phases of activity, generally labeled as analysis, design and development, implementation, and evaluation (see Figure 2.6). How have teachers fared by using ID? Martin and Clemente (1990) summarized teachers' perceptions of instructional design as follows:

- Teachers believe that they, not instructional materials, are instrumental in student learning. Teachers prefer teaching approaches that maintain their high influence on student achievement and relationships with students.
- Planning may include objectives, but not always.

- Planning and ID are time consuming and may not be worth the investment, particularly if some goals valued by the teacher are not addressed in the plans.
- Assumptions underlying ID, such as systems theory, behavioral theory, information-processing views of cognition, and the use of technology, may not match teachers' theories and beliefs.

The promise behind ID is that if the design guidelines are followed, then learning outcomes will result. In the training field, where certain outcomes must be achieved, ID has achieved its greatest success. As we have discussed, ID models are problem-solving approaches that address an instructional problem. However, some aspects of teaching may not be viewed by teachers as ordered or rational, such as the unpredictability of learning activities and student behavior during classroom teaching. All possible events in the classroom cannot be covered by an instructional design. As Martin and Clemente (1990) observed, some teachers perceive instructional design as an overly prescriptive process that counters their reliance on improvisation to adjust to changing conditions.

Another example of the rational emphasis of ID is the use of *learning objectives*. Such a behavioral focus may be at odds with some teachers' beliefs that learning outcomes cannot be fully specified in behavioral terms. Some of these learning outcomes are discussed in Chapter 3 as dimensions of learning, including creativity, moral development, and social learning. Rather than formal design, where all the outcomes and options are specified, emergent design may appeal more to teachers, as they react to continual changes in the learning setting (see Senge, Kleiner, Roberts, Ross, Roth, & Smith, 1999). However, with increased accountability for student learning, being clear about learning outcomes will help teachers adjust to changing classroom conditions while supporting learning for all students.

Benefits of instructional design

Do these benefits of instructional design appear useful to you as a teacher?

- *Pragmatic* tool to systematically help you develop and reflect on lesson and unit development. Reduces anxiety.
- *Responsive* tool to help you to address issues of learning outcomes, learners, content, teaching options (and the use of technology), and learning context and to overall keep learning in the forefront of your thinking and actions.

- *Research* tool to help you learn about students, teaching, and assessment options.
- *Accountability* tool for teacher reflectivity and self-study of your teaching. Supports the INTASC standards for beginning teachers.

To summarize, instructional design provides a tool to help teachers make responsive teaching decisions, ones that keep learning as the primary focus.

Responses to instructional design for teachers

As with planning, there are downsides and criticisms by teachers using instructional design. In Figure 2.7, we summarize some of these objections and responses.

FIGURE 2.7. Criticisms of Instructional Design and Responses.

Responses to Criticisms of Instructional Design	
Downside of ID for Teachers	**Response to Criticism**
Takes too much time for all lessons	Pre-lesson thinking raises awareness about issues of content, students, and context (see Section III)
Does not take into account realities of classrooms	Any process cannot account for all possibilities
My teaching is successful now	Teaching requires ongoing examination, reflection, and adjustments
I don't like objectives	One must be clear on what students are to learn; teachers are being held accountable to state learning standards

Qualities of a good instructional design

- *Keeps learning* in the forefront of teaching decisions
- *Reflects goals* for the school year
- *Prompts teacher decisions* within lessons, units, and curriculum about the content to be taught and learned, the learners, teaching and assessment options, and the reality of the setting
- *Records on paper* your thinking and decisions at the unit and curriculum level, so that these decisions can guide you in planning lessons, units, and curriculum in line with your goals and the goals of the school
- *Achieves an alignment* between learning, teaching approaches, and assessment
- *Ensures that technology use* supports student learning
- *Documents and evaluates teaching* by using the ID plan as a guide in terms of overall curriculum and unit goals and what students learn

Summary of differences between planning and ID

Figure 2.8 summarizes differences between teacher planning and instructional designing. The basis for any activity must support student learning. Clear written statements of learning outcomes for units can be supplemented with supporting learning objectives in lessons. A clear focus for student learning enables clear decisions on student activity. Initially, lessons need to be written out in detail. Over time, lesson plans become shorter and personalized.

FIGURE 2.8.
Differences Between Planning and Instructional Designing.

	Planning	Instructional Designing
Focus	Content, activities, state standards	Goals and objectives
Format	Mental, minimal	Written, detailed
Basis	Teaching practice	Learning principles, theory based
Process	Personal	Systematic
Novice	Lessons, student behavior	ID component procedures
Expert	Units, flexible frameworks	Nonlinear, context-specific

Figure 2.9 summarizes how ID can be used to help new teachers become better teachers.

FIGURE 2.9.
Summary of Benefits of ID for Teachers.

	How ID Can Help Teachers
Focus	Learning focus for teacher and student activities supported by specific objectives that specify what students will learn; improved clarity on teaching and assessment choices
Format	Initially, written detail, then less detail over time and with experience
Basis	Develop frameworks of teaching based on personal experience, teacher inquiry and improvement, and learning principles (theory based)
Process	Personalized approaches that evolve over time
Novice	Lessons, student behavior
Expert	Units, flexible frameworks, wider views on assessment, increased repertoire of teaching strategies

INSTRUCTIONAL DESIGN MODELS

ID Models for teachers

One ID model may be more suitable for teaching design, and another model may work better for firms developing a product (see Branch & Gustafson, 2002). We provide four examples of ID models for teachers.

Reiser and Dick systematic planning model

Reiser and Dick (1996) proposed a model with seven steps that lead from one to another (see Figure 2.10). In this model, goals are known up front, and there is no analysis step to determine the instructional goals. Goals provide overall direction for teachers. Objectives are specific student learning outcomes, several of which might support a goal. Objectives are typically specified in individual lessons.

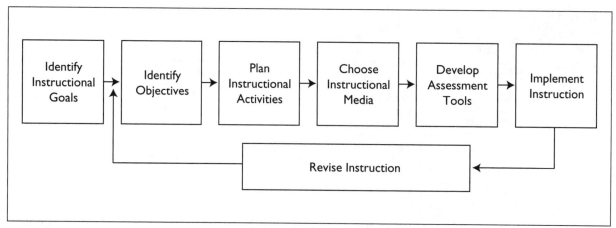

FIGURE 2.10. Reiser and Dick Systematic Planning Model (1996).

From Robert A. Reiser and Walter Dick, *Instructional Planning: A Guide for Teachers*, 2e. Published by Allyn and Bacon, Boston, MA, Copyright © 1996 by Pearson Education, reprint by permission of the publisher.

The model does not provide a step for selecting a teaching strategy, as a variety of teaching approaches could be used. At first, a model such as this will require some time and experience to use, despite its simplicity. However, this ID model helps to keep learning in the forefront of choices, activities, and revisions.

Zook's systems model

Another variation of the systematic model is from Zook (2001). Note the similarities with the Reiser and Dick model. An important difference is that Zook identifies an explicit activity related to content, namely, "identify and analyze content" (Figure 2.11). In addition, this activity is conducted in tandem with determining teaching goals. Another difference that matches the decision-making approach used in this text is that assessment procedures are determined prior to choosing teaching strategies. An important addition in the Zook model is an explicit "diagnosis of learner difficulties." Note also the location of the feedback loop.

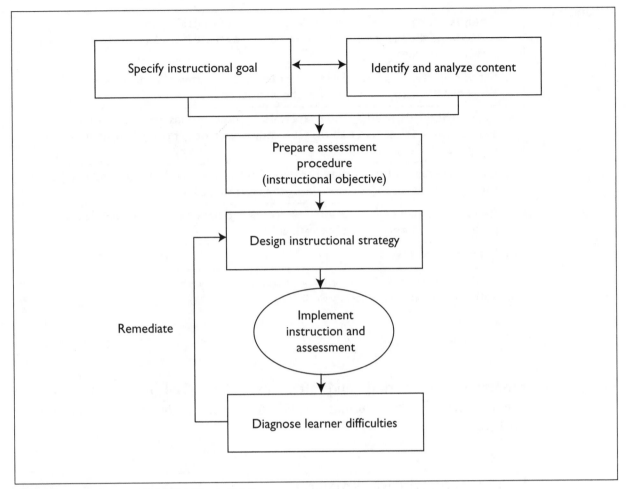

FIGURE 2.11. Systems ID Model (Zook, 2001).

Zook, Kevin, B., *Instructional Design for Classroom Teaching and Learning.* © 2001 by Houghton Mifflin Company. Used with permission.

ASSURE media development model

The ASSURE model selects and implements instructional technology and media within learning activities (Smaldino, Russell, Heinich, & Molenda, 2005). This model assumes that instructional issues inherent to the use of the media materials, such as needs assessment, task analysis, and assessment of learning, have been addressed. The six stages of the ASSURE media development model denote a linear, input–output nature, with decisions made in the first stage contributing to decisions for succeeding stages (Figure 2.12).

The model specifies evaluation in terms of learner achievement, evaluation of media materials and methods, and evaluation of the entire instructional

FIGURE 2.12.
ASSURE Model
(2005).

1. **Analyze learners**.   Conduct analysis in terms of general characteristics of the learners and the specific competencies needed by these individuals, such as knowledge, skills, and attitudes.
2. **State objectives**.   State the learning objectives in terms of what the learner will know or be able to do as a result of the instruction.
3. **Select methods, media, and materials**.   Three options exist to bridge learners and objectives: select materials that currently exist, modify materials in some way, or design new materials.
4. **Utilize media and materials**.   Plan how the materials will be used, gathering the necessary materials together, and using them in instruction.
5. **Require learner participation**.   Activities and time are required for adequate practice and reinforcement of performance.
6. **Evaluate and revise**.

Instructional Technology and Media for Learning, 8/e, by Smaldino, Russell, Heinich, & Molenda, © 2005. Adapted by permission of Pearson Education, Inc., Upper Saddle River, NJ.

process before, during, and after instruction. The model is useful to teachers who need systematic guidance to make technology and media decisions.

ID as teacher decision making

Our approach to ID for teachers is a systematic decision-making process (Figure 2.13). The up-front needs-assessment component we call "Learning About Your Classroom" (Chapter 3), which prompts you to learn (i.e., analyze) about your content, students, and context of teaching. The Teacher Decision Cycle asks four questions during the design of lessons and units. The next phase of teacher decisions is to develop instructional materials, usually either through purchase, adaptation, or custom development. The implementation of teacher decisions occurs, of course, in the actual teaching, where adjustments are made and possibly action research is conducted. An end component, "Professional Development," addresses how you want to improve as a teacher.

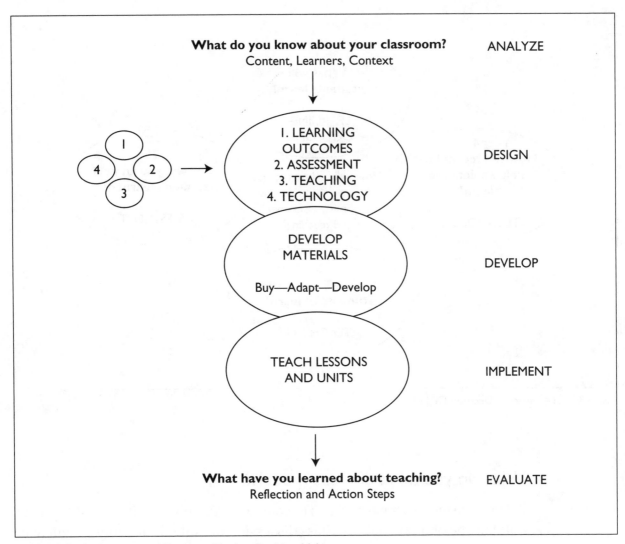

FIGURE 2.13. Instructional Design as Teacher Decision Making.

Figure 2.14 breaks out the design component, what we label as the Teacher Decision Cycle, in terms of four questions:

- What will students learn?
- How do you know if students learned?
- How will you assist students to learn?
- How might media and technology support student learning?

The technology question is ultimately a teaching decision, but we give it added emphasis in this book. In addition to enabling new forms of teaching, technology provides an overarching benefit, namely, how the use of technology provides a rethinking of decisions in questions 1 through 4.

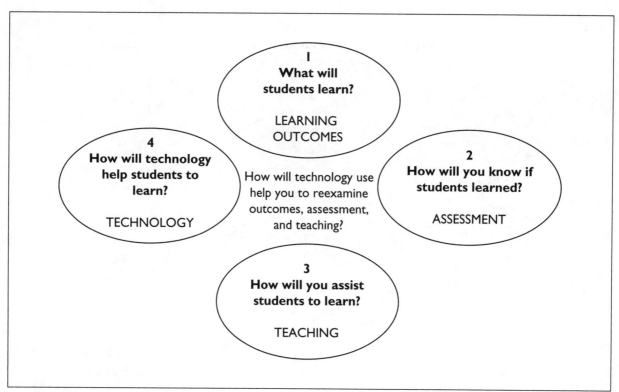

FIGURE 2.14. Teacher Decision Cycle.

What do you think of these models?

All of these models have merits. The following Design Activity prompts you to critique one of these models. Class discussion of individual critiques will help you to see the differences, downsides, and attributes of each, as well as the different ways that your peers view these models.

DESIGN ACTIVITY 7

Critique an ID Model

Task Rationale   This task asks you to critique one of the ID models for teachers in order to judge to what degree the model might be useful to you.

Task Guidelines
1. Choose one of the models in the chapter.
2. What attracted you to the model?
3. List the attributes of the model and its limitations.
4. Would you use this model for planning your lessons or units? How would you improve it?
5. What essential features should an ID model for teachers include?

Reflectivity
- Describe the thinking you did in critiquing this model.
- Do any of these models support your views of teaching that you wrote about in your mission statement?

Recapping Section I: Making Connections

- Section I focused on building connections. Chapter 1 viewed the historical evolution of learning theories, views of teaching, and views of the teacher. You can still find educators, parents, or politicians who subscribe to each of the views discussed in this chapter.
- Chapter 2 contrasted the differences between planning and instructional design. Although planning occurs through different cycles from school year to daily lessons, planning typically involves daily teaching details. Instructional design, meanwhile, looks at a bigger picture and helps the teacher think about content, students, teaching, assessment, and technology decisions. We examined four different ID models to help teachers think more systematically about their teaching. We contributed our own representation of ID for teachers, one that involves a continual cycle of teacher decisions.

Common wisdom suggests that one walks before one can fly. According to Rowland, Fixl, and Yung (1992), designing instruction is not about learning to walk but about learning to fly. It does no good if we "coax you to the edge and then push you over" without sufficient preparation. One virtue to "flying" is that you envision possibilities. We have already begun "learning to fly" in the first two chapters by examining your beliefs about teaching and learning and by making the case that instructional design will help you become a better teacher.

Reflective Teaching

"But It's Called a Planning Period, Not an Instructional Design Period!"

Using instructional design in place of traditional planning may seem to be a radical shift in the teaching paradigm. After all, teachers have a planning period, not an instructional design period, right? Beginning teachers may look at instructional design as an overwhelming task. How are they supposed to worry about the goals for the entire year when it is so difficult to get through one day? The veteran teacher may view instructional design as an overwhelming waste of time. Veteran teachers have been writing tried-and-true lesson plans for years. What is this "new and improved" method for instructional planning being thrown at them now? Even though both beginning and veteran teachers may approach instructional design with apprehension, once they embrace it, they may soon discover the benefits that instructional design has to offer. By using a systematic process that forces learning to remain at the forefront of all teaching decisions, teachers might find choosing appropriate assessments, incorporating technology, and self-reflecting to be easier tasks, based on the instructional design model they have chosen to follow or develop themselves.

Teacher Inquiry

- A research focus could study the differences in teacher planning between you and your peer. In such a study, you could analyze the differences in how one plans, teaches, and makes adjustments improves teaching.
- Another possibility is for experienced teachers to develop a mentoring system for new teachers and study its implementation over time.

REFERENCES

Branch, R. M., & Gustafson, K. L. (2002). *Survey of instructional development models* (4th ed.). Syracuse, NY: ERIC Clearinghouse on Information Resources. (ERIC Document Reproduction Service No. ED477517)

Bullough, R. V., Jr. (1989). *First-year teacher: A case study.* New York: Teachers College Press.

Council of Chief State School Officers (CCSSO). (1992). *Model standards for beginning teacher licensing, assessment and development: A resource for state dialogue.* Washington, DC: Author. www.ccsso.org/content/pdfs/corestrd.pdf

Clark, C. M. (1983). Research on teacher planning: An inventory of the knowledge base. In D. C. Smith (Ed.), *Essential knowledge for beginning educators* (pp. 5–15). Washington, DC: American Association of Colleges for Teacher Education.

Clark, C. M. (1995). *Thoughtful teaching.* New York: Teachers' College Press.

Clark, C. M., & Yinger, R. J. (1979). *Three studies of teacher planning* (Research Series No. 55). East Lansing: Michigan State University, Institute for Research on Teaching. (ERIC Document Reproduction Service. No. ED 175855)

Griffin, G., Hughes, R., Jr., Barnes, S., Defino, M., Edwards, S., Hukill, H., & O'Neal, S. (1982). *Changing teacher practice: Research design for an experimental study.* Austin: University of Texas at Austin, Research and Development Center for Teacher Education.

Mager, R. F. (1984). *Preparing instructional objectives* (2nd ed.). Belmont, CA: Fearon.

Martin, B. L., & Clemente, R. (1990). Instructional systems design and public schools. *Educational Technology Research & Development, 38*(2), 61–75.

Morine-Dershimer, G. (1979). *Teacher plan and classroom reality: The South Bay study, Part IV* (Research Series No. 60). East Lansing: Michigan State University Institute for Research on Teaching. (ERIC Document Reproduction Service No. ED191796)

Nelson, W. A., Magliaro, S. G., & Sherman, T. M. (1988). The intellectual content of instructional design. *Journal of Instructional Development, 11*(1), 29–35.

Reiser, R. A., & Dick, W. (1996). *Instructional planning: A guide for teachers* (2nd ed.). Boston: Allyn and Bacon.

Ross, E. W., & Hannay, L. M. (1992). Towards a critical theory of reflective inquiry. *Journal of Teacher Education, 37,* 9–15.

Rowland, G. (1993). Designing and instructional design. *Educational Technology Research & Development, 41*(1), 79–91.

Rowland, G., Fixl, A., & Yung, K. (1992, December). Educating the reflecting designer. *Educational Technology,* 36–44.

Schön, D. A. (1987). *Educating the reflective practitioner: Toward a new design for teaching and learning in the professions.* San Francisco: Jossey-Bass.

Senge, P., Kleiner, A., Roberts, C., Ross, R., Roth, G., & Smith, B. (1999). *The dance of change: The challenge of sustaining momentum in learning organizations.* New York: Currency Doubleday.

Shambaugh, R. N., & Magliaro, S. G. (1997). *Mastering the possibilities: A process approach to instructional design.* Boston: Allyn and Bacon.

Simon, H. A. (1996). *The sciences of the artificial* (3rd ed.). Cambridge, MA: MIT Press.

Smaldino, S. E., Russell, J. D., Heinich, R., & Molenda, M. (2005). *Instructional technology and media for learning* (8th ed.). Upper Saddle River, NJ: Merrill-Prentice-Hall.

Smith, P. L., & Ragan, T. J. (1993). *Instructional design.* New York: Merrill.

Smith, P. L., & Ragan, T. J. (1999). *Instructional design* (2nd ed.). Upper Saddle River, NJ: Merrill.

Valli, L. (1992). (Ed.). *Reflective teacher education: Cases and critiques.* Albany, NY: State University of New York Press.

Yinger, R. (1980). A study of teacher planning. *Elementary School Journal, 80,* 107–127.

Zook, K. (2001). *Instructional design for classroom teaching and learning.* Boston: Houghton Mifflin.

RESOURCES

Print Resources

Edmonds, G. S., Branch, R. C., & Mukherjee, P. (1994). A conceptual framework for comparing instructional design models. *Educational Technology Research & Development, 42*(4), 55–72.

> Organizing ID models by their function.

Klein, J. D., Spector, J. M., Grabowski, B., & de la Teja, I. (2004). *Instructor competencies: Standards for face-to-face, online & blended settings* (rev. 3rd ed.). Greenwich, CT: Information Age Publishing.

> Published in cooperation with the Association for Educational Communications & Technology (AECT) and the International Board of Standards for Training, Performance and Instruction (ISTE). This text is designed for those educators who might be thinking of working in the fields of training and development, human resource development, performance technology, and workplace learning and performance.

Web-Based Resources

Instructional Designer Competencies

Accrediation Standards for Programs in Educational Communications and Instructional Technology (ECIT).

> www.aect-members.org/standards/

AECT/NCATE. (1999). *Revised accreditation guidelines.*

> International Board of Standards for Training, Performance, and Instruction. (1999). 1998 instructional design competencies.
>
> www.ibstpi.org/

Instructional Design Models

Numerous links to ID models and learning theories.

> http://carbon.cudenver.edu/~mryder/itc_data/idmodels.html

SECTION II

Understanding Your Classroom

3 Content, Learners, and Context

Main Idea of This Chapter
The informed teacher is better prepared to help students learn.

INTASC Standards Addressed in This Chapter

Principle 3 LEARNER DIFFERENCES: The teacher understands how students differ in their approaches to learning and creates instructional opportunities that are adapted to diverse learners.

Principle 7 PRE-UNIT THINKING: The teacher plans instruction based on knowledge of subject matter, students, the community, and curriculum goals.

Focus Questions

- What do you know about the full range of content to be learned?
- How has the content been previously taught?
- What are the teaching possibilities for this content?
- How could media and technology help students learn?
- Who are your learners?
- What is the reality of the learning setting?

Design Activities

DA 8: Thinking About Content
DA 9: Learner Profile
DA 10: Context of the Learning Environment
DA 11: Pre-Lesson Thinking

WHERE ARE WE IN THE ID PROCESS?

This chapter addresses the analysis component of Instructional Design, which is sometimes referred to as needs assessment (Figure 3.1). The purpose of needs assessment within the ID process is to learn more about students' instructional needs. In this book, we characterize needs assessment as a means to learn more about your classroom.

FIGURE 3.1.
Instructional Design as Teacher Decision Making.

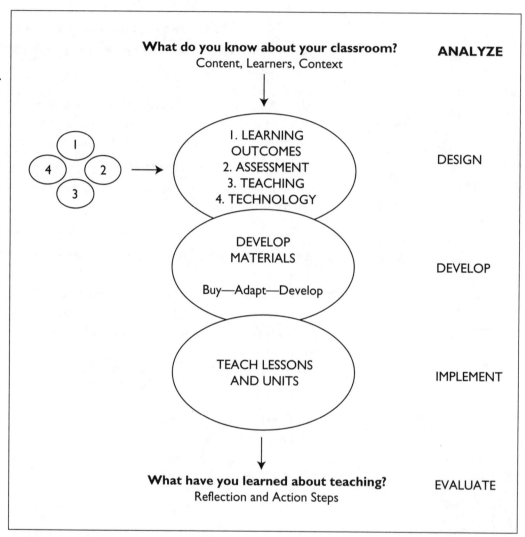

What do you know about your classroom?
Content, Learners, Context

ANALYZE

1. LEARNING OUTCOMES
2. ASSESSMENT
3. TEACHING
4. TECHNOLOGY

DESIGN

DEVELOP MATERIALS

Buy—Adapt—Develop

DEVELOP

TEACH LESSONS AND UNITS

IMPLEMENT

What have you learned about teaching?
Reflection and Action Steps

EVALUATE

WHAT THIS CHAPTER IS ABOUT

We characterize needs assessment as a means to learn more about your classroom in three ways:

- Identify the full range of *content* to be learned by your students.
- Learn more about your *students*.
- Increase awareness of the *context* of the classroom setting.

The topic sequence for this chapter is visualized in Figure 3.2.

FIGURE 3.2.
Visual Organizer
for Chapter 3.

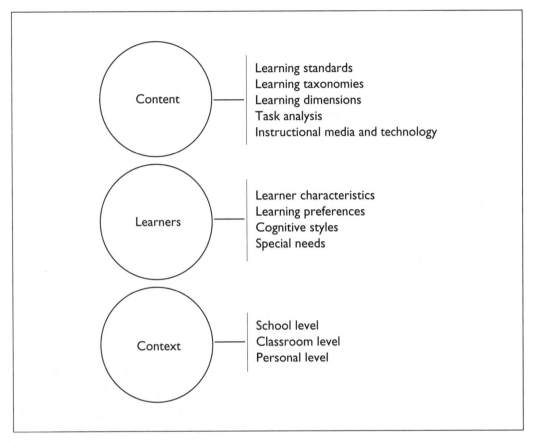

WHAT "CONTENT" IS TO BE LEARNED?

The word *content* is placed within quotes here to signal the full range of content to be learned in lessons, units, and curriculum. Learning frequently involves more than just subject matter learning. Many professional organizations specify what students should know in their respective content areas. In addition, states prescribe learning standards. Translating these requirements into instruction poses a daily challenge to teachers. Individual schools or school districts may concentrate on specific learning goals for the school year to address deficiencies in students' performance on statewide tests. Individual teachers or groups of teachers may implement integrated lessons and units, in which a broad range of learning outcomes is addressed.

To understand the full range of "content" to be learned we provide five ways to view it: learning standards, learning taxonomies, learning dimensions, task analysis, and media and technology (Figure 3.3).

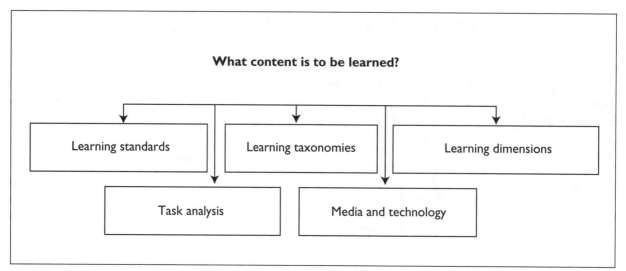

FIGURE 3.3. Five Ways to View "Content."

Learning standards

Professional organizations have developed learning outcomes in content areas such as science, mathematics, social studies, art, writing, reading, and physical education. Chapter 9 looks at several of these areas.

Many professional organizations have reexamined expectations for learning in terms of literacy. In the case of science, the issue becomes "What does it mean for a K–4 student to be literate in science?" Professional science organizations have developed standards that characterize science as inquiry or actual investigation. The way to learn science is to actively participate in scientific practices and to learn facts, concepts, and theories through focused discovery. The nature of the "content" is developing scientific expertise in students and giving them opportunities to experience what the community of scientists actually does. This is an example of teaching through the use of "authentic" activities and through an apprenticeship in terms of thinking like a scientist.

Both traditional subject learning and broader views of learning may be accounted for within these content-area standards. For example, National Science Education Standards for grades 5 through 8 have been developed by the National Research Council (1996). These content standards are organized around the following categories: unifying concepts and processes, science as inquiry, physical science, life science, earth and space science, science and technology, science in personal and social perspectives, and history and nature of science. Social learning and affective learning are not addressed in these standards, although in the category of science as inquiry, the "abilities necessary to do scientific inquiry" suggests that social behavior and affective skills would be useful to participate in the community of scientists.

Another example of supplementary learning in science for both grades K through 4 and 5 through 8 addresses the "abilities of technological design." The science standards recommend that students learn five abilities in order to design solutions to problems: identifying appropriate problems, designing a solution, implementing the design, evaluating the design, and communicating the process used. Such a set of abilities suggests that creativity and communication might be useful components of "content" for science teaching.

Although these standards itemize what students should know, they do not always provide suggestions for teaching. One strategy might adopt the science learning cycle, which involves stages of exploration, explanation, and application (Renner, 1982). However, keeping the standards in front of you can aid in organizing the design of lessons and units and evaluating how textbooks address one's state standards. The idea here is to keep in mind that other forms of learning, not always addressed by the standards, may be involved and necessary to teach. These other views of learning are addressed in the following sections.

Learning taxonomies

Another way to view learning is by characterizing the primary capability to be learned. Three types of learning have been analyzed and represented: *cognitive* (thinking), *affective* (valuing and appreciating), and *psychomotor* (physical movement). These three types of learning have been characterized through the use of a taxonomy. In a taxonomy, learning is represented by different levels, one learns at one level before advancing to the next level, and mastery of a higher level depends on the ability to learn at the lower level.

Cognitive learning taxonomy

Each taxonomy uses an organizing principle that describes how learning levels are determined and how each level is related to the others. The most common taxonomy is the *cognitive taxonomy* (Bloom, 1956). The organizing principle for the cognitive learning taxonomy is the *degree of complexity of thinking processes*. The cognitive taxonomy consists of six levels of learning, the lowest level being knowledge, followed by comprehension, application, analysis, synthesis, and evaluation, the highest cognitive level of learning (Figure 3.4).

If student learning involves the recall of new information, then the cognitive level of learning is "knowledge." As one moves up the taxonomy, the complexity of thinking grows more challenging. For example, to "comprehend" new knowledge, the next cognitive level, one must be able to recall, recognize, acquire, and identify the "knowledge." For the "application" level, a student must be able to recall learned knowledge *and* comprehend its meaning in order to apply this knowledge in a new problem. The analysis

FIGURE 3.4.
Learning
Taxonomies.

Cognitive	Affective	Psychomotor
Evaluation	Characterization by value or value set	Nondiscursive communication
⇧ Synthesis	⇧ Organization	⇧ Skilled movements
⇧ Analysis	⇧ Valuing	⇧ Physical activities
⇧ Application	⇧ Responding	⇧ Perceptual
⇧ Comprehension	⇧ Receiving	⇧ Basic fundamental movement
⇧ Knowledge		⇧ Reflex movements

level involves breaking apart ideas in terms of structuring and classification. The next level, synthesis, requires an ability to combine ideas in a paper or a project. The uppermost level of the thinking taxonomy is evaluation, the capability to compare and contrast, to argue, and to decide. In developing lessons and units, it is helpful to look at one's choice of student learning outcomes and see where they lie on the taxonomy. You get a sense for what you are expecting students to learn and can then make informed choices on teaching and assessment.

Affective learning taxonomy

If your "content" includes developing attitudes or values, then the affective taxonomy can help you understand the development of this type of learning (Krathwohl, Bloom, & Masia, 1964). Until recently, the teaching of affective learning goals has been limited because of a focus on student achievement in other areas, a lack of assessment methods, and the belief that affective learning is a private matter. The affective taxonomy is organized according to the *degree of personal internalization* of a new idea or issue (see Figure 3.4).

Here a person's attitude shifts from general awareness of an issue to an attitude that consistently guides one's behavior. In other words, a new idea is adopted by the user and used. To achieve the valuing of an issue, for example, a student must first pay attention to the topic, listen, and suspend judgment ("receiving"). To begin to appreciate an issue, the student needs to "respond" to the issue by spending time with and becoming involved with the issue. Further up the learning levels in the affective taxonomy, the student must come to "value" the topic, idea, issue, or activity. This can be achieved through a student's increased proficiency in use, ongoing debate, or other support of the issue. Further up the taxonomy, the student "organizes" aspects of the new idea or issue, and teachers look for ways in which the student can discuss, theorize, and examine all sides of an issue.

Psychomotor learning taxonomy

If your "content" includes physical skills, the psychomotor domain may be helpful. Although there are different forms of psychomotor taxonomies, the one developed by Harrow (1972) serves our purposes to illustrate how physical skills can be deconstructed and better understood, so that teachers can appropriately support student learning in these skills. The psychomotor taxonomy is organized by the *degree of physical coordination* required in a task (see Figure 3.4).

The psychomotor learning taxonomy may have more application than just physical education curriculums—any activity that requires physical skill use and coordination. Any hands-on activities may require specialized skills that should be included in your learning outcomes, and assessment is usually demonstrated, either through observation of a performance, such as dance or gymnastics, or in a product, such as a sculpture. General physical capabilities are usually not specified in learning outcomes, such as walking and being able to hold objects. However, basic physical capabilities may be a significant learning issue for some students. Issues of special needs—an example of the dimensions of human learning not well addressed in the taxonomies—is discussed later in the chapter.

Combining taxonomies

Some learning tasks, such as writing a paper or developing a science fair project, may require the use of all three taxonomies. To write a paper requires a range of thinking capabilities, plus the physical skills to use a keyboard, pencil, or pen. Good papers tend to be written by people who value the writing process. The cognitive and affective taxonomies figure prominently in the performance of any high-level critical thinking or problem-solving task. Gagné combined all three taxonomies to create his "Learned Capabilities" taxonomy to help educators think about the relationships between the three taxonomies (Gagné, Wager, Golas, & Keller, 2005) (Figure 3.5).

Once you know that student learning involves one or more learning types, you can sequence lessons in units roughly according to the taxonomy (Figure 3.6). Teachers frequently characterize teaching as a flow of activity, but this flow is usually based on some rationale, such as simple concepts or skills to more complex concepts or skills. Understanding the nature of what students will learn, possibly using the hierarchical arrangement provided by a taxonomy, provides a tool to establish a learner-focused rationale to the flow of teaching.

FIGURE 3.5.
Five Types of
Learned
Capabilities
(Gagné, Wager,
Golas & Keller,
2005).

Capability	Examples of Performance
Intellectual skill	• Identifying the diagonal of a rectangle • Demonstrating use of objective case of pronoun following a preposition
Cognitive strategy	• Using an image link to learn a foreign equivalent to an English word • Rearranging a verbally stated problem by working backward
Verbal information	• Stating the provisions of the Fourth Amendment to the U.S. Constitution • Listing the events of instruction
Attitude	• Choosing to read science fiction • Choosing running as a regular form of exercise
Motor skill	• Jumping rope • Printing the letter E

From *Principles of Instructional Design*, 5th edition, by Gagné/Wager/Golas/Keller. © 2005. Reprinted with permission of Wadsworth, a division of Thomson Learning: www.thomsonrights.com. Fax 800 730-2215.

FIGURE 3.6.
Sequencing
Principles for
Gagné's
Combined
Taxonomy.

General Sequencing Principles for Gagné's Combined Taxonomy

Intellectual skills: new *procedure* preceded by basic skill, simple *concept* elaborated by detailed concepts, simple *principles* to more complex principles

Cognitive strategies: simple recall to complex use of knowledge

Verbal information: conceptual organization, relate to meaningful content

Affective: gaining attention to actually using and advocating; adequate time is needed to support

Psychomotor: practice of simple movements to mastery of complex behaviors

Learning dimensions

A third way to view content is to take into account the different dimensions of learning that are not addressed by content area standards or taxonomies. One way to appreciate this idea is to think about what capacities you would like to support in your students. Do the standards or taxonomies address these capacities? What one values in what is to be taught is a central issue in the development of curriculum, the topic of Chapter 9. The word *dimensions* is used here to characterize the full character of what it means to be human. As you read the next sections, think about how these dimensions may exist or could become a feature in your lessons and units (Figure 3.7).

FIGURE 3.7.
Human Learning
Dimensions.

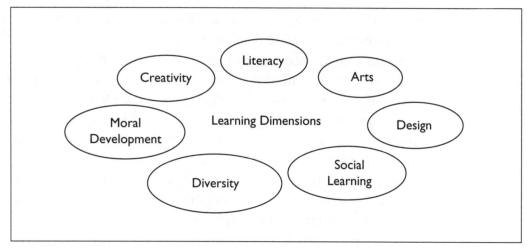

Literacy

Reading is at the heart of literacy, and the purpose of teaching is "getting meaning from print" (Zemelman, Daniels, & Hyde, 1998, p. 30). However, *literacy* can be defined as the ability to read, write, speak, listen, and communicate visually (Arends, Winitzky, & Tannenbaum, 2001). Generally, reading and writing have been shown to promote the development of each other. In schools, literacy is addressed by standards for English language arts (see National Council of Teachers of English and International Reading Association, 1996). A common strategy is providing learners with comprehension skills so they understand what they are reading. A complementary teaching strategy to support literacy is the creation of a *literate environment* in schools and in homes, where both reading and writing take place continually and are modeled by teachers and parents (Arends et al., 2001).

The traditional view of literacy as reading and writing has broadened to include speaking and listening (Valmont, 2003). Visual literacy has taken on greater emphasis, owing to the strong influence that the media have on humans. We see literacy useful as a strategy to view all learning. What does it mean to be technologically literate? Scientifically literate? Visually literate? What it means to be literate can form the basis of curriculum for many content areas (Shambaugh, 2000; also see Chapter 9), as educators debate and decide on what it means to be "literate" in almost any content area or endeavor.

Arts

Eisner (1998) expressed the value of arts as a way of knowing what words cannot express. Thus, the arts provide students with a means of demonstrating understanding that complements or even rises above what words can provide. The scope of what the arts can be for students is addressed in their own set of standards (National Committee for Standards in the Arts, 1994). Although these standards provide accountability for learning in the arts, the idea of the *arts* as a human learning dimension can be a way of rethinking outcomes and assessing those outcomes and as a form of teaching. Eisner (1998) says that "not only cannot all outcomes be measured, they frequently cannot be predicted. When humans work on tasks, they almost always learn more and less what was intended" (pp. 67–68). This tension regarding clear learning outcomes is integral to the learning dimensions that are profiled here. Literacy development requires actual involvement in literate activities, most notably reading and writing, but in other ways as well. The arts require genuine and sustained activity over time in creating works in a variety of forms. Integrated curriculums, discussed in Chapter 9, benefit from the use of the arts as a strategy for curriculum design. Imagine how the content areas can be integrated into the arts, rather than the other way around. Imagine what schools would be like if the arts were central to the curriculum.

Design

The purpose of design is to address human needs (Norman, 1990). We defined design in Chapter 2 as a process that helps one improve upon an existing situation. Design contributes to a better world and consequently qualifies as a dimension of learning, but it is not always addressed in content areas. Design solves practical problems and is a unique form of thinking, with its own set of problem-solving processes (see Rowe, 1987). Design is inherent in our ability to use, manage, understand, and assess technology. One of the problems with design is that we think we know what it is, that it has something to do with aesthetics and the creation of new products and structures. However, there is no one agreed-on definition of design. One professional organization, the International Technology Education Association (ITEA), addresses design in its Technology for All Americans Project (ITEA, 1996), a set of technological literacy standards for public schools. Design, like the arts, can provide an organizing strategy for curriculum. What would schools look like if design was prominently featured in curriculums? Students who become motivated by design find a way to seek out more design opportunities. Where in school will they find them?

Social learning

Piaget (1969) identified three types of knowledge that children acquire in their development. *Physical knowledge* involves knowledge about objects in the world, knowledge acquired through a child's active use of perceptions, such as sight, touch, hearing, or smell. *Logical-mathematical knowledge,* a mental invention of patterns, is acquired through handling objects. These mental inventions or understanding of numbers, volume, class, time, and weight, among others, are based on a child's initial experience but can be applied to other objects.

Social knowledge can be learned only through interactions with people. Note the common ingredient in all three forms of knowledge is children's action, action with objects, and action with people. Human interactions produce moral rules, values, cultural understanding, history, and symbol understanding (even language).

One difficulty in promoting social learning is not being able to teach and assess social knowledge with the same degree of precision as logical-mathematical knowledge. School curriculums have traditionally focused on logical-mathematical abilities. However, human learning does not end with logical-mathematical forms of learning; "our intellect is not meant to stop working when it comes to social relations. On the contrary, history tells us that the farthest-reaching effects of intellectual achievements eventually become manifest in a change of society's view of the human person" (Furth, 1970, p. 129). Promoting citizens of a global society, then, requires attention to social learning, which is culture-specific.

Social learning is learning about ourselves as well as others (Woolfolk-Hoy, 2005). Social learning can include cooperative skills, self-concept (perceptions about ourselves), and self-esteem (values we place on our characteristics) within the family, the community, and the school. Social learning in schools requires attention to how students relate to each other and how they become familiar with the views and beliefs of other children, parents, teachers, and other members of the community (i.e., socialization). Learning about our place in the world with others also involves issues of gender, ethnicity, and special qualities.

The important idea here is that educators value social learning, and we should acknowledge its development in learning outcomes. In elementary grades, issues of classroom management become an anchoring structure for teachers and students who learn the rules, policies, and procedures of the classroom and getting along. As students grow older, they are exposed to additional opportunities in schools to learn from each other and to communicate, such as class projects and extracurricular activities. It is commonplace to witness the value that society places on teamwork in the workplace. A worthwhile question to ask is: "How will schools support student learning of social skills?"

Diversity

The basic ideas behind cultural diversity are that every culture is unique, no culture is better than another, and all people are characterized to some extent by a particular culture (Janzen, 1994). Snowman and Biehler (2000) identify several learning differences based on these ideas. Different cultures have different verbal communication patterns, which can be seen in terms of how one student quickly questions a teacher, while another student is culturally bound to not question the teacher. Different forms of nonverbal communication are present, such as eye contact and interpersonal distance. Different cultures react in different ways to the notion of time and timeliness. Different cultures have different social values, such as reactions to individual performance, competition in the classroom, and cooperation. Cultural groups may also react differently to the forms of instructional activity, such as group work, testing, debating, memorization, and physical performance.

Diversity is included here as a learning dimension because "difference" is another opportunity for learning that is not addressed by content area standards and taxonomies. Diversity takes advantage of human differences as a means for students' overall development as human beings. Diversity, however, can be viewed as "add-on" pieces to lessons, rather than integrated into learning activity. Instead of viewing diversity as a supplementary issue to address, diversity can become central to one's teaching decisions.

One school response to diversity involves individual students who need specialized instruction through the use of pull-out programs, such as federally funded Title 1 programs. A second response to diversity for special needs students is *inclusion*, in which all students are educated together in a regular classroom. Schools that adopt inclusion require all educators in these schools to become familiar with the requirements of federal legislation, such as *individualized educational plans* (IEPs) and *least restrictive environment* opportunities for special needs students.

A third response of schools to diversity is multicultural programs. The view of America as a great melting pot in which immigrants from different countries and cultures blended into an American society has been superseded in educational circles by multiculturalism. The goal of multiculturalism is to promote understanding of cultural diversity and develop student skills in handling cultural situations and prejudice. Those involved in multicultural curriculums also see these programs as change agents to correct injustice. Some teachers report that no cultural diversity exists in their schools, and what they mean is that there is no obvious racial diversity. However, numerous opportunities exist for raising students' awareness of the differences in homogeneous classrooms, as well as understanding differences outside the classroom or community.

A fourth response from schools to diversity is in language programs of instruction such as limited English proficiency (LEP) and English as a second language (ESL). These programs are quite different from traditional foreign language instruction, which some students take as options in school. Instead of foreign language, we suggest "world languages" to eliminate the "foreign" label from such learning. World language could be taught at an early age by elementary teachers, although most teachers would require in-service assistance to do so.

Moral development

Another dimension to the development of humans beyond our emphasis on thinking is the idea of moral development. Different views exist on how morals, or standards of conduct, develop in humans. A classic view comes from Kohlberg (1975), who divides moral reasoning into three levels. The first level is known as *preconventional*, when a child's judgment stems from personal needs. The second level is *conventional*, when one's judgment is influenced from the approval of others. The third level is labeled as *postconventional*, when judgment is based on an individual sense of what is right. Postconventional judgment, according to Kohlberg, is composed of both a "buy-in" to views of social contracts (government) and one's personally developed set of values that may lie outside the views of others.

Gilligan (1993), who worked with Kohlberg, proposed a sequence of ethical development using "care" as the sequencing principle. Rather than a focus on the individual as in Kohlberg's stage theory, Gilligan's research identified the need for women to connect and care for others, while men think about equality, reciprocity, and rights (Gilligan, 1988). In an ethic of care, people begin with acting in a *self-interest mode*, then move to *commitment to others*, embracing *relationships*, and *care of all people*. To put this viewpoint into practice, we can consult Noddings (1992), who identified four requirements for an ethic of care. The first requirement for the teacher is to model ethical and caring behavior to students. A second requirement is dialogue, which is characterized by open-ended conversation and the suspension of judgment, for the purpose of learning about each other. A third requirement is practice and providing opportunities for an ethic of care to take hold and develop within oneself and for others. Finally, a fourth requirement to an ethic of care, according to Noddings, is confirmation, the practice of encouraging the best in others.

Creativity

Humans value creativity within families and in society, but little of creativity is formally addressed in schools as part of the curriculum. This may be due to the difficulties of knowing what creativity is and how to teach and assess it. Views of what humans are capable of may differ widely and limit how innovation and creation are directly supported in schools. However, one way to acknowledge creative capacity in humans is to at least acknowledge the different views of human creativity (Gardner, 1982; Goodman, 1976). How might schools help students to find their creative niche or outlet? One way would be to provide diverse opportunities for student self-expression, as well as to introduce students to different forms of expression. One aspect of creativity is developing a sensitivity to the works of others, while developing a capacity to express ourselves in creative works. Teacher modeling of the creative act and taking risks would be a key strategy.

Summary

We hope that this section provided some food for thought in terms of the range of what "content" means. We have reconfigured our earlier visual by placing the idea of diversity in the center to suggest that learner differences provide a comprehensive strategy for making teaching decisions (Figure 3.8). The idea of learning dimensions acknowledges the full range of what it means to be human. If schools and educators value these capabilities and sensibilities, then lessons and units should identify them as learning outcomes. Defining clear outcomes with these dimensions is not a simple matter, but your efforts may provide students and teachers with opportunities to learn together what it means to be human.

FIGURE 3.8.
Human Learning Dimensions Reconfigured.

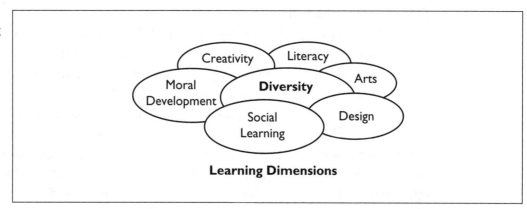

Task analysis

Task analysis provides another way to view "content." A *task analysis* is a tool with which you determine what it means for a learner to perform a task, then write a set of learning outcomes, and finally choose teaching strategies to help a student learn the task (Figure 3.9). In classrooms, task analysis is useful when students will be faced with a new and challenging task or when students are experiencing difficulties with a task. Task analysis provides an analysis method to discover where students might be having problems.

FIGURE 3.9.
Task Analysis Steps.

Task Analysis and Teaching Requirements
Step 1: Analyze the learning task. *Knowing what it means to perform the task.*
Step 2: Write performance objectives. *This is what you want students to do.*
Step 3: Specify teaching strategies. *How will you help students learn the objectives?*

In the training world, task analysis is a major activity. Trainers and instructional developers use task analysis to know how to teach a skill by first learning more about what it means to learn the skill. There are many tools used in task analysis, depending on the type of learning to be performed (Jonassen,

Tessmer, & Hannum, 1999), so the first question to ask yourself is "What is the type of knowledge and skill to be learned?"

Step 1: Conduct the task analysis

Step 1 breaks down the task into subtasks. List the physical or mental steps in the order it takes to do them or think them through and the required skills or thinking that would be necessary to master the task. Actually doing the task yourself can reveal the performance that is needed. Ask other teachers or experts for advice if the task is particularly complex. Observe students and make adjustments for future teaching. Ask students about their experiences. They may be able to tell you strategies they used or problems they experienced that cannot be easily observed. A combination of physical and mental steps may be necessary for some tasks. What content knowledge is needed to perform the task? What social requirements are needed? In many lessons, it may be necessary that some knowledge and skills be acquired before new learning can take place. Prerequisites are skills that must be mastered to learn the new material or the desired objective. These skills may include understanding concepts, procedures, and principles.

Here are some guidelines for step 1:

- What types of learning are desired? Consult the professional standards, learning taxonomies, and learning dimensions for assistance.
- List procedural steps, knowledge, and skills needed. Flowcharts can be used to document the process and to create a set of instructions or procedures to perform a task
- For mental operations, list mental steps and skills needed. What are the thinking requirements in each step? One strategy is to list the mental steps that one uses to perform a skill. Sometimes conducting a *think-aloud* with an expert can be helpful.
- Determine the *prerequisites*, or what must be learned first.
- Tables are useful to document the tasks involved in higher level skills, such as problem solving, rule learning, and concept learning.
- For verbal information, outlines are common data-gathering formats.
- Attitudes use any format that documents the behavior and demonstrates that an attitude is learned.

Step 2: Write performance objectives

Knowing the steps or subskills that make up the skill enables one to write *performance objectives*, which are learning outcome statements that explicitly describe student performance requirements. This detailed articulation guides you in the development of learning activities and serves as a basis for ongoing assessment or final assessment by the instructor. The purpose of performance objectives is to clearly spell out what you want learners to learn from instruction. Performance objectives need to be observable and measurable and specify a level of performance. Thus, well-written performance objectives should include the following:

- Observable: Students must demonstrate performance in some form.
- Measurable: You should be able to determine how well students perform this task.
- Specify a level of performance: How well should students perform the task?

Step 3: Specify instructional needs

With the information on what you know about the task and what you want students to be able to do (i.e., performance objectives), you can now specify teaching strategies. What does the instructor need to know to support student learning of these performance objectives? This step is sometimes referred to as *instructional analysis*, and the questions raised in this step include the following (Seels & Glasgow, 1998):

- What are the possible learning difficulties?
- How frequently will the skill be used?
- How immediate is the performance?
- Is any assistance required to learn the skill?
- What do instructors need to learn to make this happen?
- How might students help each other?
- How much time is needed to learn the skill?
- What are the consequences of not learning the skill?
- What is the *decay rate* of the skill?

Determining entry-level skills informs you of what level of learning you need to design instruction for. Some subskills may not need further teaching if students are already skilled in the task or have had previous experience. You may realize that you as a teacher need to learn more the procedures, knowledge, and skills to better assist the student. Having students work through the task will provide you with the differences in student reactions to the task, your instructions, and their performance. Pilot-testing of a new activity is worthy of a lesson to uncover this information, as a well-written lesson plan can never guarantee an effective lesson. From the actual teaching, you can adjust the task for reteaching, or use next time.

In summary, a *task analysis* determines what it means for a student to perform a learning task. An *instructional analysis* provides information on what it means to teach the task to students. Conducting a task analysis examines a skill closely so that you can sequence teachable subskills and identify related physical and affective aspects.

Media and technology

The use of media and technology is based on a need to give students experiences they could not have otherwise. Visiting Brazil would be the better choice, as the actual experience would surely be the best way for students to appreciate the country's culture, but the use of technology to "visit" Brazil through correspondence with Brazilian students or building a multimedia profile of the country provides an alternative.

Another way to view "content" is to see how others teach with media and technology. Look for ways that media and technology have been used in the classroom or other learning environments. Teachers are sometimes frustrated by not finding materials that exactly fit their needs. For example, you may be looking for cooperative learning strategies for kindergarten use but instead find resources from the elementary grades literature. Having a developmental understanding of children in kindergarten, you could make adjustments to what you find. Sometimes excellent sources can be found in content areas, such as science, and possibly adapted for other content areas.

In your reading, look for why the instructor used media and technology. How did its use promote student learning? Were learning outcomes clearly spelled out? Be wary of articles that tout an innovation without a clear explanation of why it was used. Many articles, due to space limitations, cannot fully describe the context of the use of media or technology. Look for the author's email address and write to that person for more details. What roles do teachers and students play in using the technology?

Thinking about content

Figure 3.10 lists prompts for thinking about "content" and learning more about what it means for learners to learn this content.

FIGURE 3.10.
Prompts for Thinking About "Content."

Prompts for Thinking About "Content"
• Identify learning outcomes using state standards, professional content area standards, or learning taxonomies.
• Identify other forms of learning (i.e., human learning dimensions) that may be necessary to learn other aspects of human development.
• Consider how the content has been taught previously. Consult with other teachers, peers, experts, and written sources.
• Conduct a task analysis if the learning is new, complex, or troublesome to students.
• Given the full range of "content" to be learned, does the teaching approach need to change? What teaching strategies need to be included?
• How can media and technology support learning? How different are learning outcomes, teaching, and assessment of teaching using media and technology?

Thinking About Content

Task Rationale   Use a lesson to think about content.

Task Guidelines   1. Content area learning outcomes? What state standards apply to this lesson? Other learning?

Content   2. How has this content been taught before, and how might you teach this content?

3. What options exist for media and technology support? How do these options prompt you to rethink your teaching?

Reflectivity   • How did this activity help you in deciding the full range of "content" to be learned?

• Reflect on the difficulty of performing this task. What would a task analysis of this Design Activity look like?

WHO ARE YOUR LEARNERS?

The more you know about your students, the easier it will be to make appropriate teaching decisions. In this section, we briefly examine different ways to view students.

Learner characteristics

"Learner characteristics" is an educational psychological approach to describing your students. These characteristics can include age, sex, educational level, achievement level, socioeconomic background, learning preferences, verbal ability, relevant experience, attitudes toward subject, role perceptions, and perceived needs, among other possibilities (Seels & Glasgow, 1998). The next Design Activity will give you practice in compiling this information in terms of learner characteristics.

Learning preferences

Educators frequently use the term *learning styles* to characterize different ways that students learn. A learning style is a student's general approach to learning and studying. Two major differences of learning styles have been noted. Some students favor a *deep-processing* approach in which they see learning for the sake of learning and regard teaching materials and activities as a means for understanding. Other students favor a *surface-processing* approach to learning and are motivated by grades and external evaluation (Woolfolk-Hoy, 2005). What most people regard as learning styles, educational psychologists label as *learning preferences*. Learning preferences characterize the individual learner in terms of specific ways of performing a task, taking notes, listening to music while studying, reading rate, drawing pictures, or working to deadlines. There are analytical instruments that attempt to assess students' learning preferences, but these have been criticized for lack of reliability and validity.

Cognitive styles

Educational psychologists have another term that is backed by more reliable and valid research, that of cognitive styles. *Cognitive styles* are the differences in how an individual perceives, organizes, and acts on information. One set of cognitive styles is *field dependence* and *field independence* (Witkin, Moore, Goodenough, & Cox, 1977). Field-dependent individuals perceive visual patterns as a whole, while field-independent learners separate and analyze parts of a whole visual pattern. This cognitive style is evident in students' note-taking practices. Field-dependent learners tend to take notes that mimic the structure, sequence, and wording of the teacher. Field-independent learners take notes in a manner of their own choosing. Another implication of this cognitive style difference is that field-dependent students will have difficulty with tasks or materials that are not well organized, whereas field-independent learners are motivated to make sense of the task and materials with their own meaningful structures (Figure 3.11).

FIGURE 3.11. Characteristics of Field-Dependent and Field-Independent Learners.

Field Dependent	Field Independent
Visual patterns perceived as a whole	Visual patterns perceived as separate visual parts of the whole image
Notes mimic the instructor	Notes constructed to fit the individual
Require well-organized tasks	Enjoy making sense of the task and impose unique interpretations

Another cognitive style set is *impulsive* and *reflective* (Kagan, 1964). Some students tend to be impulsive in their responses to questions and learning tasks, and others are more reflective and require time to speak or write. In problem-solving tasks, impulsive students move quickly to a solution and look for less information; the reflective student spends significant time in searching for information and mulling on its relevance and use (Morgan, 1997).

Special needs

Society has responded to the special needs of some individuals. The "graded school" was based on a customary group of students who were ability-sorted and graded. With compulsory school, larger and larger numbers of students entered public school, including increasing numbers of students who fell outside the customary expectations of school administrators and teachers. The federal government responded with a series of laws that culminated in the Individuals with Disabilities Education Act (IDEA, PL 101-476). See Resources for an update on the Individuals with Disabilities Education Improvement Act of 2004. The purpose of IDEA is to ensure that all individuals (birth–21 years) who have an identifiable disability receive public education that meets their needs. Placement within an educational program requires a preplacement evaluation, multidisciplinary development of an *individualized education program* (IEP), and placement in the *least restrictive environment* that the disability will allow for student success. For some students, this environment is the regular classroom, and others require specialized assistance.

The legislation recognizes twelve different categories of disabilities, which are used in some way by all of the states. These categories are designed to cover students with physical and sensory challenges, such as seizure disorders, cerebral palsy, hearing impairment, and vision impairment. Communication disorders include a range of speech impairments, such as articulation disorders, stuttering, and voicing disorders. Other forms of disorders covered include emotional or behavioral disorders, such as hyperactivity and attention disorders. One large category is classified as *learning disabilities*, which involves possible lifelong problems with language, including listening, speaking, reading, writing, reasoning, or mathematical abilities (Friend & Bursuck, 1996).

Some students with special needs are not addressed in special education laws, such as students who are gifted or talented. State funding, however, may address the needs of those with exceptional intellectual ability, creativity, athletictalent, or visual and performing arts skills. Some students may receive services under different legislation than special education. One example are those students with attention-deficit/hyperactivity disorder (ADHD). ADHD students have been diagnosed with an inability to attend to learning tasks for any length of time and may exhibit excessive physical activity or impulsive behavior. Some students may be slow learners and do not have a learning disability. Special programs, such as those for reading, may be available in some schools.

The important idea here is to learn all you can about your students, so you can better understand their learning needs. One of the challenges for today's teacher is the wide range of learner differences in students.

The next Design Activity provides an opportunity to record what you know about your learners.

DESIGN ACTIVITY 9

Learner Profile

Task Rationale	The more you know about your students, the more responsive your teaching will be.
Task Guidelines	1. Course? 2. Grade? 3. Level? 4. Ages? 5. Gender?
General Background of Students	1. Socioeconomic backgrounds, community, family, parental issues? 2. School and classroom history? 3. Developmental characteristics? 4. Special needs requirements? 5. Social issues: How do students get along and interact with each other?
Students and Content	1. Range of student knowledge and skills? 2. Differences in how students learn? 3. Attitudes and motivational issues? 4. Challenging area for teaching?
Profile Tools	1. Who and/or what did you consult on this profile? 2. What observations have you made?
Reflectivity	What did you learn about your students that you did not know before?

WHAT IS THE CONTEXT OF THE LEARNING SETTING?

"Content" and "learners" make sense, but what is context? People, rules, expectations, beliefs, and realities surround teaching. Teaching is immersed in rich surroundings that educators call context. We have organized context across three levels: the school level, the classroom level, and the personal level.

All of these concerns at these three levels interact to characterize the quality of your learning environment. Frequently, we look at context as a set of limitations that constrain teaching. However, context also should include resources we have at our disposal, resources that contribute to student learning.

School level

All classrooms and any learning environment are part political, part physical, part personal, part social, and part psychological "spaces" for learning. The first level of context involves the school. No classroom acts independently of the school. This level of context can be studied during initial visits to the school and even as early as during hiring interviews. Some of this information may be provided during an official school orientation for new teachers. Issues to be considered in the school level of context include the following:

- School district policies and initiatives: grading, homework, field trips, extracurricular activities, inclusion
- School policies and goals: achievement targets, classroom management, parental communication, special education teachers
- School calendar, including testing and grading schedules
- Department organization, hierarchy, and relationships among teachers
- Use of school areas for teaching use: hallway walls, auditorium, cafeteria, computer labs, media centers, library

Classroom level

The contextual issues at the classroom level can be organized by the following categories: physical space, furniture and equipment, instructional materials, teaching assistance, and classroom management (Figure 3.12).

The issue of the physical space is frequently left out of contextual analysis. In reality, we "inherit" physical spaces for a classroom or a lab or a lecture hall, and on the surface it appears that not much can be done. However, a teacher can improve the learning environment or at least attempt some compromises to make the best out of the current situation.

By furniture, we typically think of student desks, but a classroom may involve students at tables, lab benches, or computer workstations. What furniture and equipment will you need in your teaching?

Instructional materials used to mean construction paper, textbooks, maps, globes, and lab materials. Instructional materials can also include materials to construct or assemble, such as handouts and activity sheets. Computer-based and Internet-based instructional materials have enlarged this category significantly, to the point where significant teacher time and attention may shift to computer and web resources.

Physical Space	Furniture and Equipment	Instructional Materials
Location within the school	Student and instructor desks, tables, chairs, counters	Blackboards, whiteboards
Entrance and exits	Computing and Internet access	Textbooks, books, and publications
Physical dimensions, volume	Computing infrastructure (networking, archiving, server)	Laboratory materials
Physical surfaces, treatments	Classroom objects (displays)	Art materials
Displays	Storage equipment	Bulletin boards, student displays
Natural, artificial lighting, heating	Communication (telephone)	Handouts
Heating and air conditioning	Audiovisual	Media materials (maps, audiovisual)
Acoustics		Computer-based and Internet-based materials
Mechanical noise, exterior noise		
Activity areas		
Storage areas		
Walkways		

FIGURE 3.12. Physical Issues at the Classroom Level.

Teaching assistance

The classroom level of context involves more than the arrangement of desks and distribution of textbooks. Teaching increasingly calls for team teaching, specialists, teacher aides, student teachers, and parents. Each school will have policies involving these individuals as volunteers.

- Co-teaching
- Special education and reading specialists
- Media, computer center, library assistance
- Student teachers and teacher aides
- Parents
- Student assistance

Classroom management

Classroom management involves the physical preparation of learning areas, the posting of student work, and student behavior (Wong & Wong, 2001) (Figure 3.13). Learning areas include the available floor space and work areas for teacher and students. The wall space is an important resource.

Posting student work involves strategies for alerting students to daily activities and assignments. These postings should be placed where students can read or see them, along with reminders early in the school year on what the postings mean. As time is at a premium, taking roll can be accomplished when students are working, rather than using valuable learning time.

Student behavior includes rules, procedures, and routines. General rules should be few in number, and the list should be posted. Procedures and routines will differ according to the type of task, but students should be clear as to what they mean in specific circumstances. Specific rules, procedures, and routines should be noted on a lesson plan when you are first teaching or documented in a classroom management plan, which may be useful to show administrators, parents, and other teachers.

Rules	Procedures	Routines
School and district rules	Entering classroom	How class is dismissed
School classroom management plan	Starting work	How unnecessary noise is treated and student attention is maintained
General rules: directions, permission to speak, stay in seat, teasing, cursing, fighting, keep objects to yourself	What to do when bell rings	How to have students begin work when the bell rings
Specific rules for grade level	What to do when pencil breaks	How students are to ask for help
Specific rules for playground, cafeterias, and other areas	What to do when the emergency signal sounds	How students pass in papers
	What to do when work is finished early	
	What to do when students have a question	
	What to do when students need to go to the restroom	
	Where to find today's assignments	

FIGURE 3.13. Rules, Procedures, and Routines at the Classroom Level.

Students should be aware of what the *rules* are and what the consequences are for not following the rules. Rules document how students should behave (Wong & Wong, 2001). These rules should be determined before the school year begins and before you walk into the classroom. The number of rules should be limited to five, as too many rules are hard to remember and set the wrong tone for the classroom. To communicate the rules, the list can be posted and talked about in class. During school, the consequences of not following the rules should be immediate with positive feedback. Your responses to student behavior must be predictable and consistent.

Meanwhile, procedures and routines can be general, to cover specific activities during the school day or specific procedures during learning. *Procedures* document how things are done; *routines* document how things are done on a regular basis without supervision (Wong & Wong, 2001). Procedures and routines can be communicated by using explanation, rehearsing, and reinforcing. Explanation is defining a procedure in concrete terms and demonstrating. Rehearsing gives students practice in conducting the procedure. Reinforcing involves reteaching, praise, or corrective feedback.

Personal level

Contextual issues at the personal level involve issues that influence your attitudes and motivation to be in schools and classrooms and work with students. Consider your personal attributes and areas for improvement. Your health and well-being require paying attention to your physical, social, and psychological needs. Your professional habits model appropriate behavior for peers and students.

Time becomes a major issue. We have come to view time as a constraint rather than a resource. Time is usually viewed as a limiting factor, as we do not have an unlimited amount of time to work with. Adequate time is necessary for planning, teaching, administration, and other school duties. Look at time as a resource to be used carefully, and this self-evaluation will dictate much of what you can accomplish.

Use the next Design Activity to think through the contextual issues that will influence how your students learn.

DESIGN ACTIVITY 10

Context of the Learning Environment

Task Rationale   Describe the context to learning, using the following suggested topics.

Task Guidelines

School level
1. School or departmental requirements or initiatives?
2. School policies and calendar?
3. Statewide standards and testing?

Classroom level
1. Physical space of the classroom or other location (lab, school property)?
2. Furniture and equipment?
3. Instructional materials?
4. Teacher assistance (volunteers, etc.) needed?
5. Classroom management (rules, procedures, routines)?

Personal level
1. Physical, social, and psychological issues of students or teacher(s)?
2. Your personal style and the style of colleagues?
3. How do you respond to student dynamics?
4. Time?

Reflectivity
- In what ways did this Design Activity raise your awareness of the learning environment?
- If, in Chapter 1, you wrote about "creating a positive learning environment for students," explain what you mean by this. What decisions will you make that ensure such an environment?

SUMMARIZING YOUR LEARNING IN PRE-LESSON THINKING

The following Design Activity asks you to apply what you have learned about your classroom in terms of content, learners, and context.

Pre-Lesson Thinking

Task Rationale   Identify one lesson you plan to develop and teach. Use this activity to ready your thinking for teacher decision making.

Task Guidelines
Content
- What is the content area learning to be addressed by the lesson?
- What other types of learning might be involved in the lesson?
- How has this content been taught before?
- How might you teach this content?
- What options can you see for media and technology support?

Learners
- What do you know about your learners?

Context
- What resources do you have to teach this lesson?
- What limitations do you have to work around in the teaching of this lesson?

Reflectivity
- How did this pre-lesson thinking help you?
- What occurred during the actual teaching of this lesson?
- What did you learn from your teaching? What adjustments do you need to make?

Looking Ahead to Section III

The analysis or needs assessment phase of ID helps you learn more about the classroom in terms of "content," learners, and context. This new teacher knowledge will now be used to make your first instructional decisions in lessons. Section III begins the Teacher Decision Cycle and developing lessons (Figure 3.14).

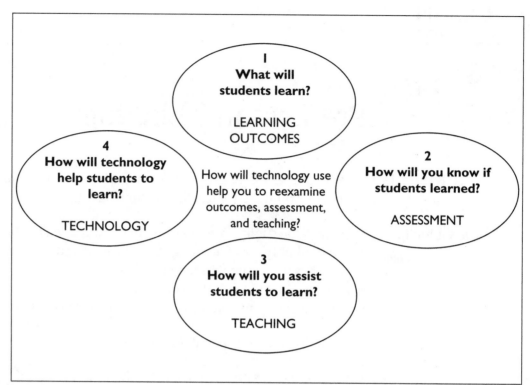

FIGURE 3.14.
Teacher
Decision Cycle.

Much of teaching is learning from students who they are and what they know. The more you know about the diversity of students in your classroom, the better your teaching decisions will be in helping them learn.

Reflective Teaching

"The Call to Collaborate"

Needs assessment can be a scary endeavor for both beginning and veteran teachers. In fact, this may be one area in which veteran teachers may feel that beginning teachers have the upper hand. Beginning teachers have recently emerged from college teacher-preparation programs with a wealth of knowledge concerning the latest research and (for better or for worse) the latest trends in special education, multiculturalism, and diversity issues. Many veteran teachers haven't attended higher education courses in many years; therefore, they have not had this same exposure to these prevalent issues—even though they are dealing with them on a daily basis within their own classrooms. This scenario provides the perfect opportunity for the beginning teacher and the veteran teacher to form a collaborative effort. If both teachers feel that conducting a needs assessment is a worthy and worthwhile task, it makes sense that the two can merge their individual resources and expertise to formulate needs assessments that are effective, practical, and user-friendly. The beginning teacher can describe the issues and research from a "this is what I learned in my college classes" point of view, and the veteran teacher can describe needs assessment from a "this is what I see and have seen with my students" point of view. By collaborating, each teacher is provided with a unique look into what the other knows to be true. The underlying goal in conducting a needs assessment is for all students to learn and experience success to their maximum potential. It makes sense for the beginning teacher and the veteran teacher to work collaboratively and combine their strengths, opinions, and insights to work toward this common goal.

Teacher Inquiry

- We suggest a teacher study involving one or more of your classmates or fellow teachers who might be teaching the same subject but in different schools. Based on this chapter, your study could document the different ways of teaching, using the categories of content, learners, and context to organize your inquiry and findings.

REFERENCES

Arends, R. I., Winitzky, N. E., & Tannenbaum, M. D. (2001). *Exploring teaching: An introduction to education* (2nd ed.). Boston: McGraw-Hill.

Bloom, B. S. (Ed.) (1956). *Taxonomy of educational objectives: Handbook I: Cognitive domain.* New York: McKay.

Eisner, E. W. (1998). *The kind of schools we need: Personal essays.* Portsmouth, NH: Heinemann.

Friend, M., & Bursuck, W. (1996). *Including students with special needs: A practical guide for classroom teachers.* Boston: Allyn and Bacon.

Furth, H. G. (1970). *Piaget for teachers.* Englewood Cliffs, NJ: Prentice-Hall.

Gagné, R. M. (1985). *The conditions of learning* (4th ed.). New York: Holt, Rinehart, & Winston.

Gagné, R. M., & Driscoll, M. P. (1988). *Essentials of learning for instruction* (2nd ed.). Boston: Allyn and Bacon.

Gagné, R. M., Wager, W. W., Golas, K. C., & Keller, J. M. (2005). *Principles of instructional design* (5th ed.). Belmont, CA: Wadsworth/Thomson.

Gardner, H. (1982). *Art, mind & brain: A cognitive approach to creativity.* New York: Basic Books.

Gilligan, C. (1988). Remapping the moral domain: New images of self in relationship. In C. Gilligan, J. V. Ward, & J. M. Taylor (Eds.), *Mapping the moral domain* (pp. 3–20). Cambridge, MA: Harvard University Press.

Gilligan, C. (1993). *In a difference voice: Psychological theory and women's development.* Cambridge, MA: Harvard University Press.

Goodman, N. (1976). *Languages of art.* Indianapolis: Hackett.

Harrow, A. J. (1972). *A taxonomy of the psychomotor domain.* New York: McKay.

ITEA. (1996). *Technology for all Americans: A rationale and structure for the study of technology.* Reston, VA: International Technology Education Association.

Janzen, R. (1994). Melting pot or mosaic? *Educational Leadership, 51*(8), 9–11.

Jonassen, D. H., Tessmer, M., & Hannum, W. H. (1999). *Task analysis methods for instructional design.* Mahwah, NJ: Erlbaum.

Kagan, J. (1964). Impulsive and reflective children. In J. D. Crumbolz (Ed.), *Learning and the educational process.* Chicago: Rand-McNally.

Kohlberg, L. (1975). The cognitive-developmental approach to moral education. *Phi Delta Kappan, 56,* 670–677.

Krathwohl, D. R., Bloom, B. S., & Masia, B. B. (1964). *Taxonomy of educational objectives: Handbook II: Affective domain.* New York: McKay.

Morgan, H. (1997). *Cognitive styles and classroom learning.* Westport, CT: Praeger.

National Committee for Standards in the Arts. (1994). *Dance, music, theatre, visual arts: National standards for arts education.* Reston, VA: Author.

National Council of Teachers of English and International Reading Association. (1996). *Standards for the English language arts.* Urbana, IL: Author.

National Research Council. (1996). *National science education standards.* Washington, DC: National Academy Press.

Noddings, N. (1992). *The challenge to care in schools: An alternative approach to education.* New York: Teachers College Press.

Norman, D. A. (1990). *The design of everyday things.* New York: Doubleday.

Piaget, J. (1969). *Science of education and the psychology of the child.* New York: Viking.

Renner, J. (1982). The power of purpose. *Science Education, 66*(5), 709–716.

Rowe, P. G. (1987). *Design thinking.* Cambridge, MA: MIT Press.

Seels, B., & Glasgow, Z. (1998). *Making instructional design decisions* (2nd ed.). Upper Saddle River, NJ: Merrill.

Shambaugh, R.N. (2000, August). What does it mean to be x-literate? Literacy definitions as tools for growth. *Reading Online,* 4(2). - Retrieved March 18, 2005. From www.readingonline.org/newliteracies/lit_index.asp?HREF =/newliteracies/shambaugh/index.html

Smith, P. L., & Ragan, T. J. (1993). *Instructional design.* Upper Saddle River, NJ: Merrill.

Snowman, J., & Biehler, R. (2000). *Psychology applied to teaching* (9th ed.). Boston: Houghton Mifflin.

Valmont, W. J. (2003). *Technology for literacy teaching and learning.* Boston: Houghton Mifflin.

Witkin, H. A., Moore, C. A., Goodenough, D. R., & Cox, R. W. (1977). Field-dependent and field-independent cognitive styles and their educational implications. *Review of Educational Research, 47,* 1–64.

Wong, H. K., & Wong, R. T. (2001). *The first days of school: How to be an effective teacher* (2nd ed.). Mountain View, CA: Harry K. Wong Publications.

Woolfolk-Hoy, A. E. (2005). *Educational psychology* (9th ed.). Boston: Allyn and Bacon.

Zemelman, S., Daniels, H., & Hyde, A. (1998). *Best practice: New standards for teaching and learning in America's schools* (2nd ed.). Portsmouth, NH: Heinemann.

RESOURCES

Print Resources

Bennett, C. I. (1999). *Comprehensive multicultural education: Theory and practice*. Boston: Allyn and Bacon.

Driscoll, M. P. (2000). *Psychology of learning for instruction* (2nd ed.). Boston: Allyn and Bacon.

> A readable survey of educational psychology. Written by one of Gagné's students. See Chapter 10 on Gagné's Theory of Instruction. See Chapter 12, "Toward a Personal Theory of Learning and Instruction" if you are serious about developing your own instructional foundation, and as food for thought.

Eisner, E. W. (1998). *The kind of schools we need: Personal essays*. Portsmouth, NH: Heinemann.

> All of the readings connect with this chapter in some way, particularly "content" and different ways of knowing. Contains four readings on the role of arts in education.

Goffin, S. G., & Wilson, C. S. (2001). *Curriculum models and early childhood education: Appraising the relationship*. Columbus, OH: Merrill Prentice Hall.

Jonassen, D. H., Tessmer, M., & Hannum, W. H. (1993). *Task analysis methods for instructional design*. Mahwah, NJ: Erlbaum.

> Description of the different tools for analyzing tasks including classifying knowledge and tasks; job, procedural, and skills; instructional and guided learning; cognitive tasks, activity-based methods (e.g., critical incident); subject matter, and knowledge elicitation (think-alouds, observations).

Kennedy, M. M. (Ed.). (1991). *Teaching academic subjects to diverse learners*. New York: Teachers College Press.

> Part I looks at teaching science, mathematics, history and social studies, and writing. Part II addresses learning theory teachers should know and students' cultural backgrounds.

Norman, D. A. (1993). *Thinks that make us smart: Defending human attributes in the age of the machine*. Reading, MA: Addison Wesley.

> This book will help you rethink how you design tasks for humans. Reframes task analysis as a way of fitting the task to the person.

Valmont, W. J. (2003). *Technology for literacy teaching and learning*. Boston: Houghton Mifflin.

> Using technology to promote a range of literacies: reading and thinking; word recognition, vocabulary, reference, and study skills; writing; listening and speaking; and graphic and visual literacy. Includes a chapter on using technology with children's literature.

Welch, M. (1996). Teacher education and the neglected diversity: Preparing educators to teach students with disabilities. *Journal of Teacher Education, 47*(5), 355–366.

> This article provides a background on the different approaches educators take in regards to teaching students with disabilities and different ways that teacher education programs can address this topic.

Wong, H. K., & Wong, R. T. (2001). *The first days of school: How to be an effective teacher* (2nd ed.). Mountain View, CA: Harry K. Wong Publications.

Web-Based Resources

American Association for the Advancement of Science (1989). *Project 2061: Science for all Americans*. Washington, DC: Author. Retrieved March 18, 2005 from http://www.project2061.org

> Project 2061 was funded by The American Association for the Advancement of Science (AAAS) and provided recommendations for what all students should know and be able to do in science, mathematics, and technology by the time they graduate from high school.

Biological Sciences Curriculum Study (BSCS) www.bscs.org

> BSCS is a nonprofit organization that has developed integrated science programs for elementary and middle schools and biology

programs for high school and college students. BSCS provides professional development and conducts research and evaluation of reform-based science programs.

The Collaborative for Academic, Social, and Emotional Learning (CASEL)
www.casel.org

Raises your awareness to the whole person, including self-awareness, social awareness, self-management, responsible decision making, and relationship skills.

Individuals with Disabilities Education Improvement Act (IDEA) 2004
www.ed.gov/policy/speced/guid/idea/idea2004.html

The Individuals with Disabilities Education Improvement Act of 2004 (IDEA) aligns IDEA

closely to the No Child Left Behind Act (NCLB), helping to ensure equity, accountability, and excellence in education for children with disabilities.

Office of Special Education Program (OSEP)
http://www.ed.gov/about/offices/list/osers/osep/index.html

The Office of Special Education Programs (OSEP) is a federal office under the U.S. Department of Education aimed at improving results for infants, toddlers, children, and youth with disabilities ages birth through 21 by providing leadership and financial support to assist states and local districts.

SECTION III

Developing Lessons

4 Determining Learning Outcomes

Main Idea of This Chapter
What will your students learn?

INTASC Standards Addressed in This Chapter

Principle 3 LEARNER DIFFERENCES: The teacher understands how students differ in their approaches to learning and creates instructional opportunities that are adapted to diverse learners.

Principle 4 TEACHING REPERTOIRE: The teacher understands and uses a variety of instructional strategies to encourage students' development of critical thinking, problem-solving, and performance skills.

Focus Questions

- How do you specify what students will learn?
- Do you have sources for lesson ideas?
- Do you know how to evaluate existing lessons?
- What lesson plan format do you use?
- How do you identify student learning outcomes in your lesson plans?

Design Activities

DA 12: Learning Topics and Learning Outcomes
DA 13: Lesson Search and Evaluation
DA 14: Lesson Plan Draft

WHERE WE ARE IN THE ID PROCESS

This chapter begins Section III, which examines teaching decisions for lessons. Chapter 4 introduces the process of building lessons by using a Teacher Decision Cycle, which consists of four questions to help you make lesson decisions. This cycle of questions and decisions is used again when developing units. The four questions approximate the design phase of instructional design (Figure 4.1). Question 1 within the Teacher Decision Cycle asks: "What will students learn?" Your decisions here identify student learning outcomes, which are the focus of this chapter.

FIGURE 4.1.
Instructional Design as Teacher Decision Making.

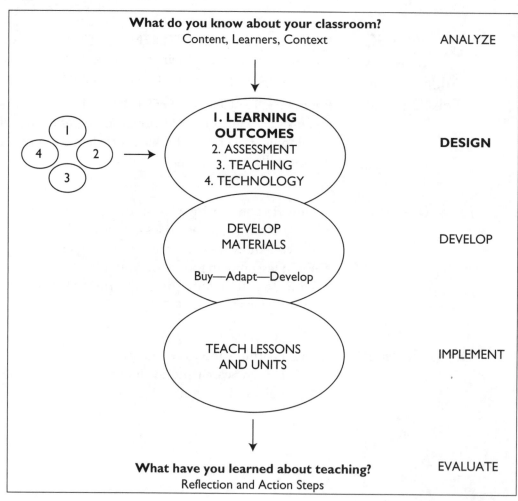

SCOPE OF THIS CHAPTER

Chapter 4 begins with an overview of the Teacher Decision Cycle. Next, we discuss learning outcomes at three levels of decision making: *learning goals, learning focus,* and *learning objectives.* Overall learning goals are specified in curriculums; the learning focus and specific learning objectives are noted in units and lessons. We will discuss four tools to help you think about the nature of these learning outcomes. The first three, state standards, learning taxonomies, and learning dimensions, were discussed in Chapter 3. The tool discussed in this chapter is facets of understanding. Collectively, these tools will help you think through what you are asking students to know, value, or do.

The second half of Chapter 4 provides an overview of our lesson plan format, particularly for new teachers but also for experienced teachers who wish to document their teaching for National Board® certification or share with other teachers. We conclude this chapter with a lesson plan example. The visual sequence for Chapter 4 is found in Figure 4.2.

FIGURE 4.2.
Visual Sequence for Chapter 4.

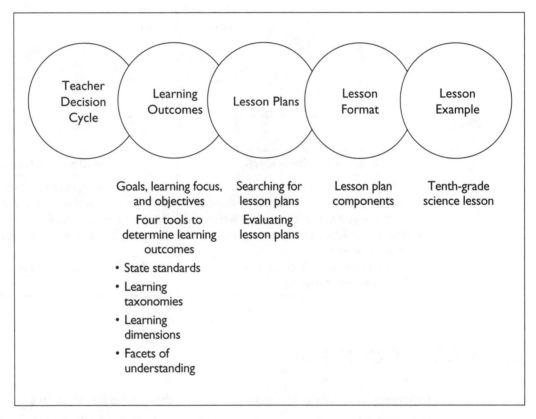

TEACHER DECISION CYCLE: QUESTION 1

The Teacher Decision Cycle consists of four questions. The first question to be asked is: *"What will your students learn?"* Teachers are responsible for translating state standards into learning outcomes. Knowing these learning outcomes, a teacher can proceed to make subsequent teaching decisions along the cycle. The cycle of teacher decisions and the corresponding text chapters are visualized in Figure 4.3.

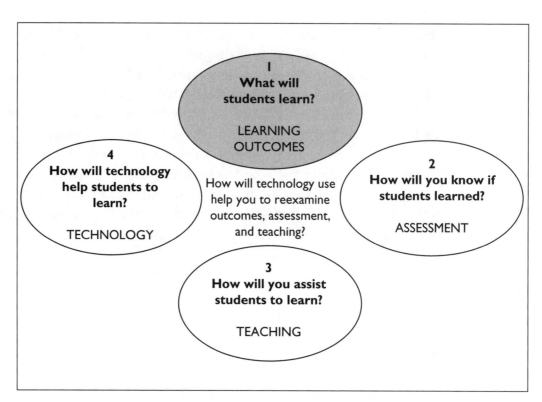

FIGURE 4.3.
Teacher Decision Cycle and Text Chapters.

Teacher Decision Cycle	Section III Chapters
1 What will students learn?	Chapter 4: Determining Learning Outcomes
2 How will you know if students learned?	Chapter 5: Exploring Assessment Options
3 How will you assist students to learn?	Chapter 6: Exploring Teaching Options
4 How will media and technology help students learn?	Chapter 7: Exploring Technology Options
How will technology decisions help you rethink previous decisions?	WRAPUP: Completing Your Lessons

LEARNING OUTCOMES

Learning outcomes is a broad category that includes learning goals and learning objectives. Determining learning outcomes is necessary before one can make decisions on assessment and teaching strategies.

Defining goals and objectives

Educators differ in their views on these terms, but here are some operational definitions. *Learning outcomes* is an overarching term that involves how you, your school, your school district, or your state specifies what students will learn. *Learning goals* provide broad directions for student learning and probably incorporate many subgoals. Goals are useful to summarize learning for curriculum and instructional units. Curriculum goals may be imposed or suggested or may be determined by groups of teachers. Individual teachers or groups of teachers usually determine goals for units, and commercially available packages will also specify these.

For individual lessons, we use the term *learning focus* to clearly identify the learning purpose of a lesson, rather than just recording the activity or topic. Although a descriptive title helps to depict the nature of the activity, a learning focus identifies the learning purpose of the lesson. Within each lesson, one or more types of learning may be the focus. Generally, *learning objectives* apply to these learning types, such as the taxonomies discussed in Chapter 3. Visually, Figure 4.4 organizes these terms to denote differences in learning outcomes.

FIGURE 4.4.
Differences in Learning Outcomes Across Instructional Use.

Learning Outcome	Instructional Use
Learning goals Learning focus Learning objectives	Broad learning outcomes for curriculum and units Overall learning purpose for lessons Specific learning specified by learning types, learning dimensions, and/or state standards

The lesson plan format introduced in this chapter incorporates a learning focus and specific learning objectives matched with state standards. Later in this chapter, we have provided a sample lesson from a teacher candidate who designed and taught this lesson during her internship. Figure 4.5 summarizes how she identified these different forms of learning outcomes.

FIGURE 4.5.
Example of Different Levels of Learning Outcomes.

Learning Outcome	Instructional Use
Learning goals	The lesson is part of a unit for tenth-grade honors science called "Changing Ecosystems." The overall learning goal was "an understanding of ecological principles."
Learning focus	"Interactions Among Organisms"
Learning objectives	• Identify how energy flows through a system • Analyze interactions among organisms in a food chain and food web
State standards	• Engage in active inquiries, investigations, and hands-on activities for a minimum of 50 percent of the instructional time • Use computers and other electronic technologies

Tools to determine learning outcomes

The following tools can be used to help determine learning outcomes:

- State standards
- Learning taxonomies
- Learning dimensions
- Facets of understanding

State standards

State standards are organized in different ways, so you need to be familiar with the standards that apply to your school. Individual schools vary in terms of how teachers meet these state standards, which are assessed by state testing. Having access to these standards can help you prioritize standards in your classroom. Usually, teachers have the freedom to translate standards to their units and lessons, although schools and groups of teachers may determine overall curriculum goals for schools, depending on the unique needs of schools and their respective students. What usually occurs is a more fluid situation in which the teacher's choice of units and lessons drives the determination of specific learning outcomes for these units and lessons.

Learning taxonomies

Student learning, as expressed by the lesson's overall learning focus and/or specific learning objectives, may include one or more levels of the cognitive, affective, and psychomotor taxonomies. Identifying learning levels for each of your learning objectives can help you choose appropriate assessments. Figure 4.6 provides some examples of verbs that can be used to formulate specific learning objectives in your lessons.

These verbs act as "indicators" in your assessment plan as you devise ways of scoring or evaluating your assessment tasks. For example, if the focus of your learning objectives is knowledge, the recall of learned material (and the lowest level of the cognitive taxonomy) is of primary concern, and assessment tools need only match this instructional purpose. If, however, your intent is at the higher cognitive levels, then your assessment purpose requires different forms of assessment.

How then do we go about assessing upper-level learning performance that involves critical thinking or problem solving? One technique instructional designers use is to look at the nature of the intellectual activity and conduct a task analysis (see Jonassen, Tessmer, & Hannum, 1999), which was discussed in Chapter 3. Examining the nature of the intellectual tasks—through task analysis of key tasks, by consulting experts, and from what you know from

Level	Activities	Learning Objective Verbs
Evaluation	Judge work of peers Develop criteria for projects	Judge, evaluate, rate, assess, choose, compare, appraise
Synthesis	Write a paper Design a lesson Compose a lyric	Compose, propose, construct, design, create, manage
Analysis	Discuss pros and cons of issue List causes Dissect earthworm Analyze interactions among organisms in a food chain and food web	Discuss, debate, question, analyze, experiment, diagram, examine
Application	Solve problem Demonstrate application Use computers	Apply, use, practice, demonstrate, illustrate
Comprehension	Explain functions of object Translate sentence Identify how energy flows through a system	Describe, explain, identify, translate, report, tell, review
Knowledge	Define key terms List major military campaigns Label moving components	Define, list, label, name, recall

FIGURE 4.6. Learning Objective Verbs for Cognitive Taxonomy (Bloom, 1956).

teaching these tasks—can help you determine appropriate ways to assess whether these intellectual skills have been learned.

Learning dimensions

In addition to the taxonomic views of learning, other forms of learning may be important in your curriculum, units, and lessons. In Chapter 3, we identified some examples of what we called "learning dimensions," which are more complex than the taxonomies (Figure 4.7).

FIGURE 4.7. Learning Dimensions.

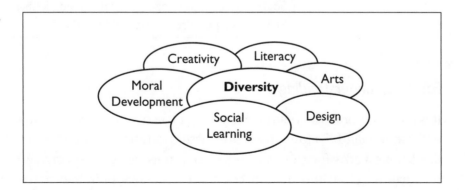

Each of these dimensions challenges the teacher to write appropriate goals, learning focuses, and objectives for instruction, as some aspects of these learning dimensions may not be served well by performance objectives. For example, design, arts, and creative learning may benefit from a statement of general learning intent, as students' performance may be rather broad and emergent. If these dimensions are important, then teachers must still document intent for learning so that appropriate teaching and assessment decisions can be made. As is suggested by Figure 4.8, the idea of diversity or human differences can provide a powerful teaching strategy. Figure 4.8 summarizes some resources to investigate for specifying a clear learning focus to your lessons.

FIGURE 4.8.
Resources for Identifying Learning Outcomes for Different Learning Dimensions.

Dimension	Resource
Literacy	Reading and writing: International Reading Association (IRA) Visual: International Visual Literacy Association (IVLA) Technological: International Technology Education Association (ITEA) Computer: International Society for Technology in Education (ISTE)
Arts	National Committee for Standards in the Arts (1994)
Design	Interior design: American Society of Interior Designers (ASID) Instructional design (training): International Board of Standards for Training, Performance, and Instruction (IBSTPI) Instructional design (instructional technology): American Educational Communications and Technology (AECT)
Social learning	Social knowledge: actions with people, Piaget (1969) Cooperative learning: Johnson, Johnson, & Holubec (1990) Self-concept: Canfield & Wells (1994)
Diversity and multiculturalism	Cultural differences: Snowman & Biehler (2000) Limited English proficiency: ESL Legislation: e.g., IDEA
Moral development	Levels: Kohlberg (1975) Ethic of care: Gilligan (1993)
Creativity	Multiple intelligences: Gardner (2000) Sources of thought, languages of the mind: John-Steiner (1997) Play in young children: Chenfield (2002)

Facets of understanding

It is common practice to write a learning objective that specifies that "the student will understand." How does one assess student understanding? Using the illustrative verbs for the learning taxonomies helps to specify what you mean by learning verbal information, cognitive strategies, or intellectual skills, but what about understanding? Are there illustrative verbs that help here? Yes, but the choice of verbs, such as *recognize, know,* or *comprehend,* presents a new set of interpretative problems. However, teachers have to be clear about what students will learn; otherwise, it will be difficult to know if a student has learned anything. What, then, are we left with? Should we avoid the word *understanding?*

Some people have been characterized as multifaceted, meaning that there are many sides to these individuals. The idea of understanding is also multifaceted. Wiggins and McTighe (2001) characterize the interconnected facets of understanding as the ability of a student to explain, interpret, apply, have perspective, empathize, and have self-knowledge (Figure 4.9).

FIGURE 4.9.
Facets of
Understanding.

Facets of Understanding	
Can *explain*	Can *interpret*
Can *apply*	Have *perspective*
Can *empathize*	Have *self-knowledge*

From *Understanding by Design,* by Grant Wiggins & Jay McTighe (2001). Copyright © by the Association for Supervision and Curriculum Development, 1703 N. Beauregard St., Alexandria, Va. Reprinted by permission.

The different facets help teachers design assessment and teaching that support student understanding. Many forms of understanding are likely to require more than one of these facets. Writing, for example, may require the ability to empathize with an audience and write in ways that interest the reader. Effective writing may require the ability to depict characters and situations. The writing act itself requires very developed abilities to be disciplined, to evaluate one's writing, and to trust one's capacities to accomplish one's intentions or to learn more. Next, we briefly explain each of these facets of understanding.

Can explain

Learning goals that ask for student understanding are a far cry from having students recall facts. Recall of information, facts, and concepts may be an important prerequisite for understanding, but how this information is used becomes an important issue. Explanation is one facet of understanding in which students are asked to explain what facts mean. Assessment involves more than answers; it includes explanations and support for these explanations. Teaching for understanding uses themes and problems to provide the central organizing structure in lessons and units (Figure 4.10).

Can interpret

Interpretation enhances student understanding beyond "explanation." Most information is not value-free, meaning that not all people will see information in

Facet	Evidence	Instruction
Can *explain*	Knowledgeable and justified accounts of events, actions, and ideas	Overarching themes and problems
Can *interpret*	Interpretations, narratives, and translations that provide meaning	Activities that encourage students to develop their own interpretations through pictures, stories, and role play
Can *apply*	Knowledge used in different situations	Near authentic problems and performance
Has *perspective*	Critical and insightful points of view	Use of guiding questions that invite multiple points of view
Can *empathize*	Appreciation of other points of view	Genuine experiences where students must face the consequences of their decisions
Has *self-knowledge*	Self-awareness of what one knows and does not know, and implications of one's actions	Self-reflection and draft versions of student work with periodic feedback

FIGURE 4.10. Teaching for the Facets of Understanding.

From *Understanding by Design* by Grant Wiggins & Jay McTighe (2001). Copyright © by the Association for Supervision and Curriculum Development, 1703 N. Beauregard St., Alexandria, Va. Reprinted by permission.

the same way. To "interpret" could involve telling a story that depicts what knowledge means, based on the student's experience. Teaching uses activities in which students develop their own interpretations through pictures, stories, or roles as examples. Here student activity combines both teaching and assessment.

Can apply

With "understanding" outcomes, students demonstrate a grasp of concepts, perspectives, and ideas in order to use this knowledge on a problem of interest. Application allows students to demonstrate their understanding. A challenge for teachers is not only giving students challenging problems but also allowing students the freedom to apply what they know. Teaching decisions involve the choice of relevant problems, authentic to the extent that they are appropriate to children's developmental needs and classroom realities. Teachers then come to know what students know and what they don't know. In addition, students develop an awareness of what they know through these application activities.

Have perspective

Gaining perspective helps students develop the capacity to see and voice different viewpoints. Evidence for this learning involves student activity in which students experience different points of view through listening, writing, speaking, or some other type of performance. This experience can include students in class, guests, or the use of media to visually depict different views on a topic. Teachers can also use guiding questions and encouragement to bring everyone into these activities. Developing an appreciation for cultural diversity can be addressed within this facet of understanding.

Can empathize

Building empathy or the ability to understand someone's feelings and point of view requires direct human experience rather than a mere description of how to appreciate others. Evidence of empathy can include what students say and do, through writing, role play, projects, or other actions. Students can develop these experiences with peers, but sometimes building empathy with new acquaintances may further improve students' empathetic capacities in the classroom and the community.

Have self-knowledge

Helping students develop self-knowledge is not always a learning outcome. Allowing students time to reflect and including reflectivity as part of an assessment plan give teachers information on how self-knowledge is developing in a student. Ask students for their reactions and feelings. Sometimes this can be done in the classroom, through writing activities, or with personal conferences. Sometimes peer sharing of this self-knowledge can be very powerful, whether you set this up formally in learning or you provide opportunities during the school day for this to happen.

For example, many people acknowledge their poor writing skills. In addition to knowing grammar and composition, a writer must understand the nature of writing as a human activity. Having self-knowledge means valuing writing as human expression, sharing common fears, submitting drafts, and learning from feedback. Students view writing as a private act. Students come to believe that what they hand in is a final version. Sharing drafts of work requires periodic, consistent, and responsive feedback from the instructor.

DESIGN ACTIVITY 12

Learning Topics and Learning Outcomes

Task Rationale   Practice identifying learning outcomes for learning topics and making the connections between learning outcomes across curriculum, units, and lessons.

Task Guidelines
1. Choose a learning topic that you would like to teach, a lesson that will include "understanding" as a specific learning outcome
2. Identity the **curriculum title** and **goal, unit title** and **goal,** and **lesson title, learning focus,** and **learning objectives**. To do this, you will have to think about learning outcomes at the curriculum, unit, and lesson level.

Learning Topic:

Curriculum Title:
Curriculum Goal:

Unit Title:
Unit Goal:

Lesson Title:
Learning Focus of Lesson:
Specific Learning Objectives for an Activity:

     For one learning objective that specifies student understanding, identify ways to assess this understanding. Refer to the facets of understanding discussed earlier to help you.

Reflectivity
- What questions or issues occurred to you as you were working through the different levels of outcomes?
- At what level(s) was understanding specified?
- What would be the possible ways in which student understanding would be assessed?

SEARCHING FOR AND EVALUATING LESSON PLANS

There are many web-based resources for lesson ideas and for adapting them to your teaching. The Educator's Reference Desk site is particularly useful (www.eduref.org). It includes a question-and-answer archive, 2,000 lesson plans, and 3,000 links to education information, organized by counseling, educational levels, educational management, educational technology, evaluation, family life, general education, librarianship, reference, specific populations, content areas, and teaching.

There are many sources for lesson plans, but not everything you discover in publications or online warrants use without evaluation. Here are some questions to ask yourself:

- Is a source to the lesson identified, so you can credit its use in your lesson plan?
- Is the site commercial or noncommercial? If the site is commercial, you should scrutinize the motives of the lesson to use some proprietary approach or software.
- Does the lesson clearly identify the educational level of the learner and the learning outcome(s)? Many lessons are procedures for student activity and are not always clearly connected to student learning.
- Does the lesson provide a means to assess student learning?
- Are the assessments appropriate to the learning being asked of the student?
- If rubrics are provided, are they constructed well, including adequate categories of performance and meaningful ranges of performance?
- Does the lesson merit application to a different educational level, developmental level, or content area?
- Are you limiting your search to looking for a specific grade and content area?
- What degree of effort will it take to find the materials needed? Do you have adequate expertise, or do you need to learn some skills to teach this lesson?

Many teachers are interesting in trying out new lessons, and they are equally eager to share them with others. The next Design Activity involves searching for lessons to review and evaluate.

Lesson Search and Evaluation

Task Rationale   Search the Internet for lesson plan ideas and evaluate their usefulness.

Task Guidelines   Consult the follow web site:
www.eduref.org/
Lesson plans in the Educator's Reference Desk are organized by arts, computer science, foreign language, health, information literacy, interdisciplinary, language arts, mathematics, philosophy, physical education, science, social studies, and vocational education. You can also search by grade levels. Including Pre–K, Kindergarten, Grades 1–12, Higher Education, Vocational Education, and Adult/Continuing Education.

1. Identify three lessons from the database that interest you.
2. For each lesson summarize the following:
   - Why you chose the lesson
   - Learning focus
   - Teaching strategies
   - Assessment
3. Evaluate each lesson by using the following criteria (record Y/N or make a brief note):

Lesson title:	URL:
Why you chose the lesson:	
Learning focus:	
Teaching strategies:	
Assessment:	

EVALUATIVE CRITERIA	Y-N
Student level and learning outcomes identified?	
Appropriate assessments provided?	
Value in translating lesson to other grade levels and content areas?	
Materials listed?	
Do I have sufficient expertise?	
Lesson developer identified?	
Commercial connections?	

Reflectivity   How did this search help you to think about new ways to teach your lessons?

LESSON PLAN COMPONENTS

As discussed in Chapter 2, experienced teachers plan at different cycles: yearly, grading periods, units, and lessons. Experienced teachers use different formats as well. Some teachers use very detailed approaches, similar to our suggested format. Some create their lesson plans on computer and store them digitally, performing a "save as" function on the files to develop new versions, a technique that enables you to document your teaching and share your ideas with others. This archival habit will be helpful if you elect to earn National Board Certification®, which is discussed in Chapter 10. Other teachers keep the details in their head, and most teachers use a format somewhere between the two. Many teachers make brief notes in the grid or table format found in classroom assignment notebooks. As no one format works for all teachers, you will need to develop your own system.

The following lesson plan format combines many features of lesson plans (Figure 4.11). We organize the lesson plan into categories to illustrate specific functions, which include the following:

- Title
- Identification
- Learning focus
- Teaching and assessment overview
- Teaching procedures
- Post teaching

This lesson plan format appears complex and daunting. The format is labeled and structured to illustrate the major features and benefits of this information. Not all lesson plans have this detail, but all effective lessons are based on thinking about and making decisions on these items. It is unreasonable, given the time constraints faced by teachers, to expect all lessons to be written out in this detail. The purpose of the format in this book is to help new teachers see the complexity of their decisions and understand that effective teaching requires attention to the issues raised by the items in the lesson plan. This format enables experienced teachers to "unpack" their teaching decisions. Another benefit is that the plan provides structure to document some of the lessons that teachers believe represent their teaching. These plans could become exhibits for national certification.

Descriptive title of lesson

Describe the lesson with a title that captures the essence of the lesson. The title could include words that describe both student learning and the teaching approach. An example would be "Acting Out: Using Puppets in the Writing

Descriptive Title of Lesson

IDENTIFICATION SECTION

Teacher Candidate:

School: **Grade level:**   **Date(s):**

Cooperating teacher:

LEARNING FOCUS SECTION

Subject Unit: **Time Estimate:**

LEARNING FOCUS:

OVERVIEW SECTION

Materials:

Objectives:

- What will students learn in this lesson?
- Match with appropriate state standards

Teaching and Assessment Overview:

- Briefly describe teaching and assessment strategies

TEACHING SECTION

Procedures:

- Introduction or opening activity or review
- Instruction/activities
- Transitions
- Closure: review, assignments
- Classroom management rules or procedures that apply to this lesson
- Teacher inquiry procedures (data gathering of teacher and student activity)

POST-TEACHING SECTION

Lesson plan reflective questions:

- What did the students learn during your lesson, and how do you know?
- What would you do differently the next time you teach this lesson and why?
- What went well during this lesson, and how do you know?
- What did you learn about teaching?
- What did your cooperating teacher (or peer) say about your teaching?
- How well did you incorporate issues of diversity, special needs, and technology? Could these become a central strategy in your activity?

Modifications or reteach strategies:

FIGURE 4.11. Suggested Lesson Plan Format.

Process." The use of puppets communicates a role-play teaching strategy in helping students learn one phase of the writing process. The title also may provide thematic continuity between related lessons. A compelling title attracts others to read and use your lesson. Titles that read "Lesson One,"

"Lesson Two," and "Lesson Three" are not too compelling. Titling your lessons also contributes to the development of your "teacher voice" and professional identity.

Identification section

The identification section identifies you, your cooperating teacher, and the school where you are teaching. This information will be helpful to others who might review your lessons. If you are specializing in special education, you may be placed at two different schools and grade levels to gain experience in elementary and secondary school settings. Entering the date or dates is useful to keep the lessons in chronological order. The date section is also useful if a lesson covers several days. For example, a science lesson may last the entire week, depending on the scope of activities. Additional lessons may be needed to give students practice or for reteaching.

Learning focus section

The learning focus is the most important section of the lesson plan. Without a clear focus for student learning, your subsequent decision making will be activities that may have nothing to do with your intended learning outcomes. Knowing the learning focus of the lesson will require appropriate activities, teaching strategies, assessment, and technology. Delete or revise decisions that do not help students to learn.

Subject and student learning

The subject line records the content area(s) you are teaching. With related lessons found in units, identifying the subject will connect the lesson plans. You could, for example, record: "American Literature—Poetry Unit—Living the Life of a Soldier." The learning focus for this lesson might be: "Understanding how poets depict the human dilemmas of their day and time." The learning product from this lesson could be the submission and presentation of a poetry portfolio. The learning focus reminds the teacher to frame the focus of the lesson on what students will learn, not merely on what students do.

Time estimates

Estimating the time needed for a lesson comes with experience. You may plan more activity than you have time for, or your teaching could be interrupted by some event. The lesson can become two lessons. Some activity in the lesson may need to be changed or deleted. One concern of new teachers is running out of instructional activities. Students tell us that this is one of the worst things that you can experience. Having a supplementary activity, then, is useful in this case, particularly until you become used to improvising and adjusting on the spot. Another option is to include in your classroom management plan "what happens when students finish." Include this in the teaching section. It is also useful to estimate time requirements for individual activities within the lesson procedures.

Overview section

This brief section records the learning materials you will need, the specific learning objectives that support the student learning focus of the lesson, and an overview of the teaching and assessment strategies used in the lesson. This information clearly communicates that you are clear as to student learning, as well as how you are teaching and assessing.

Materials

List the materials you need. A list acts as a checklist to ensure that you have everything you need and may alert you to preparations you need to make before class. Review the list to see what you might have to modify or develop and decide if you have sufficient lead time to complete these preparations.

Objectives

Keeping the learning focus in mind, list the specific objectives of what students will know, understand, value, or be able to do in the lesson. When you list learning objectives, identify the type or level of learning. Is the learning objective an information recall objective? Is it a thinking strategy? Is your objective a complex combination of cognitive, affective, and psychomotor? Is your objective one of promoting "understanding," or is your objective supporting one or more dimensions of learning?

Match the learning objective with one or more state standards, if this is required in your school. This match of objective and state standard helps you become acquainted with the standards and signals to lesson reviewers, administrators, and other teachers your understanding of state accountability standards.

Teaching and assessment overview

This subsection is not usually found in lesson plan formats. What you achieve here is a brief description of the teaching and assessment strategies to be used. A brief statement of these strategies helps you and others see your overall teaching and assessment approach and helps you judge if your decisions are appropriate to your learning focus and specific learning objectives.

Teaching section

This is the heart of the lesson plan, the procedures you will use in teaching. Listing the steps is the simplest and most straightforward way of documenting your intent for teaching. Over time, you will probably reduce or even eliminate the details here, as you become familiar with implementing the flow of instruction. It is sometimes helpful to group the procedures in some logical way if a long list is developed.

The teaching section lists procedures for instruction and activity, which may be teacher directed, student focused, or a mix of the two. In our lesson plan format, the flow of instruction includes an introduction or review, instruction, and activities, including what media, materials, or technology is used. We also suggest, if you are conducting teacher research, that procedures for gathering data be listed here. In this way, data collection becomes a part of planning your teaching, much like gathering and using media materials. Finally, we suggest including in the teaching section whatever procedures for closure, review, or homework assignments are needed. Time estimates for particular activities help to gauge the time needed for instruction.

Introduction procedures

The beginning of teaching usually involves an opening activity, which is designed to gain students' attention and ready them for instruction. New teachers tend to be interested in developing these activities to motivate students, as they are concerned with student behavior and student reactions to what they say and do. As a result, they may spend a good deal of effort on the opening activity, but the rest of the instruction shifts back to less compelling strategies. Frequently, a rich, compelling opening activity can provide the basis for a strong lesson. Gaining student attention is a useful purpose to an opening activity, as the time can be used to review a previous lesson or focus students' attention on a new topic. Like an opening chapter to a novel, an interesting opening activity may trigger student curiosity, questions, and activity and, like a good book, motivate one to read further.

Instructional procedures

Your opening activity should lead directly to learning new topics and may stimulate students' curiosity or point out major ideas to be elaborated on. "Teaching" at this point may use different teaching strategies. Our customary view of teaching is that you present new material to be learned and that this knowledge is "given" to students in the form of a presentation, lecture, or demonstration.

However, teaching may involve student activity in which they discover, research, debate, role play, simulate, problem solve, brainstorm, or question. Student activity may be individual or may involve pairs (dyads) or small groups. This part of the lesson plan records instructor and student activity. The flow of teaching may shift between teacher and student or be equally shared.

Another customary view of teaching is that one "teaches" first and then evaluates. In the flow of instruction, one can assess student learning *as* one teaches. In many situations, ongoing assessment of student learning may involve observing and commenting on students' work or responding to their questions. Sometimes a checklist provides an assessment tool to document important behaviors. The checklist records a list of performance items and should support the learning objective. If, for example, you are "promoting communication in group problem solving," then your checklist will include behavior and communication indicators. Generally, this form of assessment is known as "formative assessment," and its purpose is to monitor student learning during instruction. Assessment information of this type helps you adjust your teaching to provide review, better examples, or additional practice or to work with individual students.

Transition guidelines

Instructional procedures can include guidelines for critical procedures, implementation, or transitions between activities or lessons. This section can suggest ways to help students understand the meaning behind an opening activity, review previous learning, or ask questions to prompt student attention. These details can be noted after the lesson has been taught one or more times. Guidelines can also be suggested from a peer, a mentoring teacher, or an outside source.

Classroom management

Record any classroom management rules or procedures that apply to the lesson. Classroom management is more than just behavior. Classroom management includes everything you need to organize students, space, time, and materials so that learning can take place. Classroom management involves the physical preparation of learning areas, posting of student work, and student behavior (Wong & Wong, 2001).

Teacher inquiry procedures

In action research or any formal teacher inquiry, you will be gathering "data." You are probably already gathering data. The purpose for this section is to remind you to collect student work so that it can be assessed for student learning and incorporated in your teacher research. You may already be collecting student work to provide formative assessment, but an additional procedure may remind you to photocopy student work, for example, so that you can analyze it more carefully.

Closure procedures

Identifying ways to end the lesson provides a time for reviewing student performance, clarifying conceptual problems, or briefing students on what is due for "next time." Closure may be a necessary component of a particular teaching strategy. For example, having group members report back to the class on their findings provides closure to an activity. Closure may also include housekeeping functions, such as cleaning up an activity area.

Post-teaching section

The post-teaching section is filled out after teaching. The purpose of this section is to reflect on your teaching, comment on what happened, and determine what changes need to be made the next time the lesson is taught. Guidelines, suggestions, or caveats for teachers may be included. Alternative teaching strategies or activities might also be suggested.

Reflection

In our lesson plan format, we have listed suggested questions to reflect on after a lesson is taught. The important questions are: "Did your students learn, and how do you know?" and "What do you now know about the differences in how your students know the content?" Responses to the reflective section further document your teaching in ways that a lesson plan by itself may not address. Reflectivity should prompt action and adjustments in daily teaching. Reflective habits usually take time to develop and may serve different purposes across one's teaching career, and their form may take on very individualistic patterns similar to personalized forms of planning.

Modifications

What changes do you need to make in this lesson? Making these change notes increases the value of your lesson plan for the next time you or someone else uses it. Recording notes on improvements or additional guidelines for teaching the lesson helps you grow your teaching at the lesson level.

LESSON PLAN EXAMPLE

The following section includes a lesson plan written by a fourth-year teacher education student in an undergraduate instructional design course (Figure 4.12). The lesson was pulled from a four-lesson unit that was required at the end of the course. Lessons two through four will be featured in Chapter 8 on unit development. The text that follows this example describes and comments on what the student designed.

Web Your Appetite: Discovering Interactions

IDENTIFICATION SECTION

Teacher Candidate: Whitney Hatcher

School: County H.S. **Grade level:** Tenth-Grade Honors Science **Date(s):** Two periods

Cooperating teacher: [name withheld]

LEARNING FOCUS SECTION

Subject-Unit: "Changing Ecosystems" **Time Estimate:** Two 50-minute periods

LEARNING FOCUS: Interactions among organisms

OVERVIEW SECTION

Materials:

Individual: copies of computerized presentation file and printout, Section 5.1 from the textbook, activity summation questions

Group: organism index cards, string, "Web Your Appetite" activity

Objectives: Students will be able to:

1. Identify how energy flows through a system.
2. Show interactions among organisms within a food chain and a food web, and analyze those interactions.

State Standards:

- Engage in active inquiries, investigations, and hands-on activities for a minimum of 50 percent of the instructional time.
- Use computers and other electronic technologies.

Teaching and Assessment Overview:

- This lesson makes use of direct instruction, cooperative learning, and discussion. The computer-based presentation is a form of direct instruction, and the activity is a form of cooperative learning.
- Asking questions at end of presentation, individual summation questions, and questions at the end of Section 5.1.
- Class discussion.

TEACHING SECTION

Procedures:

<u>Introduction or opening activity or review</u>

- Teacher outlines main ideas of Section 5.1.

<u>Instruction/Activities</u>

- Computer-based presentation on the interactions among organisms. Ask the students for examples of organisms that fit the vocabulary words (15 min.)

- "Web Your Appetite" group activity (35 min.)
- Summation questions from the activity (20 min.)
- Questions at the end of Section 5.1 in the book (15 min.)
- Discuss answers to both sets of questions (15 min.)

Media, materials, or technology used

- Computer and video projector

Teacher inquiry procedures

- Record in journal reflective observations on this lesson.

Closure: Review, assignments

- Review the summation questions and Section 5.1 questions. Ask students for any questions.

POST-TEACHING SECTION

Modifications or reteach strategies:

If the students do not understand the activity or answer the questions with 100 percent accuracy, then go back over the material they seem to be having trouble with.

FIGURE 4.12. Lesson Plan Example.
Adapted from Whitney Hatcher. Reprinted with permission.

Identification section

Identifying school, grade level, and date helps the teacher organize the lessons for a portfolio or future use.

Learning focus section

Subject and student learning

This lesson is the first of a four-lesson unit for tenth-grade science honors students, "Changing Ecosystems." The teacher has planned two continuous fifty-minute periods for this lesson, and the purpose for the lesson is "interactions among organisms."

Overview section

Materials

The materials list was divided in terms of materials for individual students and groups.

Objectives

The first objective has students learning to identify how energy flows through a system. The second objective asks students to show and analyze interactions. Lessons frequently include student activity and assessment in the objective statement. A third objective could be added to this lesson, such as assessing student behavior in cooperative groups. Cooperative behavior and performance could join the understanding of energy flow in organisms as another aspect to the "content," and a matching learning objective included.

Teaching and assessment overview

The teacher identifies direct instruction, cooperative learning, and discussion as the teaching strategies. She sees the presentation as a variation of direct instruction. If you look at the bulleted list under instruction, you will see that the teacher has provided suggestions within the presentation to "ask the students for examples." The presentation could integrate other teaching approaches. For example, a computer-based presentation does not have to be solely new material but can also include student activity in the form of responses to teacher questions, simulations, or video clips embedded within the presentation that are designed to provide examples. Also, hyperlinks within the presentation can connect to other sources, such as live web chats with experts. These suggestions would upgrade this low-level use of instructional technology from teacher directed to student centered. Another factor in this decision is the time available for this lesson and the scope of activities. Direct instruction provides time efficiency in this lesson and allows more time for the intended activity. A higher level of instructional technology activity would be most likely the major activity in the lesson.

Cooperative groups are used for the "Web Your Appetite." The teacher developed separate activity sheets on which she included much of the detail for its implementation. In other words, she created in her unit a set of lesson plans and a set of activities. A benefit to this approach is that if the teacher posted her lesson plans to the web, she could link from the lesson plan web page to the activity web page.

Assessment included the group activity and summation questions, text questions, and closure discussion. The formative evaluation of student performance is addressed by student activity—in this case, the demonstration of energy flow and analysis of this flow.

Teaching section

Introduction procedures

The lesson is introduced with an outline of Section 5.1 of the textbook. The outcome can be written on the board or included in the computer presentation.

Instructional procedures

The sequence of teaching in this lesson spans two lessons. The flow of activity represented here visually illustrates the mix of teacher and student activity.

Mix of Teacher–Student Activity		
Teacher	15 min.	Computer-based presentation
Both		Student response to questions during presentation
Group	35 min.	"Web Your Appetite"
Students	20 min.	Activity summation questions
Students	15 min.	Text questions
Class	15 min.	Discussion

This flow of activity mixes teacher activity, student activity, and joint activity. Student activity includes a mix of class participation, peer interactions, and individual performance. Note also the mix of lecture and presentation with student activity. Options for this activity might be to rethink the use of text questions for assessment. Perhaps textbook questions that supplement "Web Your Appetite" would be more appropriate. These questions should address biological energy flow in other examples, so as to assess student understanding of energy flow in organisms. Removal of the text questions would provide more time to the activity and the discussion that follows. In addition, removing the text questions activity directly connects student activity with the class discussion!

Teacher inquiry procedures

Developing a habit of journal writing about what happened in class is a valuable activity for any teacher. Record your entries as soon as possible after the lesson is taught. You will forget many details if you wait until the weekend to record what happened in class the previous week. This activity might supplement other forms of data that are being used to answer one or more research questions conducted by formal teacher inquiry. Teaching and learning are heavily influenced by the learning context. Having a record of your teaching, student reactions, and performance, as well as the other details that characterized your teaching for that day, will document a more accurate accounting of what influenced student learning.

Closure procedures

In the class discussion for lesson closure, the teacher learns to summarize what she sees in class in terms of student performance and reactions to the learning activities. Closure can include a teacher's assessment of what was learned, as well as point out conceptual issues and direct student attention to future assignments or what the next lesson will be about.

Post-teaching section

Modifications

Experience with the activity and feedback from students will improve the structure of any activity. It takes time to explain what an activity is about and to provide clear instructions, so this time may need to be estimated and included in the overall plan. Writing instructions on the board may be necessary or, for older students, providing instructions on paper can reinforce oral instructions. When you look at developing a unit, a meaningful lesson may help students become acquainted with an activity or a new form of teaching, particularly if the lesson leads to significant student performance, such as discussions or peer projects.

LESSON DRAFTS

The following Design Activity repeats our suggested lesson plan format and gives you an opportunity to draft a lesson. Although the lesson plan format looks daunting, once you complete a few lessons, you will become familiar with the level of detail you need to teach the lesson.

Lesson Plan Draft

Task Rationale   Here is a suggested lesson plan format to record teaching decisions.

Task Guidelines   Respond to the following prompts to help you think through your first lessons.

TITLE OF LESSON

IDENTIFICATION SECTION

Teacher Candidate:

School: **Grade level:**   **Date(s):**

Cooperating teacher:

LEARNING FOCUS SECTION

Subject – Unit: **Time Estimate:**

LEARNING FOCUS:

OVERVIEW SECTION

Materials:

Objectives:

- What will students learn in lesson?
- Match with appropriate state standards, if applicable

Teaching and Assessment Overview:

- Brief statement on teaching strategies and how you assess learning

TEACHING SECTION

Procedures:

- Introduction or opening activity or review
- Instruction/Activities
- Transitions
- Closure: review, assignments
- Classroom management guidelines
- Teacher inquiry procedures

(continued)

Lesson plan reflective questions:

- What did the students learn during your lesson, and how do you know?
- What would you do differently the next time you teach this lesson, and why?
- What went well during this lesson, and how do you know?
- What did you learn about teaching?
- What did your cooperating teacher say about your teaching?
- How well did you incorporate issues of diversity, special needs, and technology?

Modifications or reteach strategies:

Reflectivity   What features of this lesson plan format worked for you, and why? What else is needed?

TEACHER DECISION CYCLE

With a clear decision on student learning outcomes, we can continue along the Teacher Decision Cycle (Figure 4.13), providing assistance to help you make teacher decisions on assessment, teaching, and technology (Chapters 5, 6, and 7, respectively).

FIGURE 4.13. Teacher Decision Cycle.

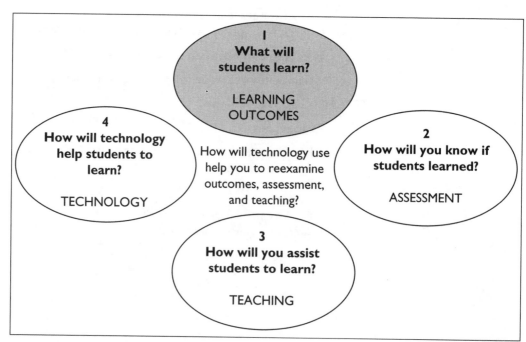

*An Idea
Worth
Thinking
About*

Design learning experiences based on
what students can imagine.

A common and sensible educational practice is to design learning experiences based on what students know and to build on this existing knowledge (Donovan, Bransford, & Pellegrino, 1999). Egan (2003) proposes a less restrictive principle. Rather than design to what students *know*, design learning experiences to what students can *imagine*. Building on what students know, according to Egan, is based on much research, but children's minds are not restricted to content knowledge and the gradual buildup of content. "Where children are" involves their imaginative engagement with the world. This is why teachers are fond of using stories, which are not constructed on what children know but on possibilities in the world. Stories also provide the basis for helping students understand various affective concepts such as good and bad or rich and poor. Many concepts are amenable to relating them to what students know, such as hot and cold, but more affective issues such as safety and fear concerns cannot be addressed in this manner. However, children readily understand these notions through characters, dreams, stories, and pictures.

The use of metaphor in stories, art, music, dance, and other expressions of human creation can form the basis for lessons and units. Relating new learning to what the student knows *and* can imagine is worth contemplating (Figure 4.14).

FIGURE 4.14.
Organizing a
Lesson Around
Imagination.

Incorporating Imagination as a Lesson Organizing Idea	
Providing logical and sensitive flow	Relating the student's world to the outside world
Organizing around key ideas	Topics and themes that may not have any conceptual basis but are critical for children's development
Providing compelling titles	Themes that attract student interest but record student learning and teaching strategy
Designing in interest	Student-developed stories, drawings, music, art
Designing in flexibility	Learn from your students; provide choice

Reflective Teaching

"How Do I Fit My Learning Objectives, Materials Needed, and My Assessment Strategies into That Tiny Little Box?"

It is no secret that a teacher candidate's lesson plan looks dramatically different from lesson plans produced by many veteran teachers. The stringent requirements placed on teacher candidates as they submit lesson plans may seem like cruel and unusual punishment. However, the beginning teacher may find that trying to adapt their lesson plans to fit into the typical "box by box" format of most lesson plan books is a most challenging task as well. Many teacher candidates go out into the world and think to themselves, "I will *never* write lesson plans like *that* again as long as I live!" Yet, when they actually get the job and are faced with turning in their lesson plan books to the principal for the first time, it may feel like Lesson Planning 101 all over again. How does a teacher fit everything into those tiny little boxes? Taking a peek at a veteran teacher's lesson plan book might be of little help. In fact, many veteran teachers will admit that their lesson plan books would make little sense to anybody but them. The beginning teacher is then faced with a dilemma. How do they find the "happy medium" between pages upon pages of detailed lesson plans and the minimalist version of only indicating a page number and a teacher manual reference? Thus begins the empowering journey of the beginning teacher. Now it is the beginning teacher, not the college professor or advisor, who is in control of learning how to construct meaningful lesson plans that follow a format that the beginning teacher can use productively and efficiently.

Teacher Inquiry

- Given a particular learning focus, different teachers, either individually or in groups, could develop very different lessons and units. Topics for inquiry could include the different ways that teachers view content and the different teaching and assessment strategies they use.
- Facets of understanding could be the focus of inquiry into the development and teaching of new units of instruction.
- Specific learning outcomes, such as problem solving, multiculturalism, creativity, and moral development, could be the focus of unit development across grade levels in a school. Inquiry could involve the different ways that teachers designed instruction and how students learned.

REFERENCES

Bloom, B. S. (1956). *Taxonomy of educational objectives: Handbook 1: Cognitive domain.* New York: McKay.

Canfield, J., & Wells, H. C. (1994). *100 ways to enhance self-concept in the classroom* (2nd ed.). Boston: Allyn and Bacon.

Chenfield, M. B. (2002). *Creative experiences for young children* (3rd ed.). Portsmouth, NH: Heinemann.

Donovan, S. M., Bransford, J. D., & Pellegrino, J. W. (1999). *How people learn: Bridging research and practice.* Washington, DC: National Academy Press.

Egan, K. (2003). Start with what the student knows or with what the student can imagine? *Phi Delta Kappan, 84*(6), 443–445.

Gardner, H. (2000). *Intelligence reframed: Multiple intelligences for the twenty-first century.* New York: Basic Books.

Gilligan, C. (1993). *In a difference voice: Psychological theory and women's development.* Cambridge, MA: Harvard University Press.

John-Steiner, V. (1997). *Notebooks of the mind: Explorations of thinking* (rev. ed.). New York: Oxford University Press.

Johnson, D. W., Johnson, R. T., & Holubec, E. J. (1990). *Circles of learning: Cooperation in the classroom.* Edina, MN: Interaction Book Company.

Jonassen, D. H., Tessmer, M., & Hannum, W. H. (1999). *Task analysis methods for instructional design.* Mahwah, NJ: Erlbaum.

Kohlberg, L. (1975). The cognitive approach to moral education. In P. Scharf (Ed.), *Readings in moral education* (pp. 36–51). Minneapolis, MN: Winston Press.

National Committee for Standards in the Arts. (1994). *Dance, music, theatre, visual arts: National standards for arts education.* Reston, VA: Author.

Piaget. J. (1969). *Science of education and the psychology of the child.* New York: Viking.

Snowman, J., & Biehler, R. (2000). *Psychology applied to teaching* (9th ed.). Boston: Houghton Mifflin.

Wiggins, G., & McTighe, J. (2001). *Understanding by design.* Upper Saddle River, NJ: Merrill–Prentice Hall.

Wong, H. K., & Wong, R. T. (2001). *The first days of school: How to be an effective teacher* (2nd ed.). Mountain View, CA: Harry K. Wong Publications.

RESOURCES

Print Resources

Bloom, B. S. (1956). *Taxonomy of educational objectives: Handbook 1: Cognitive domain.* New York: McKay.

Classic source for the cognitive taxonomy.

Gunter, M. A., Estes, T. H., & Schwab, J. (2003). *Instruction: A models approach* (4th ed.). Boston: Allyn and Bacon.

A practical survey of different teaching strategies, including variations, steps in their use, and a scenario for each. The book is prefaced with a discussion of goals and objectives and organizing lessons and units.

A set of unit case studies provided for kindergarten, middle school, and high school.

Jonassen, D. H., Tessmer, M., & Hannum, W. H. (1999). *Task analysis methods for instructional design.* Mahwah, NJ: Erlbaum.

Explanation of different types of learning tasks, including procedural, learning hierarchy, thinking tasks, critical incidents, and conceptual, among others. Includes a chapter on ways to elicit knowledge from experts, through analysis of documents, observations, surveys, interviews, think-alouds, focus groups, and the Delphi technique.

Web-Based Resources

Americans for the Arts

www.artsusa.org

Standards, research, and professional development on art education and child outcomes.

American Educational Communications Technology (AECT)

www.aect.org

American Society of Interior Designers (ASID)

www.asid.org

Children's Music Web

www.childrensmusic.org

Incorporating music into the curriculum, songs, and links.

International Board of Standards for Training, Performance, and Instruction (IBSTPI)

www.ibstpi.org/

International Reading Association (IRA)

www.reading.org

International Society for Technology in Education (ISTE)

www.iste.org

International Technology Education Association (ITEA)

www.iteawww.org/

International Visual Literacy Association (IVLA)

www.ivla.org

National Art Education Association (NAEA)

www.naea-reston.org

Lesson Plans

Copyright and Fair Use

http://fairuse.stanford.edu/

The Fair Use Doctrine provides for limited use of copyrighted materials for educational and research purposes without permission from the owners. This site provides background information on the evolving issue of copyright and fair use.

EDSITEment

http://edsitement.neh.gov/lesson_index.asp

Lesson plans on art and culture, literature and language arts, foreign languages, and history and social studies.

Educator's Reference Desk

www.eduref.org

The Educator's Reference Desk site includes a question-and-answer service, a collection of 3,000 resources organized by counseling, educational levels, educational management, educational technology, evaluation, family life, general education, librarianship, specific populations, content areas, teaching, and a reference section. The site also includes more than 2,000 lesson plans.

Lesson plans in the database are organized by subject, including arts, computer science, foreign language, health, information literacy, interdisciplinary, language arts, mathematics, philosophy, physical education, science, social studies, and vocational education. The site also solicits contributions.

Individuals with Disabilities Education Act (IDEA)

www.ed.gov/offices/OSERS/Policy/IDEA/

Intel® Teach to the Future

www97.intel.com/education/teach/index.htm

Unit plans using technology. Organized by grade/age levels and subject (mathematics, science, language arts, social studies, interdisciplinary).

Library of Congress

http://memory.loc.gov/learn/

Lesson plans organized by theme, topic, discipline, and era. Includes topics in civics and government, literature, and poetry.

5 Exploring Assessment Options

Main Idea of This Chapter

Assessment provides teachers with information about students and student learning.

Principle 4 TEACHING REPERTOIRE: The teacher understands and uses a variety of instructional strategies to encourage students' development of critical thinking, problem solving, and performance skills.

Principle 8 ASSESSMENT: The teacher understands and uses formal and informal assessment strategies to evaluate and ensure the continuous intellectual, social, and physical development of the learner.

Focus Questions

- What are your views on assessment?
- What are the different purposes for assessment?
- What are some of the tools for assessing student learning?
- What is a rubric?
- What assessment tools did you choose for your lessons?

Design Activities

DA 15: Views on Assessment
DA 16: Matching Learning Outcomes with Assessment Tools
DA 17: Develop a Rubric
DA 18: Assessment Overview

EXPLORING ASSESSMENT

Without assessment, how will you know that your students are learning? This question asks you to consider the value of assessment in educational settings, particularly for your primary focus on helping students learn. People react differently to the term *assessment*, and to appreciate the value of assessment, it is necessary to get your views on the table. In this chapter, we will ask you to write about your views of assessment. Assessment can be used for different purposes, the most important one of which is addressed in this chapter—namely, to assess student learning. The main idea in this chapter is that once you are clear on your purpose(s) for assessment, you can then make decisions on appropriate assessment tools. The remainder of the chapter describes these tools.

The sequence of Chapter 5 is visually represented in Figure 5.1.

FIGURE 5.1.
Visual Sequence for Chapter 5.

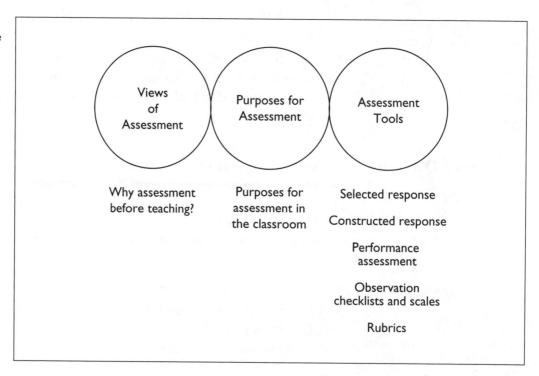

TEACHER DECISION CYCLE: QUESTION 2

At the lesson level, a teacher has to make a decision on what students will learn. This was question one in the Teacher Decision Cycle. Subsequent decisions include choices for assessment, teaching, and media and technology use. Chapter 5 discusses ways in which you document student learning.

How will you know if students learned?

This book is designed to guide you through a thinking process that supports teaching decisions. Figure 5.2 visually depicts the questions in the Teacher Decision Cycle and where we are in the cycle.

FIGURE 5.2.
Teacher
Decision Cycle:
Assessment
Question.

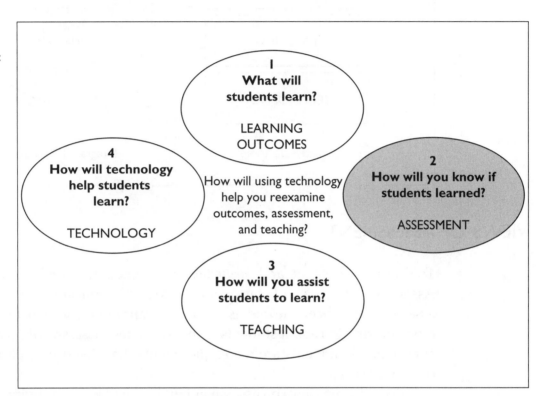

Why assessment before teaching?

We address assessment before teaching strategies, because you need to determine the purpose of assessment *before* you propose a teaching method to support the desired learning. Otherwise, your thinking favors "what students will do in the activity" without being clear as to *why* they are engaged in a particular activity.

Over time, a teacher becomes adept at making decisions about what is to be learned, how to assess student learning, and how to create learning environments. Chapters 4 through 7 deconstruct this skilled, very personalized form of teacher thinking into categories of teacher decisions that help you see the connections between the three. Decisions involving learning outcomes, assessment, teaching, and technology options become more integrated over time (Figure 5.3).

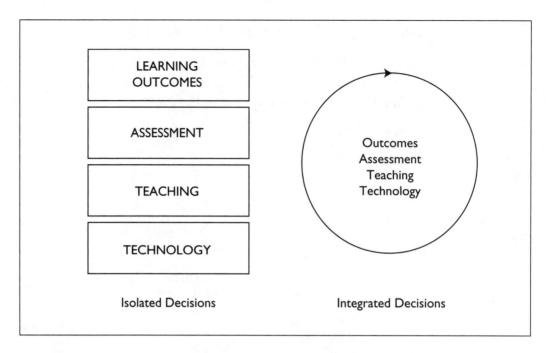

FIGURE 5.3.
Isolated Versus
Integrated
Decisions.

VIEWS OF ASSESSMENT

The terms *assessment* and *evaluation* are sometimes used interchangeably. Assessment covers a wide range of ways to learn about students. Traditionally, assessment has been viewed as evaluation, although assessment can provide more information about students than just grades. Assessment becomes evaluation when judgments are made, judgments that determine, pass, or certify (Eisner, 1994).

Record your views on assessment in the next Design Activity.

Views on Assessment

Task Rationale Make visible to yourself and others your views on assessment.

Task Guidelines

1. When you hear the term *assessment*, what comes to mind?
2. Describe a personal experience with "assessment"?
3. How do you see using assessment in your teaching?

Reflectivity

What did you think about in your writing, and what prompted your choice of a personal assessment experience?

PURPOSES FOR ASSESSMENT

In Chapter 4, we asked you to *record* student learning outcomes in your lesson plan in two ways. At the lesson level, we suggested recording a *learning focus* for your lesson, rather than merely recording "student activity." This keeps learning as the focus of the lesson rather than just student activity. Within the lessons, *learning objectives* detail specific student performance.

Our focus in this text is to describe assessment options used in classroom instruction. Assessment in the classroom can serve four different purposes: placement, diagnostic, formative, and summative assessment (Linn & Gronlund, 2000).

How assessment is used in the classroom

Assessments for *placement* purposes prior to instruction help to identify prerequisite knowledge and skills, mastery of content, or some evidence that demonstrates a student's placement in a particular instructional setting, such as small groups or individual work. Assessments for placement include tests of readiness, aptitude tests, pretesting, and observations by teachers or guidance counselors (Figure 5.4).

Meanwhile, assessment can serve a *diagnostic* purpose. For example, published diagnostic tests and careful observations provide the basis for determining learning difficulties.

FIGURE 5.4.
Purposes for Classroom Assessment and Assessment Tools.

Assessment Purpose	Assessment Tools
Placement: What do students know, and where should they be placed for instruction?	Pretesting, aptitude tests, observations
Diagnostic: What areas are students having difficulty with?	Published tests, observations
Formative: What learning progress are students making?	Observations, work sheets, quizzes, practice, draft papers, speeches, discussion, group activity
Summative: What grades have students earned?	Tests, projects, papers, science fair projects, portfolios, performances

Teacher-made assessments frequently assess *formative* student learning during instruction. Formative assessment tools are numerous, including observations, work sheets, and quizzes that help the teacher assess what students know. Observation is a major assessment tool for teachers. Observation checklists and rubrics can be used to help record observations.

Formal measurements of student learning, or *summative* assessments, include teacher-made tests and results from performance activities, such as hands-on projects, lab work, and physical performance (e.g., physical conditioning tests, musical performance, art exhibitions). Summative products, for the purpose of assigning a grade, can also include portfolios, essays, and demonstrations.

ASSESSMENT TOOLS

Traditionally, assessment has been viewed as testing, with tests being the principal way that students are evaluated. Wiggins (1989) recommends that we not shy away from "testing"—the test is central to instruction—but that we must carefully decide on what is a true test of learning. What is the *purpose* behind this true test? Choosing one or more "true tests" depends on knowing the learning outcomes. Testing, along with other forms, can be viewed as "techniques serving assessment. . . . Tests may contribute to the [assessment] program, but they should not define it" (Chittenden, 1990, p. 24).

Assessment tools can be divided into three types (Figure 5.5): asking your learners to choose from among choices, producing *selected response* assessments; allowing students to provide their own responses, producing *constructed response assessments*; and having students demonstrate their learning in *performance assessments*.

FIGURE 5.5.
Assessment
Tools.

Selected Responses (Students choose from choices)	Constructed Responses (Students provide their own responses)	Performance (Students demonstrate their learning)
Multiple choice Matching True-false	Short answer and essays Interviews with students Self-assessments	Projects Portfolios

Selected response assessments

Selected response assessment methods require that students select from a choice of answers. Common examples include multiple choice, matching, and true-false questions. These assessments can be used to determine a student's mastery of a large body of content and, with careful construction, can be useful to assess a wide range of cognitive capabilities (Popham, 2005).

The obvious advantage to selected response assessments is the ease with which they can be scored, and they are frequently used in situations where a large number of students must be taught and/or there is little time for scoring and student feedback. Another advantage is that an adequate number of questions can be asked to assess many skills and a great deal of knowledge. This reduces high scores from merely guessing. The major disadvantage is that students must make a choice rather than produce their own answers.

Multiple choice

One of the strongest selected response assessments is multiple choice, because one can construct selection options, or alternatives, that vary in their correctness, as compared with matching and true-false. Two ways in which multiple-choice items are constructed are through a direct question or an incomplete sentence. Students are asked to select the correct answer or the best answer.

Matching

Matching assessments consist of two lists, with the student attempting to match items from one list to items on the other according to the operating premise described in the assessment's directions. Items in each list are similar or homogeneous such that items in the first column, for example, are all dates, while items in the second column are all historical events. Matching items are frequently used in conjunction with other assessment options.

True-false

True-false assessments measure a student's ability to discern right-wrong answers. Increasing the number of items reduces the likelihood that guessing will produce a large number of correct answers. True-false questions require a short time to answer, so they can be used to cover a lot of content. Constructing them requires care that they are not worded so that they are obviously true or false.

Constructed response assessments

Selected response assessments require that students choose among options, but constructed response tests ask the student to supply or construct an answer. Such questions may have one right answer, such as a "fill-in-the-blank" question, or be more open-ended, such as an essay, where a range of responses may be correct based on some criteria.

If you are looking for the learner to produce a correct answer to a question, then constructed response tests are the choice. They become more difficult to score as the response lengthens, as in short-answer and essay assessments. A rubric that specifies criteria for an acceptable response must be constructed to ensure scoring reliability. How rubrics are developed is discussed later in this chapter. The trade-off here is scoring accuracy versus a better match between the assessment method and the desired skills.

Short answer quizzes and essays

Short answer quizzes and essays are constructed-response assessments that assess learning through writing by describing, analyzing, explaining, and summarizing (Gronlund, 1982). In fact, essays can be used to assess learning at all levels of Bloom's (1956) cognitive taxonomy, as well as the facets of understanding (Wiggins & McTighe, 1998). Essays can also be used to assess understanding, communication, and self-reflection skills. In addition to Bloom's cognitive skills, essays help to assess how one organizes responses and communicates them in writing. The subskills of composition—spelling, syntax, grammar, and sentence and paragraph structure, as well as mastering various essay forms, such as informative or persuasive essays—can also provide criteria for assessment.

Essays can be used to record and examine affective capabilities, such as being open to new views, responding to needs, valuing one's own ideas and the ideas of others, and resolving conflicts of inner speech and transforming the results into writing. Good items for essays can be difficult to prepare, and their scoring is subjective, difficult, and less reliable than objective tests (Gronlund, 1982). Rubrics can be useful to reduce the subjectivity and interpretation.

Interviews with students

Interviews are process forms of performance assessments that can be conducted prior to, during, and after instruction. During instruction, individuals or groups can be interviewed, depending on the structural details of the instructional event. Interviews can be either informal or formal. They can be held as needed during instructional sessions or scheduled with a list of questions that help instructors structure the sessions and obtain a consistent range of responses. These sessions give learners feedback, advice, encouragement, and prompting for further understanding. In addition, teachers have information from which to make adjustments to subsequent instruction. They may also provide insight as to the real reason behind competencies and learning difficulties.

Learning debriefing sessions give a teacher information not usually obtained from other assessment methods. Debriefing asks students to respond to questions while the instructor records the answers. For example, students might verbalize on how they solved problems and managed class require- ments. They reflect on what they have learned and what they would like to learn and provide feedback on the instructional methods and materials used. Interviews can also be used to elaborate on portfolios and projects. In second- language learning, for example, teachers use conversations with students as a major assessment tool.

Self-assessment

Self-assessment allows students to assess themselves. Here both instructors and students can see how student learning is progressing. Self-assessment can be either a *process assessment* or a more formal *product assessment* coupled with performance assessments, such as projects and portfolios. Self-assessment can take the form of logs and journals; self-evaluations (oral and written) include debriefing interviews on student demonstrations, investigations, and projects. All of these may require rating criteria for scoring purposes, depending on how the self-assessment activity figures into the overall assessment plan. Instructional time may be needed to introduce learners to this type of activity, as well as time in class to record their responses.

Performance assessment

Performance assessment can also take both process and product forms, giving students the opportunity to demonstrate performance as they learn and as a means to demonstrate final mastery (Wiggins, 1998). Projects and portfolios are the most common form of performance assessment.

Projects

Projects are assessment products that are comprehensive demonstrations of skills or knowledge. Projects usually address a broad range of competencies and scoring and can be assessed by teacher, panel, or self-assessment (Rudner & Boston, 1994). Projects can be individual or group efforts and can include objectives for social skill development. Students need to select meaningful subjects for investigation, relevant to their interests, and suitable to address the goals of the instructional activity.

With projects, participants learn about the dynamic nature of group problem solving and communication. Students tackling an authentic task re-create many of the same problems and challenges found in real life, such as misreading what someone means or says, the different motivations between participants, and navigating the sometimes rough waters of power and partnerships. These authentic learning opportunities model real-world team building, social interaction, and responsibility for assigned work. Group work conducted at the elementary level should usually be done in class, so parents do not have to find ways to bring students together. Group work at middle and secondary levels can usually be done inside and outside the classroom.

Scoring can be improved through the use of clear criteria that support learning goals and objectives. The rules for this scoring should be clearly communicated to learners. Projects are usually completed out of class; however, in-class time may be needed to introduce particular aspects of the content or skills supporting a project or to give the instructor an opportunity to observe individual or group performance.

Portfolios

The overall purpose of a portfolio is either to document learning development, a *developmental portfolio*, or demonstrate competence, a *showcase portfolio*. The portfolio provides both student and teacher with a formative learning assessment as the portfolio expands with student work. The portfolio could be used as a summative assessment if the final version of the portfolio demonstrates student competence over time. In an elementary classroom, portfolios can archive and document student activity and performance across the school year. Portfolios can demonstrate mastery of a grade level (a summative purpose for assessment) or, in some schools, provide the basis to enter a higher grade level or course section (a placement purpose of assessment). In secondary classrooms, portfolios could represent student work across a subject, such as writing, social studies, or art.

A teacher education program may require physical and/or digital portfolios that document student work at different stages in the program. In some programs, a formal portfolio review is necessary for advancing in the program. A teacher education program may characterize its program along particular competencies, whereas a teaching position may have similar but different categories of competence. Portfolios serve a developmental purpose across the program with periodic review points. The portfolio becomes a showcase portfolio when students present their best work in the program keyed to required competencies in the program, such as the INTASC core standards.

The portfolio can become instrumental in hiring decisions for teaching positions. For experienced teachers, portfolios become useful in demonstrating their competence to administrators, parents, and school boards. They can be used in professional development work to help other teachers. Portfolios become essential components in National Board Certification® efforts (discussed in Chapter 10).

In summary, portfolios will look different based on their different purposes. To develop a portfolio, one needs to understand its purpose and have an organizing strategy based on the categories of performance. Different portfolios require different strategies for organization, storage, and presentation. For example, a course portfolio could be organized around learning task requirements, such as tests, papers, presentations, problem sets, and whatever activities comprised the subject over a length of time, which could be across a unit or across the entire school year. A portfolio for a teaching position (or any other type of position) should be organized around categories identified in the position announcement, such as education, skills, job experience, capabilities, and work samples.

Storage can take the form of physical means, such as file folders, sorting bins, or three-ring notebooks. Many portfolio requirements include digital storage, either CD-ROM or DVD or archived on a web site. Physical (analog) and digital forms of storage and documentation have their own means of organizing the materials within them. Physical portfolios, such as a three-ring notebook, could include a tab system for organizing the categories, a means to label items within the tabs, annotations to explain each submission, and examples of student work.

Digital portfolios can be storage media and folders. Digital portfolios require deciding how to name files, organizing the files into folders, and choosing strategies for browsing and searching the portfolio. Digital files can include hyperlinked text "pointing" to other files on the storage media, whether a web site or local digital media.

For classroom use as a performance assessment tool, a points total or a percentage of the final grade might be assigned for the portfolio. A rubric would probably be necessary to assess student performance on various aspects of student performance.

Observation checklists and scales

Observations are rich sources of information and are probably the most common type of assessment for teaching. Observations, when recorded, document student performance and provide data for teacher–student interactions. If you are assessing student behavior, a checklist gives you a developmental record. Formatted in a table, the checklist can include a range of behaviors across the top of the table, with student names or group names running down the left side of the table. In some "content" learning, behavior is an important component. For example, using inquiry and cooperative learning strategies, group behavior and individual roles and responsibilities are important aspects of what students must learn. In elementary-level lessons, student behavior becomes an integral part of the "content" and crucial to its success. If you know the specific behaviors you are looking for, then a scale can be an efficient assessment tool. Scales are a list of performance criteria attached to a numerical (e.g., 1–5) or qualitative (poor-to-excellent) scale.

You try it!

Use the next Design Activity to match the assessment tool to learning outcomes.

Matching Learning Outcomes with Assessment Tools

Task Rationale The purpose for this activity is to examine one of your lessons, record the learning outcomes and assessment tools, and evaluate to what extent there is an appropriate match.

Task Guidelines Take one of your lessons or lesson drafts and record in the following table the lesson's overall learning focus, the specific learning objectives, and the assessment tool(s) you will use to assess each objective.

Lesson title:	
Learning focus of lesson:	
What is to be learned in your lesson? LEARNING OUTCOMES	**How will you know if students learned this?** ASSESSMENT TOOL(S)
1. 2. 3. 4.	

Reflectivity
- Explain why there is an appropriate match between learning outcome (expressed most likely as an objective) and assessment tool(s).
- What questions do you have on assessment choice, development, and use?
- What types of assessment have you observed in your school?

Rubrics

For some learning tasks where completion of a number of requirements is the prime objective, a checklist or a scale is an adequate assessment tool. If the learning requires more complicated performance, a rubric may be necessary to provide fair assessment. A rubric is an assessment tool used to evaluate a range of student performance across several categories of performance. Examples of complicated performance may include projects, writing, portfolios, and public performance. If learning performance requires interpretation, development of a rubric can be a useful exercise to be clear on what constitutes an overall performance, as well as the range of performance across the categories. Groups of teachers may be involved in assessing portfolios, for example. A rubric is necessary to communicate to the reviewers the required categories and levels of performance. Portfolios, in particular, can include rubrics that specify whether students are cleared for advancing in an program or graduating from a program.

Categories of Performance

Rubrics take time to develop because one has to first identify the categories of performance and then describe the different levels of performance in each category. For example, having students write up a case study may require the following categories to assess student performance:

- Background
- Problem
- Response
- Recommendations
- Writing
- Format

How will a teacher know what is an acceptable performance or an unacceptable performance or something in between? To answer this question, the teacher needs to determine the different levels of performance (Figure 5.6).

Levels of Performance

To indicate the range of performance, you could establish scores of 1, 2, 3, or 4, but this would not tell you much. You might understand what level of learning occurred assigning a 1 or a 4, but no one else would understand what this number meant. This approach would not be fair to the students. To reduce the ambiguity, you must think through the different levels of performance for each category and be able to describe this performance in words.

In Figure 5.6, note that categories 1 through 4 address the content of a write-up of a case study for medical or legal purposes. Categories 5 and 6 address writing mechanics and organization. Both the content of the case study and how it is written and organized constitute the purpose of the learning task. However, different levels of performance may occur across the task. These levels are based somewhat on your experience with the activity.

Range → Category ↓	Unacceptable	C	B	A
1. CONTENT: Background	Insufficient	Some but missing important details	Adequate range but lacks details in some areas	Helps reader to understand the case.
2. CONTENT: Problem identification and issues	Did not include problem statement	Identified the wrong problem	Identified the essential problem but needs clarification	Identified the critical problem and component issues
3. CONTENT: Response or strategy	Did not supply a response to problem or response does not address problem	Inappropriate response to problem	Mix of appropriate strategies but not prioritized	Clear list of responses; match of responses to problem
4. CONTENT: Recommendations	Did not include	Some items outside the problem; not backed by the facts of the case	Appropriate list but too long or too broad	Prioritized list that addresses areas of the problem
5. MECHANICS: Writing	Wouldn't show to anyone	Needs editing	Inconsistencies across document	To the point, consistent writing
6. ORGANIZATION: Format	Did not use a format	Used a different format but did not justify in cover letter	Used some of the format	Included all sections and formatted consistently

FIGURE 5.6. Rubric Example.

Interpretation may still be necessary in many of the cells, but a rubric reduces the subjectivity. A rubric must be used to identify its weaknesses. Developing an ideal rubric the first time is difficult unless others, including peers and students, have evaluated and improved it with repeated use. Showing a draft to a colleague for suggestions and improvements can help. Students can be a productive source of feedback on what constitutes performance. By involving students in rubric development, they have invested themselves in the success of the rubric and its strength to accurately assess their performance.

Caveats for rubric use

- Keep the overall performance in mind when you use a rubric. See that the categories support this overall learning and that the assessment does not become overly dependent on isolated performance of individual rubric cells.
- Rubrics can be used to track development of performance across time (across the semester or an academic program). You must build into your schedule adequate time for periodic and responsive review and student feedback.

- You have to decide what constitutes a grade or point reward for each level of performance. In this example, a letter grade was assigned to each, but you could use a four-point system, and the total performance across all categories would be given a grade, based on the number of points.
- Try to share the rubric development with students. This gives students an investment in the activity, and students are more apt to be clear as to the expected performance. Students may identify categories that you had not considered.
- With rubrics you have already prepared, ask students if they understand your categories and levels of performance.

Developing confidence with rubrics requires hands-on use and a willingness to invest the time. "Yes, I've developed a rubric" is an accomplishment worth working toward. Developing a rubric is the goal for the next Design Activity.

DESIGN ACTIVITY 17

Develop a Rubric

Task Rationale This Design Activity asks you to identify the purpose for a rubric, categories of student performance, and levels of student performance.

Task Guidelines Use the following table as a template to record your decisions.

Task 1: Rubric Purpose • Identify a learning task that might be suitable for a rubric and describe its use in your teaching. What does the rubric intend to assess overall?

Task 2: Performance Categories • Identify the different categories of performance that make up the learning task.

Task 3: Levels of Performance • For each category, write brief statements that characterize different levels of performance for each category.

Assessment for:			
Description of use:			
	Levels of Performance:		
Category	Level A	Level B	Level C

Task 4: Rubric Evaluation • How will student performance equate into a grade? Does the rubric assess overall learning?
• Have you identified adequate performance categories? What is missing, or what can be consolidated?
• Have you written out appropriate statements for levels of performance?

Reflectivity Describe your experiences and the thinking you did in developing your rubric. What improvements need to be made?

ASSESSMENT IN YOUR LESSONS

What you write in the next Design Activity can be used to summarize the "Teaching and Assessment Overview" section in the lesson plan format.

Assessment Overview

Task Rationale Determine assessment tools in your lessons based on an appropriate match with learning outcomes.

Task Guidelines Choose a lesson you have taught or one that you plan to teach.

1. Identify student learning outcomes for this lesson.
2. Write a brief paragraph describing each assessment tool, and how and why it is appropriate to use.
3. Update the "Teaching and Assessment Overview" section in your lesson plan to indicate what assessment tools are being used in the lesson(s) you are developing.

Reflectivity • What experience and concerns do you have with your choice of assessment tools?
• What assessment tools do you want to learn more about?

SUMMARY

• Assessment is viewed differently by people. Understand what others mean by this term and how assessment is being used and why. Your beliefs and attitudes toward assessment may be heavily influenced by your personal experiences.

- The main idea in this chapter is that you choose assessment tools based on your purpose(s) for assessment.
- Your view of assessment may also divide assessment options into two types: traditional and alternative. We have come to label traditional assessment as "testing" and alternative assessment as "performance." Rather than setting up this value system, we advocate a clear purpose for assessment and then choice of the appropriate assessment tools.
- Wiggins (1989) has said that "we should not shy away from testing—the test is central to instruction—but that we must carefully decide on what is a true test of learning."
- Continue to ask yourself the question: "What will students learn and how will I know if they have learned this?"

An Idea Worth Thinking About	"The virtues involved in not knowing are the ones that really count in the long run. What you do about what you don't know is, in the final analysis, what determines what you will ultimately know." *(Duckworth, 1987, p. 68)*

Children learn quickly that "knowing the right answer" is what teachers value. Providing an environment in which "not knowing" is equally valued provides opportunities for teachers to help students learn. Duckworth (1987) suggests that "accepting surprise, puzzlement, excitement, patience, caution, honest attempts, and wrong outcomes" (p. 69) provides, in fact, moments when students move forward.

Reflective Teaching

"Basal Beware!"

You have landed your first full-time job as a second-grade teacher, and you are so excited. You are still in the process of identifying your teaching style and creating a classroom management system that works well for you. You may even be incorporating as many of the research-based instructional strategies (that you learned in college) into your lessons. You are discovering how to be an individual while learning how to work and collaborate with your colleagues. One caveat of your position that you were anticipating is that all second-grade teachers at your school must use the basal reader. Not a problem! You learned how to incorporate basal readers in many various ways throughout your teacher preparation process. So, you select a story that you just know your students will love from the basal. You do all sorts of neat activities to go along with the story. You are positive that your students know that story inside and out. They can retell the story in their own words, they can relate parts of the story to their own lives, and they can define and use each of the new vocabulary words introduced in the story. The problem? You've just made copies of the comprehension test that goes along with the story. As you look over the test, you realize your students are *not* going to do well on this test. How do you know? Because *you* also know this story inside and out, and *you* are not sure of the answers to three of the ten multiple-choice test questions! This is where your teacher-candidate days need to kick in. If you had remembered to think about what you wanted students to learn from reading this story and doing all of the neat activities, then you would have realized that the basal-provided comprehension test would not suit your purposes. Don't be discouraged! Use this experience as a learning opportunity for you and grow from it! Create your own assessment tool for the story, and remember to keep learning and how you will know students are learning at the forefront of your future instructional and assessment decisions.

Teacher Inquiry

- Assessment tools are likely to be your principle sources of data in any teacher research. What other forms of "data" might be useful?
- A data-management system may be needed to keep track of different data sources, much as you organize student records. Thus, this teacher inquiry system could become part of your current organizing system. Getting organized, however, is a learning experience in itself. Keep working on ways to keep track of student work and your work, but realize that the system that works for you is one that you develop over time.

REFERENCES

Bloom, B. S. (1956). *Taxonomy of educational objectives: The classification of educational goals: Handbook 1: Cognitive domain*. New York: McKay.

Chittenden, E. (1990). Authentic assessment, evaluation, and documentation of student performance. In V. Perrone (Ed.), *Expanding student assessment* (pp. 22–31). Alexandria, VA: Association for Supervision and Curriculum Development.

Duckworth, E. (1987). *The having of "wonderful ideas" and other essays on teaching and learning*. New York: Teachers College Press.

Eisner, E. W. (1994). *The educational imagination: On the design and evaluation of school programs* (3rd ed.). New York: Macmillan.

Gronlund, N. E. (1982). *Constructing achievement tests* (3rd ed.). Upper Saddle River, NJ: Prentice-Hall.

Linn, R. L., & Gronlund, N. E. (2000). *Measurement and assessment in teaching* (8th ed.). New York: Macmillan.

Popham, W. J. (2005). *Classroom assessment: What teachers need to know* (4th ed.). Boston: Allyn and Bacon.

Rudner, L. M., & Boston, C. (1994). Performance assessment. *ERIC Review, 3*(1), 2–12.

Wiggins, G. (1989, May). A true test: Toward more authentic and equitable assessment. *Phi Delta Kappan*, 703–713.

Wiggins, G. (1998). *Educative assessment: Designing assessments to inform and improve student performance*. San Francisco: Jossey-Bass.

Wiggins, G., & McTighe, J. (1998). *Understanding by design*. Upper Saddle River, NJ: Merrill–Prentice Hall.

RESOURCES

Print Resources

Andrade, H. G. (2000). Using rubrics to promote thinking and learning. *Educational Leadership, 57*(5), 13–18.

A frequent writer on the use of rubrics used to assess student performance.

Angelo, T. A., & Cross, K. P. (1993). *Classroom assessment techniques: A handbook for college teachers*. San Francisco: Jossey-Bass.

Although addressed to college teachers, this text describes tools keyed to knowledge and skills, attitudes and values, and reactions to instruction.

Campbell, D. M., Cignetti, P. B., Melenyzer, B. J., Nettles, D. H., & Wyman, R. M. (2001). *How to develop a professional portfolio: A manual for teachers*. Boston: Allyn and Bacon.

Guidelines organized by INTASC standards.

Eisner, E. W. (1994). *The educational imagination: On the design and evaluation of school programs* (3rd ed.). New York: Macmillan.

Written at the curriculum level, this text discusses curriculum ideologies; the explicit, implicit, and null curriculums; and a chapter on the different purposes of evaluation.

Gardner, H. (1999). *The disciplined mind: What all students should understand*. New York: Simon & Schuster.

Provides suggestions on designing compelling instruction to support student understanding. See in particular Chapter 6, "Designing Education for Understanding."

Gronlund, N. E. (2004). *Writing instructional objectives for teaching and assessment* (7th ed.). Upper Saddle River, NJ: Merrill–Prentice Hall.

A short text that is keyed to the learning taxonomies, as well as products, projects, achievement testing, performance, and affective assessment.

Howell, J. H., & Dunnivant, S. W. (2000). *Technology for teachers: Mastering new media and portfolio development*. Boston: McGraw-Hill.

A student portfolio workbook and CD-ROM. Links to articles and connected to activities.

Linn, R. L., & Gronlund, N. E. (2000). *Measurement and assessment in teaching* (8th ed.). Upper Saddle River, NJ: Merrill–Prentice Hall

A comprehensive text on issues and concepts on the tests and measurements field.

Popham, W. J. (2005). *Classroom assessment: What teachers need to know* (4th ed.). Boston: Allyn and Bacon.

A practical guide to the understanding, design, and implementation of assessment tools and procedures. Written in a personal tone.

Wiggins, G. (1998). *Educative assessment: Designing assessments to inform and improve student performance*. San Francisco: Jossey-Bass.

Practical guide for using performance assessment.

Web-Based Resources

Barrett, Helen

http://electronicportfolios.com/

A comprehensive set of guidelines and resources on digital portfolios.

CTB–McGraw Hill

www.ctb.com

Publisher of educational testing materials.

Harcourt Educational Measurement

http:harcourtassessment.com

Publisher of educational testing materials.

Northwest Regional Educational Laboratory (NWREL)

www.nwrel.org

Assessment resources, including ways to evaluate constructed-response assessments.

Riverside Publishing

www.riverpub.com

Publisher of educational testing materials.

U. S. Department of Education

www.ed.gov

Check this site frequently, and use the search capability to look for resources and materials.

WestEd

www.wested.org

A nonprofit agency that focuses on educational research and professional development.

6 Exploring Teaching Options

Main Idea of This Chapter
There is more than one way to teach.

INTASC
Standards
Addressed in
This Chapter

Principle 4 TEACHING REPERTOIRE: The teacher understands and uses a variety of instructional strategies to encourage students' development of critical thinking, problem solving, and performance skills.

Principle 5 LEARNING ENVIRONMENTS: The teacher uses an understanding of individual and group motivation and behavior to create a learning environment that encourages positive social interaction, active engagement in learning, and self-motivation.

Focus Questions

- What are your views of teaching?
- What are the basic activities in teaching?
- What options exist for teaching?

Design Activities

DA 19: Views of Teaching
DA 20: Instructional Events
DA 21: Teaching Options for Lessons

EXPLORING TEACHING

This chapter explores your teaching options, commonly referred to as teaching strategies. We first examine your views on teaching, in the belief that this self-examination clarifies how you view students and teaching. Next, we examine how most teaching strategies consist of similar activities called instructional events. We profile several teaching models that cover most teaching, followed by examples of content-specific teaching strategies and, finally, some generalized strategies that teachers frequently use. Figure 6.1 visualizes the sequence of Chapter 6.

FIGURE 6.1.
Visual Sequence for Chapter 6.

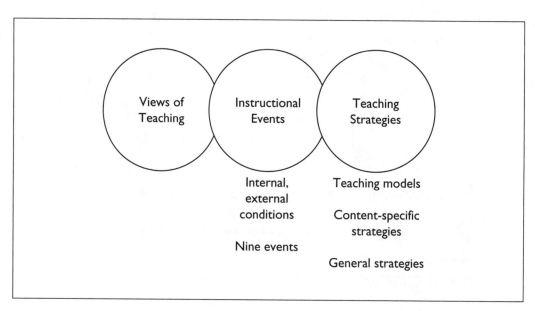

TEACHER DECISION CYCLE: QUESTION 3

In Chapter 4, we asked you to answer the question: "What is to be learned?" In Chapter 5 we asked the question: "How do you know if your students learned these outcomes?" Given this knowledge, we can ask a third question: "How will you assist students to learn?" This question addresses teaching decisions and the strategies that you use to help students learn (Figure 6.2).

How will you assist students to learn?

FIGURE 6.2.
Teacher
Decision Cycle:
Teaching
Question.

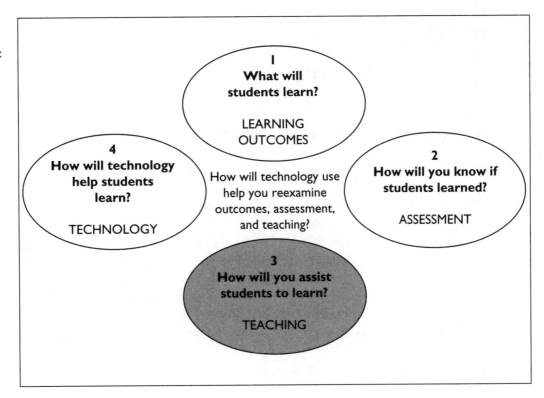

VIEWS OF TEACHING

As we did in the previous chapter on assessment, we begin this chapter by having you write about your views on teaching. Writing can reveal how you view students and how you view your overall role as an educator.

Views of Teaching

Task Rationale   You defined *teaching* in Chapter 2. It is time to revisit this question.

Task Guidelines   Please respond in writing to the following questions:

1. How do you see students?
2. How do you see yourself as a teacher?
3. How does (did) your cooperating teacher see teaching?
4. How do your colleagues view teaching?
5. How does your principal see teaching?
6. How do you want to be known as a teacher?

Reflectivity   In what ways have your views on teaching and learning evolved so far?

INSTRUCTIONAL EVENTS

Robert Gagné (1985) identified factors that relate different teaching approaches to their conceptual or theoretical foundations. Gagné called these factors "conditions of learning." According to Gagné, there are two types of learning conditions. One type involves internal conditions. These are states of mind that students bring to the learning situation, whether at school or at home or on vacation. Internal conditions include intellectual skills, thinking strategies, knowledge, attitudes, values, beliefs, and physical coordination skills.

Given that students possess these conditions, the question becomes: "How can these internal states or capacities of a learner be influenced?" Modeling behavior is one way, as students observe role models in the world. Teachers act as central role models for students. According to Gagné, instruction is a formal means to influence a person's internal states, intellectual skills, or values. *External conditions* are the second type of learning conditions. One important difference between the two types is that external conditions can be designed! Gagné, Wager, Golas, and Keller (2005) defined instruction as a set of *external* events designed to support *internal* learning processes. The purpose of designed events is to influence mental processes, such as attending, learning, remembering, appreciating, physically coordinating, and problem solving (Figure 6.3). Extending this idea to the various human dimensions of learning, these changed states of mind contribute to moral development, appreciation of diversity, creativity, design, artistic expression, and other forms of learning.

FIGURE 6.3.
Relationship Between Internal and External Conditions of Learning.

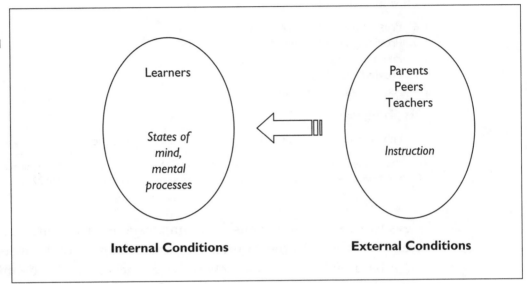

Gagné et al. (2005) also identified characteristics of all instruction (external conditions) that can assist the development of these mental processes (internal conditions). They called their list of teaching characteristics *instructional events*, which involve a set of activities roughly in the order listed in Figure 6.4.

Not all teaching includes all of these events. Some may not be needed or may be emphasized more or less, depending on the teaching strategy selected. Some of these events may overlap, such as gaining student attention, reviewing previous learning, and informing students of the learning objectives for the day. For example, when you walk into a classroom and begin writing on the board, you are completing the first two instructional events: gaining attention and informing the students of the learning objectives for the class period. Next, we explain each instructional event. As you read about each event, think how each matches up with how you teach. In Figure 6.4 we have organized the nine events into three categories: readying for new instruction, new instruction, and applying learning.

Readying for new instruction

The first three events ready the learner for new instruction. The first event serves to gain the attention of the learner. A second readying event informs the learner of the objective of the instruction, which helps to alert students to

FIGURE 6.4.

Instructional Events.

Instructional Events
Readying for new instruction
1. Gaining attention
2. Informing learner of the objective
3. Stimulating recall of prior learning or learning that is needed
New instruction
4. Presenting the new "content"
5. Providing learning guidance
6. Prompting student performance
7. Providing feedback on performance
8. Assessing performance
Applying learning
9. Enhancing retention of learning through variety of practice

From *Principles of Instructional Design*, 5th edition, by Gagné/Wager/Golas/Keller. © 2005. Reprinted with permission of Wadsworth, a division of Thomson Learning: www.thomsonrights.com. Fax 800 730-2215.

relevance, task requirements, and implications. The third readying event recalls what was learned previously and relates prior knowledge to what might be useful in new instruction. New teachers might identify this set of events as opening activities, which are designed to stimulate students' attention to the "main event" teaching activity.

New instruction

Events 4 through 8 address new instruction. Event four presents new learning. The exact presentation of new material depends on the nature of the content and the teaching model or strategy used to "present" new learning opportunities. The stimulus material could consist of case studies, examples, situations, simulations or role play, a lecture, a guest speaker, a hands-on activity, a stimulating key question, or a demonstration. A whole variety of methods exist to present the new material.

Event 5, providing learning guidance, specifies the ways in which you assist the learner. This assistance can include modeling behavior, feedback, questioning, tutoring or reteaching, reinforcing and providing encouragement, and structuring tasks (Tharp & Gallimore, 1988). Much classroom "teaching" provides one-on-one assistance during class activities.

Event 6, prompting student performance, requires active participation by the learner, demonstrating what one has learned through performance, whether it be through recall, synthesis, attitudinal change, physical skill improvement, creative expression, or some other means. The role of the teacher is to prompt the learner to demonstrate this performance in some manner, such as response to questions in class, participating in discussion, writing, projects, portfolios, or physical performance. Teaching for understanding, for example, requires that students be able to explain, demonstrate, and apply what they know.

In event 7, providing feedback on performance, the instructor responds to student performance. This response may take the form of spoken or written communication, such as individual or group feedback or written comments on student work. This event frequently overlaps with the next one.

Event 8 assesses student performance keyed to the objectives of the activity. Is the performance valid, measuring performance against a learning objective, and does the performance measure what it was designed to measure? These issues are all critical, regardless of the nature of the assessment purpose. Events 4 through 8 can occur during classroom teaching as teachers provide students with guided practice, as well as outside class in the assignment of homework.

Applying learning

Event 9, enhancing retention, is often neglected. Even 9 prompts the learner to apply what has been learned to a new set of problems. This capability is often referred to as *transfer*. Addressing this event ensures that we provide opportunities for learners to connect school tasks with the real-life application of knowledge and skills. One way in which this transfer can be accomplished is looking for opportunities across the school year in which students apply what they have learned in class projects to address school or community needs.

Trying out instructional events

In the next Design Activity, see how instructional events can be addressed in one of your lessons.

Instructional Events

Task Rationale   Apply your knowledge of instructional events to the teaching proposed for one of your lessons.

Task Guidelines   1. Identify a learning activity from one of your lessons.
2. Use the following chart to record how your activity addresses one or more instructional events.

Instructional Event	Learning Activity
1. Gaining attention	
2. Informing learner of the objective	
3. Stimulating recall of prior learning or learning that is needed	
4. Presenting the new "content"	
5. Providing learning guidance	
6. Prompting student performance	
7. Providing feedback on performance	
8. Assessing performance	
9. Enhancing retention of learning through practice	

Reflectivity   • What were your reactions to the list of instructional events?
• What events were not addressed in your lesson, and why?
• Did this activity help you think through the events you cover in your teaching?

Next, we profile several teaching strategies that can frequently be used across all educational levels and content areas. These strategies, which have been studied and have significant research behind them, are sometimes referred to as teaching models. The models profiled include direct instruction, classroom discussion, and three forms of cooperative learning.

TEACHING MODELS

Direct instruction

Direct instruction is a behavioral model suitable for the teaching of basic knowledge and skills. A sufficient base of learning may need to be taught before teaching more complex ideas, processes, or skills. Whatever fundamental knowledge can be taught *directly* is a candidate for this model. One example is when a skill needs to be taught in a particular way. Key features of direct instruction include breaking content up into learnable pieces, giving students practice, observing student behavior, and providing feedback until mastery is achieved (Rosenshine, 1983). Direct instruction is an efficient teaching model, based on the combination of direct teacher-presentation of new material and guided practice in the classroom. The procedure for using direct instruction includes the steps listed in Figure 6.5.

FIGURE 6.5.
Steps in Direct
Instruction.

Direct Instruction
1. **Review** what has been learned.
2. **State objectives** for the lesson.
3. **Present** new material.
4. **Guided practice:** assess performance, provide corrective feedback.
5. **Provide independent practice:** assess performance, provide corrective feedback.
6. **Review** practice and **provide** corrective feedback.

From Gunter, Estes, & Schwab, *Instruction: A Models Approach* 4/E. Published by Allyn and Bacon, Boston, MA. Copyright © 2003 by Pearson Education. Adapted by permission of the publisher.

The direct instruction model can incorporate other strategies. Graphic organizers can be used in step 2 to inform students of the conceptual organization of new knowledge. Organizers provide a conceptual reference point within the content of a lesson. At step 3, "present new material" (Gunter, Estes, & Schwab, 2003), the lecture or presentation is commonly used.

Presenting new material also involves the organization of the content by arranging material into smaller parts, focusing on important points, presenting content from general to specific, and taking into consideration student ages, styles, and abilities. The actual presenting of material can incorporate many other teaching models or strategies, from lectures to demonstrations, and then observing the reactions and behavior of students to what is being said, presented, shown, or demonstrated.

The steps of the direct instruction model are very similar to the events of instruction (Figure 6.6). Direct instruction is suitable for teaching basic skills,

skills that can be taught directly. Note in the model that a review is conducted before communicating the objectives of the new lesson. The order will depend on what works for you. The last instructional event, "enhancing retention," is not specified directly by the direct instruction model.

Direct instruction provides numerous opportunities for assessment and media use. "Assessing the performance," event 8, can include informal as well as formal assessment, such as when grades are needed. Media is typically introduced to present the stimulus material, but some forms of media, such as interactive technologies, may incorporate all of these events.

Instructional Event	Possible Instructor Action
1. Gaining attention 2. Informing the learner of the objective 3. Stimulating recall of prerequisite learning 4. Presenting the stimulus material 5. Providing learning guidance 6. Eliciting the performance 7. Providing feedback about performance correctness 8. Assessing the performance 9. Enhancing retention	• Demonstration • Writing on board, verbal, or handout • Teacher or student summary; questions • Teacher, student, media • Teacher provide examples on board, student attempts examples; teacher walks around • Class suggestions; individual prompting • Class examples; lab activities; homework; verbal comments on work • Verbal or written comments; marks, grades • Repeating in subsequent lessons; provide additional diverse examples

FIGURE 6.6. Direct Instruction and Instructional Events.

Discussion

Discussion is an instructional method with a long history and is a major activity for many teachers. Goodlad's (1984) observations of secondary classrooms suggest that "only one percent of teachers' questions require of students anything but the most superficial thought" (p. 161). The major feature of discussion is a dialogue that generates questions and increases the teacher's ability to engage students in higher-level thinking. In addition to guiding the planning and selection of questions used in classroom discussions, the model guides the teacher in conducting the classroom interactions during the discussion. The steps are found in Figure 6.7.

1. Read material

The first step in the use of discussion has the teacher reading the material in advance and developing factual, interpretive, and evaluative questions before class. This is done to ask more thought-provoking questions in the

FIGURE 6.7.
Steps in
Discussion.

Discussion
1. **Read** the material and prepare questions. • Factual questions: ask for specific facts in the reading. • Interpretive questions: ask what the text means. • Evaluative questions: ask about the value of the text. 2. **Cluster** basic and follow-up questions. 3. **Introduce** the model and assign the reading. 4. **Conduct** the discussion. 5. **Review** the process and **summarize** students' observations.

From Gunter, Estes, & Schwab, *Instruction: A Models Approach* 4/e. Published by Allyn and Bacon, Boston, MA. Copyright © 2003 by Pearson Education. Adapted by permission of the publisher.

classroom than might otherwise happen without preparation (Gunter et al., 2003). *Factual* questions point to a section in a book, *interpretive* questions ask what the text means, and *evaluative* questions require students to make value judgments and relate the meaning of text to the reader. Gunter and colleagues (2003) suggest wording good discussion questions precisely so that the intent of the question is clear, narrowed sufficiently to give the discussion direction, and framed in such a manner to reflect doubt, searching, and value.

2. Cluster questions

The second step using discussion has the teacher comparing ideas, reactions, and questions with another teacher, if possible. Questions are clustered by broad, basic questions that raise an issue. Clustering questions focuses the discussion and allows students to cover a basic question in depth. Follow-up questions develop the ideas behind the basic question. The key to this step, however, is to know when to deviate from your prepared questions. Careful listening to what students say should be your guide. Adjust your follow-up questions to build on and extend what students say.

3. Introduce discussion

The third step is to assign the reading, some of which could be done in class. Ask students to prepare questions for discussion, and give students adequate time to reread material before discussion. If the reading is done outside class, you may need to have students generate a summary or their own list of questions to contribute to the discussion and to hand in. You should be clear that this requirement "counts" in your assessment, or you risk that students will come to class not prepared.

4. Conduct the discussion

Conducting an effective discussion requires a nondirective role, particularly evaluating the weight given to student questions that in your view are more correct than others. When students answer questions, prompt them for evidence or elaboration on their meanings. Students should be encouraged to offer their opinions on responses, as well as listen carefully to others' opinions. Constructive discussion accommodates different frameworks of thinking and unique motivations and promotes the view that all deserve the respect to express their views and to question others.

5. Review and summarize

Finally, in step 5, students review the main points discussed and summarize what was said in the discussion. The teacher may share in this role.

In summary, the instructor and students read new material in advance, while the instructor prepares questions. The instructor introduces the discussion model in the classroom, conducts the discussion, reviews with students how the discussion fared, and summarizes student responses.

Classroom discussion is an important teaching model because frequently "the quality of those discussions . . . determines the extent and quality of students' learning" (Gunter et al., 2003, p. 176). Discussion is an excellent strategy when learning outcomes specify "understanding" because one or more facets of understanding can be supported. Classroom discussion is a good example of how flexible the events of instruction can be, depending on the steps of a particular model (Figure 6.8). The first two steps, reading the material and constructing the questions, are conducted before the instruction; however, development of questions is key to the success of the discussion. Although not explicit steps in the model, gaining attention and stimulating recall are two instructional events that the instructor can use to supplement the steps of this model. By comparing the steps of the model with the range of instruction provided by the "instructional events," one can see how much is involved in conducting the discussion.

In terms of assessment, the instructor can observe and record discussion performance according to some established criteria. For example, criteria could include participation by students and the quality of participation, including evidence offered to support claims, examples to clarify a position or idea, and tolerance of differing points of view. It is essential that the instructor involves the whole class in the discussion and exerts care in judging individual responses and individuals called on.

Instructional media may assume a major role in presenting the new material. A movie may be shown in class to introduce students to new ideas or review prior instruction. Media can also be used to promote learning transfer by asking students to respond to questions about these new media-based

Instructional Event	Possible Instructor Actions
1. Gaining attention	Walking into the classroom and writing on the board
2. Informing the learner of the objective	Writing on the board, "What we are going to do today?" and repeating verbally
3. Stimulating recall of prerequisite learning	Instructor or student summarizing previous lesson; both asking questions
4. Presenting the stimulus material	Describing an event or example to begin discussion
5. Providing learning guidance	Prompting discussion with a key question for the day; writing major topics on the board
6. Eliciting the performance	Asking penetrating questions
7. Providing feedback about performance correctness	Including all comments; writing on the board; encouraging all participants; prompting for elaboration, reasoning, and source of response
8. Assessing the performance	Recording participation and responses
9. Enhancing retention	Periodic guidance on note taking; providing key ideas; suggesting additional work

FIGURE 6.8. Classroom Discussion and Instructional Events.

examples. Instructional technology, such as video conferencing, might enable a discussion to occur with students or experts anywhere in the world.

Cooperative learning

Cooperative learning aims to create a positive environment where people learn to work together to achieve joint objectives. The model aims to create a positive working environment and to develop cooperation and understanding of others as individuals while learning together. The model may be used to supplement other forms of instruction by giving students the opportunity to teach one another, discuss in groups, or put into practice skills or information presented by the instructor (Slavin, 1995).

Think-Pair-Share

There are numerous types of cooperative learning. The simplest to implement is Think-Pair-Share. The simplicity of this model for new teachers is that you can explain the model through the words of its title (Figure 6.9).

The cooperative teaching model shares the responsibility for learning across the pair. The value of the model is improved thinking and social skills and being able to work together, discuss, listen, and contribute. Students learn they can interact one-on-one or think privately before sharing ideas with the whole class. This model can be used at different grade levels and content areas. The thinking activity can include students writing about what they are thinking

FIGURE 6.9.
Procedure for
Think-Pair-Share.

Cooperative Learning: Think-Pair-Share
1. Teacher poses a question.
2. Students think individually: **THINK**
3. Student discusses answers with another student: **PAIR**
4. Students share answers with the class: **SHARE**

From Gunter, Estes, & Schwab, *Instruction: A Models Approach* 4/e. Published by Allyn and Bacon, Boston, MA. Copyright © 2003 by Pearson Education. Adapted by permission of the publisher.

and then sharing what they have written with others. The pairing could also include larger groups of three or four students, depending on the nature of the task and the number of students in the group. The model provides some efficiency when a teacher assigns time limits to each step in the model, depending on the nature of the activity (Gunter et al., 2003).

Jigsaw

In this form of cooperative learning, students are broken up into groups. Each person has a specific role in the group and conducts research on a section of a problem. Those with the same role get together from all the groups and discuss what they have found. The original group re-forms, and each person reports on what was discovered. The purpose of the strategy is to involve everyone in the group, as all members must contribute, and to learn from other groups.

Role play

Another type of cooperative learning is role play. Role play enables students to act out an event, either a historical event or an issue of interest to students, by taking on the roles of actors. The goal is to have students enact what people in those events had to do to solve a problem or make decisions. Role play provides an opportunity to publicly experience roles and ethical dilemmas that call for taking a stand or a problem-solving approach. The procedure for role playing is listed in Figure 6.10.

Role play can be a strategy used in conjunction with another teaching model called conflict resolution. Together, role play and conflict resolution show students new ways to solve problems or conflicts in their classroom or schools or to act out community controversies. Actual problems or constructed problems can be used. Giving students near-authentic situations allows them to work with others to consider alternatives to problems. One student can act as a mediator to help peers arrive at some agreement. Each side in a conflict is allowed to tell a particular side of the issue without interruption. This strategy

FIGURE 6.10.
Procedure for
Role Play.

Cooperative Learning: Role Play
1. Teacher chooses an event or a situation in which people must make decisions.
2. Select teams.
3. Assign the problem and explain what students are to do.
4. Teams assign roles to team members.
5. Teacher assigns tasks to observers.
6. Teams act out their roles.
7. Teams discuss their performance.
8. Class and observers discuss the performance.
9. Teacher evaluates.

From Gunter, Estes, & Schwab, *Instruction: A Models Approach* 4/e. Published by Allyn and Bacon, Boston, MA. Copyright © 2003 by Pearson Education. Adapted by permission of the publisher.

allows students to talk about problems they may be having and can result in student-generated strategies to address these student problems. Role play is an effective model to turn to when current events in the world or in the school suggest a teaching opportunity.

Cooperative work groups

Working well in groups is highly valued in work environments, so it makes sense to give students opportunities to experience what it means to work together to accomplish a goal. Cooperative work, however, is not successful by merely placing people around a table. Some situations require solving a real problem rather than just acting out roles. Students assume specific team-member roles to solve the problem. A number of features have been found to be critical in this type of cooperative learning (Johnson, Johnson, & Smith, 1991) as listed in Figure 6.11.

Interdependence in a cooperative work group requires a number of features. A clear, mutual goal must be communicated and understood by members of the group, resources must be shared, and tasks must be divided, with

FIGURE 6.11.
Features of
Cooperative
Learning.

Cooperative Learning: Cooperative Work Groups
Interdependence: "sink or swim together"
One-to-one interaction: students help each other
Individual accountability: individual performance assessed and shared
Social skills: groups need social skills to function
Group processing: group reflects on what and how they are doing

From Johnson, D. W., Johnson, R. T., & Smith, K. A. (1991). *Active learning: Cooperation in the college classroom.* Reproduced by permission of Interaction Book Company. 7208 Cornelia Dr., Edina, MN 55435.

complementary roles assigned. The group should be encouraged to establish its own identity distinct from other groups.

One-to-one interaction in cooperative groups encourages students to support and help each other. Group members must willingly exchange resources so that everyone has access to the information of others, provides feedback, and gives opportunities for individuals to challenge each other's conclusions.

Individual accountability within the group can be designed into cooperative work groups. Establish small groups and rotate task assignments, such as assigning one member as team leader and another as the recorder and then rotating roles periodically to give everyone in the group shared responsibilities. In essence, individuals teach other members of the group what they learn. This strategy is useful if cooperative work groups are used across a length of time to allow role rotation. Depending on the purpose of the cooperative group, assessment can be observations of individual and group behavior, as well as individual tests and group performance.

Groups need *social skills* to function. These skills, however, are not intuitive. Within these groups, students become aware of cooperative skills. One of the issues that learners have with this model is that individuals pull their weight in the group. This concern becomes acute when the group is graded as a whole in lieu of assigning individual scores. The combination of individual accountability and group performance, however, is preferred to meet this concern.

Cooperative work groups require time to implement and perhaps several years for instructors to learn to use well, but the benefits for student learning merit the investment of time. Thinking through what makes up cooperative work in your setting gives you categories to *assess* cooperative work. A rubric can be used to assess this form of social learning (Figure 6.12).

Cooperative Criteria	Below	Meets	Exceeds
Interdependence: "sink or swim together"			
One-to-one interaction: students help each other			
Individual accountability: individual performance assessed and shared			
Social skills: groups need social skills to function			
Group processing: group reflects on what and how they are doing			

FIGURE 6.12. Assessing Social Skills in Cooperative Work Groups.

The cooperative criteria become rubric categories of performance, and some type of performance range is determined (e.g., below expectations, meets expectations, exceeds expectations), with typical performance identified for each category.

CONTENT-SPECIFIC TEACHING STRATEGIES

The teaching models profiled in the previous section provide teachers with teaching strategies that can be used across most educational levels and content areas. Some strategies have been developed that are suitable for particular content area (Figure 6.13).

Reading and Language Arts	Science	Social Studies	Mathematics
Literacy lesson	Learning cycle	Jurisprudential inquiry	Manipulatives
Guided reading	Concept maps	Role play	Word problems
Reader's theater	Graphic organizers	Conflict resolution	Visuals
Read-aloud	Simulations	Case studies	Simulations
Writing conferences	Labs and demonstrations	Debates	Tutoring
Reading-writing	Field trips	Visuals, such as timelines	Games
Word wall	Experts	Interviews and guests	
Learning centers	Service learning	Service learning	
Word pictures			
Movies			

FIGURE 6.13. Content-Specific Teaching Strategies.

Reading and language arts

Some content-specific teaching strategies may be variations of generic teaching models. Literacy lessons, for example, share several features with direct instruction. In a literacy lesson, a skill or strategy, such as identification of character traits, is introduced. The teacher then demonstrates the skill or strategy, and student practice follows. Student practice may be responding to teacher questions, shared reading, or writing. Finally, the teacher reviews the new skill or strategy.

Guided reading, another strategy, may involve a single group or multiple groups arranged according to reading levels (Fountas & Pinnell, 1996). In guided reading, a teacher and students read passages in a book and participate in some manner, depending on the reading level of the students. For example, in a second-grade classroom, students may be asked to turn to a specific page in a book. The teacher may ask students to look for a specific item while reading particular pages, such as "sh" words or nouns. After students have completed reading a passage, the question is asked again, along with other, related questions. Students are then given additional reading, perhaps for homework. The benefit of guided reading is individual performance in a social setting. Teachers can observe how each student is reading a text while students learn new reading strategies.

A unique teaching strategy is reader's theater, which is based on reader-response theory (Karolides, 2000). This theory focuses on the relationship between the reader and the text and encourages students to use their life experiences to create meaning from the text. Reader's theater does not use elaborate staging or props and instead centers on dialogue between two or more characters acted out by students. Students showcase their interpretation of the reading and invite the audience to sense characterization, setting, and story action through students' voice rather than movement. This strategy invites creativity, involvement, different interpretations, and reading for a deeper meaning.

Read-aloud is another common literacy strategy involving students, teachers, and adults. Reading specialists may assist individual students, or trained volunteers may visit schools on a regular basis. Author reading is less frequent but an effective strategy to promote reading. A local or regional author may participate, or the teacher may feature an author each month.

Science

Popular forms of teaching involve hands-on, active learning, or discovery learning, in which students directly experience the content to be learned and make sense of the world in unique ways. One teaching strategy based on these ideas is the learning cycle, which has many variations (Karplus, 1977; Renner, 1982). In general, the learning cycle involves exploring a concept, explaining a concept, and then applying the concept. The learning cycle for lesson use can take on more specifics. For example, the "engage" part of the cycle serves as an opening activity to attract student curiosity and questions. The "explore" stage gives students time to investigate without the teacher's direct supervision. An "explain" stage prompts students to show evidence and clarify their explanations. Finally, an "application" phase is necessary to have students apply their new knowledge.

A characteristic of science strategies is inquiry, which can include whatever classroom practices guide independent learning of complex questions, problems, and issues. The process of inquiry involves formulating good questions, collecting evidence, analyzing the results, presenting the results, and judging the importance of what was discovered. Inquiry can include interactive lecture, discussion, group work, case studies, problem-based learning, service learning, simulations, field trips, fieldwork, and labs.

One strategy used frequently in science is concept maps, as much of science involves understanding knowledge and how concepts are organized and connected. The structure of concept maps includes a particular concept label, usually one or more words, connected by lines, which are labeled to signify a relationship (Figure 6.14). The concepts and subconcepts are usually arranged in a hierarchy, with the most general concept followed by more specific concepts. Concept maps can be used by teachers to organize conceptual knowledge, and they provide a general-to-specific sequence for teaching. Concept maps can also be used as assessment strategies to see how students "map" their understanding before and after instruction. With concept maps, students can visualize how science facts are connected.

FIGURE 6.14.
Example of
a Concept Map.

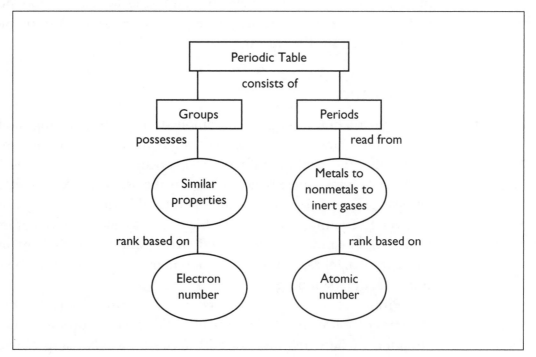

Social studies

Role play can be an effective strategy in social studies instruction. It gives students an opportunity to act out the roles of historical characters and experience important moments in history. Reporting current events has always been a long-standing strategy to involve students in studying the events of the day.

Conflict resolution, discussed earlier, enables students to confront issues and deal with events close to their concerns.

A teaching strategy known as jurisprudential inquiry is useful for examining current political and social issues that may be the focus of one or more lessons or topical units, such as foreign policy, environmental issues, racial conflicts, or health issues. Jurisprudential inquiry has students synthesizing the facts behind issues, taking a position, exploring the different viewpoints, and examining the consequences of certain stances (Joyce, Weil, & Calhoun, 2004). The choice of issues may be summarized in the use of case studies. This strategy promotes dialogue and engages students to look at different sides of an issue. The teacher's role is to guide the activity and prompt clarification of student positions. Assessment involves behavior and tolerance, but ultimately how students make the case supporting their positions is an important category of performance.

Other common teaching strategies in social studies involve the use of debates in which student groups advocate a particular position. Field trips and meeting actual government officials or people who have played a major role in history in some manner are effective strategies to bring a more human face to history. Maps, encyclopedias, pictures, and newspapers are commonly used to support social studies learning.

Mathematics

Direct instruction has been a common strategy for teaching mathematics, as its direct teaching, guided practice, independent practice, and application are well suited to learning mathematical concepts and procedures. Cooperative learning provides some benefits, such as the use of think-pair-share to involve everyone in the classroom in mathematical thinking. For early grades, manipulatives give young students a tactile means to understand mathematical concepts. Older students may benefit from simulations where mathematical concepts in algebra, geometry, trigonometry, and calculus can be visualized to promote understanding.

Problem solving has been a common feature in mathematics lessons, as the application of the concept is tested out. Word problems tap real-world situations where mathematics is needed to solve a problem. Common problem-solving strategies are the use of paper and pencil to speed up problem solving. Diagrams help students understand spatial concepts and mathematical patterns. The use of notation, such as variables representing an unknown with a single symbol, is itself mathematical strategy. Mathematical expressions reduce the cognitive and memory load in solving problems and representing relationships. Problems can also take the form of games in which mathematical concepts are designed into a situation where rules and an objective are proposed.

GENERAL TEACHING STRATEGIES

Many strategies are general approaches useful across teaching. These general strategies include reteaching, modeling, task structure and instructions, observations, feedback, homework, and study skills instruction.

Reteaching

Reteaching is a common teaching strategy needed when students are experiencing difficulties with already taught lessons and require additional instruction. This form of teaching is different from review. Review entails summarizing major points of a lesson and setting the stage for new learning. Reteaching, by contrast, involves a return to learning outcomes that were not adequately achieved in a previous learning activity. Before a student can move on, additional instruction or reteaching is needed. Repeating the original lesson is not the procedure; however, a new mini-lesson is called for, one that focuses on the topics or skills of student difficulty. Reteaching can involve the use of additional examples and explanation of difficult concepts. Other teaching strategies can be used, such as guests, rereading, new student activity, discussion, role play, grouping, or additional practice opportunities (see Figure 6.15).

Reteaching may involve a single student or a group of students rather than an entire class. As an example, Figure 6.15 summarizes a reteaching

FIGURE 6.15. Reteaching Lesson Format with Small Groups.

Reteaching Format for Small Groups
Scenario: You have taught a new concept to the entire class and assigned a task that features the new concept. Individual students complete the task. Upon reviewing the papers, you see that some students did not understand the concept.
Reteaching format: Small groups of three or four students
Reteaching procedure:
• Remind students of the new concept.
• Ask them what they know about the concept. Allow students to talk, intervening only to correct misconceptions or misunderstandings.
• Review concept with a group activity. For example, if students were to learn a set of vocabulary words and use them in context, the activity might involve a game matching these words to the correct definitions.
• Answer any questions and review the concept. Have the students respond to questions so that you see that they understand.
• If an additional activity is needed, give the group a short, individual activity. This activity may be shorter or a different version than the previous activity.
• Later in the day, try to use the small group activity with the class, so that the small group members experience success with the rest of the students.

format that is used by a Title I teacher. Reteaching in this example involves one or more small groups to address one or more reading issues. In this case, the teacher establishes a routine for the rest of the class to follow when reteaching is in place.

Teacher modeling

Teacher modeling is probably the simplest and most powerful teaching strategy at your disposal. Modeling refers to how the teacher behaves and performs. Students observe the teacher, then imitate and practice that teacher's behavior. The teacher is acting as a role model which the student is emulating. Students, of course, may assume the behavior of other role models—other adults and peers in and out of the classroom. For the classroom teacher, the important caveat is "Attend to your behavior, as students will notice."

Bandura's (1986) social learning theory suggests four elements to attend to in the use of modeling (Figure 6.16). These elements apply to whoever is doing the modeling, such as the teacher or other students.

FIGURE 6.16.
Elements of Modeling.

Modeling Elements	
Attention:	Students have to be able to see, hear or experience teacher behavior. Attention can be accomplished through voice tone, volume, emphasis, and pacing.
Retention:	Students must be able to remember what they experience. This can be accomplished through repeated modeling (rehearsal) of the behavior and providing cues through voice, actions, or media aids.
Production:	Students must practice the behavior until it matches the behavior of the teacher or peer. This can be supported through feedback and encouragement.
Motivation and reinforcement:	Continued modeling of the behavior by the teacher reinforces similar behavior by the student.

Teacher modeling requires a teacher who desires to set a good example for students. Students will not learn well from teachers who do not enjoy teaching. Enthusiasm for the content and activities goes a long way in motivating students to learn.

Task structure and instructions

Tasks engage students in meaningful learning activities for the purpose of helping them think and perform. Elementary teachers frequently use worksheets to give students guided practice in class on isolated and specific learning outcomes. Tasks, however, can address more complicated outcomes, such as critical thinking and problem solving. Designed learning tasks give students the structure that many need. The level of difficulty and complexity should be sufficient to challenge students, to be "within their reach" but not so difficult that it is beyond their reach. One of the challenges to rich learning tasks is to somehow balance the experiential quality of authentic tasks with the need to periodically support reflecting thinking (Norman, 1993). Experiential tasks challenge the student with an engaging purpose, much like games do for students outside school. Designing a compelling task requires knowing the students and adjusting an existing task to take advantage of the range of students in the classroom. Reflective tasks, such as writing and projects, complement experiential tasks, and together they provide evidence of student learning.

Whatever learning tasks are placed in front of students, should feature clear instructions. For elementary students, voicing instructions is necessary. Older students who can read benefit by reinforced vocal instructions coupled with written instructions on the blackboard. More complex tasks designed for middle and secondary-level students require that directions be written out so that all students participate with the same instructions. These written instructions will need to be reinforced through vocal instructions and any clarifications before students begin. This is particularly important before assigning homework or a project. Developing "clear" instructions is an ongoing challenge for teachers.

Observations

Observations are a common form of teaching and assessment. New teachers tend to think of assessment as worksheets and tests and underestimate the teaching value of "walking around." Observation and asking students questions provide the necessary means to check for student understanding. Observations also occur as a teacher is talking and looking at students, maintaining attention through eye contact and voice, and checking for reactions on student faces and physical behavior. Observations and ongoing adjustments to teaching suggest what Schön (1987) referred to as reflection-in-action, as opposed to reflection-on-action after teaching.

Feedback

Students deserve feedback on their work. Effective feedback should be appropriate, timely, and consistent. Appropriate feedback is comments that match the nature of the learning task. Comments and "marks" should support the students' learning and include encouragement as well as constructive criticism. Comments might also include questions asking the student to clarify or provide a stronger case for what was written or spoken. Students need to know what is required of revisions if these are features of the task. Writing is one example where written feedback is helpful, and revision may be part of the learning. Comments that include statements of "good," for example, need explanations.

Timely feedback means that students receive feedback as close as possible to their performance of the task. In-class feedback gives students immediate information on their performance and helps clarify any questions they may have. Homework requires feedback as soon as possible, as teachers need to know if students are learning and what topics or procedures need to be reviewed or retaught.

Consistent feedback requires that teachers stay aware of individual student performance and development across a grading period and over the school year. An assessment plan helps teachers record this information for the purpose of monitoring student learning and ultimately assigning grades.

Homework

Homework is sometimes a controversial topic among teachers. Its function is to provide students with an opportunity to practice new knowledge and skills or give them more time to show what they know through reflection, writing, or some other performance. Another function of homework is to read material before classroom discussion. Two suggestions are worth noting here. First, we must be clear as to the purpose of homework. If it has an instructional purpose, then, second, the homework must "count" in terms of assessment. If students are required to read material in advance of class activity, then some evidence of this reading is necessary, either through a written task or in-class performance.

The issue of homework is related to feedback, as homework provides the teacher with a source of evidence as to if and how students are learning. This information, however, must be gleaned from student work and folded back into daily teaching, including keeping students informed about how they are performing.

Study skills

Study skills can become part of the "content" in classrooms and are best supported in individual content areas. Here students make the connection between what is to be learned and the use of specific strategies that help them learn. Generally, providing study skills strategies will take some teaching time, but the results may be worthwhile in the long run.

YOUR TEACHING OPTIONS

Now, make some choices about the teaching strategies in your lessons.

Teaching Options for Lessons

Task Rationale   This Design Activity brings forward what you have learned in the previous chapters and asks you to decide what teaching strategies you will use in a lesson.

Task Guidelines   Select a lesson you have developed, and evaluate its effectiveness by using the Teacher Decision Cycle.

1. What do students need to learn? The *learning* question.
2. How will you know they learned anything? The *assessment* question.
3. What approaches to teaching will you choose? The *teaching* question.

Learning Outcomes	Teaching and Assessment Used

Reflectivity
- Comment on your thinking processes used in these three teacher decisions.
- How do your teaching strategies match up with the list of instructional events?

SUMMARY

We emphasize that teacher decision making does not generally follow this cycle of steps. However, the purpose for the visual cycle is to help you systematically think about the complex decisions for lessons and units (Figure 6.17) where these issues are interconnected.

FIGURE 6.17.
Teacher
Decision Cycle:
Teaching
Question.

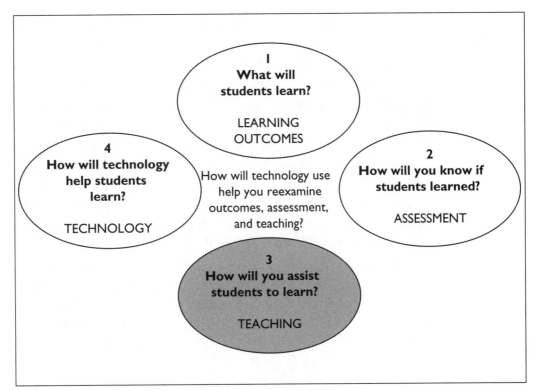

An Idea
Worth
Thinking
About

"Being and behavior are what children observe, study, remember."
(Sinetar, 1998, p. 135)

Modeling appropriate behavior is one of the strongest forms of teaching. How do you expect students to enjoy learning if you don't enjoy teaching? This quotation from a book entitled *The Mentor's Spirit* can apply to all sorts of teacher behavior. Other teaching options worth exploring include tutoring, coaching, and mentoring.

Reflective Teaching

Powerful and Endless Possibilities!

Beginning teachers and veteran teachers alike face the difficulties of having students in their classrooms who do not seem to be motivated to learn. It seems that most individuals who enter the teaching profession were at one time extremely motivated (and usually excellent) students themselves, so it seems unnatural for them to have unmotivated students within their classrooms.

However, just because a student enters a classroom with no interest in school or the learning process does not mean that the student must feel the same apathy toward learning when they exit the classroom.

The teacher has an enormous impact on the type of attitude students will have about learning—regardless of the types of learning experiences the students have had in the past. The teacher has the power to vary instructional strategies in such a way that most students will be able to experience learning success. The teacher has the power to engage students in hands-on activities that allow the students to showcase what they know in ways not dependent on paper and pencil. The teacher has the power to allow students to work in pairs or small groups to collaborate and learn from one another as they interact socially. The teacher has the power and the responsibility to use the instructional strategies that work best for the students in their classroom. When thinking about the countless instructional options that teachers have at their disposal to try, adapt, and use, the potential for reaching even the most unmotivated student does not quite seem like such a daunting and impossible task.

Teacher Inquiry

- Conduct an independent search for new teaching strategies that support the student learning for one of your lessons. Try to modify an approach used in one content area for your use. Teacher inquiry can consist of documenting how learning was originally taught and your experiences in learning and using a new strategy.
- In action research, new teachers typically try to compare differences between teaching strategies. Proving that one approach is more effective than the other is problematic and stems from our long-standing views on research. In this case, new teachers frequently believe that research must compare something. As we advocate multiple teaching strategies rather than identifying just one, a research study could describe the different ways of teaching "content" using both strategies and how the mix of the two influenced student learning.

REFERENCES

Bandura, A. (1986). *Social foundations of thought and action: A social cognitive theory.* Englewood Cliffs, NJ: Prentice-Hall.

Fountas, I. C., & Pinnell, G. S. (1996). *Guided reading.* Portsmouth, NH: Heinemann.

Gagné, R. M. (1985). *The conditions of learning* (4th ed.). New York: Holt, Rinehart, & Winston.

Gagné, R. M., Wager, W. W., Golas, K. C., & Keller, J. M. (2005). *Principles of instructional design* (5th ed.). Belmont, CA: Wadsworth/Thomson.

Goodlad, J. (1984). *A place called school: Prospects for the future.* New York: McGraw-Hill.

Gunter, A. A., Estes, T. H., & Schwab, J. H. (2003). *Instruction: A models approach* (4th ed.). Boston: Allyn and Bacon.

Johnson, D. W., Johnson, R. T., & Smith, K. A. (1991). *Active learning: Cooperation in the college classroom.* Edina, MN: Interaction Book.

Joyce, B., Weil, M., & Calhoun, E. (2004). *Models of teaching* (7th ed.). Boston: Allyn and Bacon.

Karolides, N. J. (2000). *Reader response in the secondary and college classroom.* Mahwah, NJ: Lawrence Erlbaum Associates.

Karplus, R. (1977). *Science teaching and the development of reasoning.* Berkeley, CA: University of California Press.

Norman, D. A. (1993). *Things that make us smart: Defending human attributes in the age of the machine.* Reading, M.A: Addison-Wesley Publishing Company.

Renner, J. (1982). The power of purpose. *Science Education, 66*(5), 709–716.

Rosenshine, B. (1983, March). Teaching functions in instructional programs. *The Elementary School Journal, 83,* 335–350.

Schön, D. A. (1987). *Educating the reflective practitioner: Toward a new design for teaching and learning in the professions.* San Francisco: Jossey-Bass.

Sinetar, M. (1998). *The mentor's spirit: Life lessons on leadership and the art of encouragement.* New York: St. Martin's Griffin.

Slavin, R. E. (1995). *Cooperative learning* (2nd ed.). Boston: Allyn and Bacon.

Tharp, R. G., & Gallimore, R. (1988). *Rousing minds to life: Teaching, learning, and schooling in social context.* New York: Cambridge University Press.

RESOURCES

Print Resources

Combs, M. (2002). *Readers and writers in primary grades.* Columbus, OH: Merrill Prentice-Hall.

Many teaching strategies combining reading and writing.

Cipani, E. (2004). *Classroom management for all teachers: 12 plans for evidence-based practice.* Upper Saddle River, NJ: Merrill.

Classroom management organized in three ways: classroom management as discipline, as a system, and as instruction.

Ford, M. P. (2002). Using centers to engage children during guided reading time: Intensifying learning experiences away from the teacher. *Reading Teacher, 55*(8), 710.

Many teaching strategies combining reading and writing.

Freiberg, H. J., & Driscoll, A. (2005). *Universal teaching strategies* (5th ed.). Boston: Allyn and Bacon.

A practical, clearly laid out survey of some common teaching strategies for classroom teachers.

Gunter, A. A., Estes, T. H., & Schwab, J. H. (2003). *Instruction: A models approach* (4th ed.). Boston: Allyn and Bacon.

A practical guide to instructional practice. This text offers examples and exercises that illustrate the nuances of each model.

Hardin, C. J. (2004). *Effective classroom management: Models and strategies for today's classrooms.* Upper Saddle River, NJ: Merrill.

Specific plans for classroom management.

Johnson, D. W., & Johnson, R. T. (1998). *Learning together and alone: Cooperative, competitive, and individualistic learning*. Boston: Allyn and Bacon.

A good introduction to making cooperative learning work in schools.

Joyce, B., Weil, M., & Calhoun, E. (2004). *Models of teaching* (7th ed.). Boston: Allyn and Bacon.

A classic synthesis of theory and action in articulating instruction across schooling and training settings. Models organized by "families" of purpose and theoretical foundation.

Landau, B. M. (2004). *The art of classroom management: Building equitable learning communities*. Upper Saddle River, NJ: Merrill.

Integrates management, law, and multicultural issues, while citing true case studies.

Novak, J. D., & Wandersee, J. (Eds.). (1991). Special issue on concept mapping. *Journal of Research in Science Teaching, 28*, 10.

Leading researchers in the development of concept maps and other visuals.

Slavin, R. E. (1995). *Cooperative learning* (2nd ed.). Boston: Allyn and Bacon.

A concise source of guidelines on cooperative learning.

Tharp, R. G., & Gallimore, R. (1988). *Rousing minds to life: Teaching, learning, and schooling in social context*. New York: Cambridge University Press.

A social framework for helping students and teachers learn in schools. Implements many of Vygotsky's ideas and expands the notion of teaching across many options.

Web-Based Resources

Teaching Strategies

www.adprima.com/

Advantages, disadvantages, and preparation requirements of different teaching strategies, as well as multiple links on classroom management, thinking, and IDEA.

www.iub.edu:/~teaching/handbook_2.shtml

University-developed handbook for teachers.

Concept maps and graphic organizers

www.graphic.org/concept.html

Useful site on the theory underlying concept maps from its originator, Joseph Novak, as well as guidelines for teachers.

Cooperative learning

Jigsaw.org/index.html

Overview of technique, history, and implementation of this commonly used cooperative learning model.

Inquiry

http://inquiry.uiuc.edu/

Source for units using inquiry as the teaching approach.

http://webquest.sdsu.edu/

Applying inquiry and problem based learning. Examples organized by content area and grade level.

Conflict resolution

www.courts.wa.gov/education/lessons

Using the mediation process in the primary grades.

Role play

www.oxfam.org.uk/coolplanet/teachers/literacy/bullp6.htm

Addressing bullying by using role play.

7 Exploring Technology Options

Main Idea of This Chapter

The use of media and technology is just another teaching decision.

Principle 4 TEACHING REPERTOIRE: The teacher understands and uses a variety of instructional strategies to encourage students' development of critical thinking, problem-solving, and performance skills.

Principle 6 COMMUNICATION: The teacher uses knowledge of effective verbal, nonverbal, and media communication techniques to foster active inquiry, collaboration, and supportive instruction in the classroom.

Principle 7 PRE-UNIT THINKING: The teacher plans instruction based on knowledge of subject matter, students, the community, and curriculum goals.

Principle 8 ASSESSMENT: The teacher understands and uses formal and informal assessment strategies to evaluate and ensure the continuous intellectual, social, and physical development of the learner.

Focus Questions

- What are your views on technology, and what are your technology skills?
- What do you know about technology standards?
- How do I make choices about technology in my teaching?

Design Activities

DA 22: Views of Technology
DA 23: Technology Skills
DA 24: Universal Design for Learning (UDL)
DA 25: Technology in Instructional Events
DA 26: Teaching and Technology Options in Your Lessons

SCOPE OF THIS CHAPTER

This chapter first asks you to record your views of technology and perceptions of your curriculum integration skills and technology tool skills. This chapter introduces technology standards for students and teachers. Teaching with technology involves looking at how technology can support learning outcomes, including learning levels (taxonomies), understanding, and special needs. This chapter also examines how technology can be integrated across most teaching by using the idea of instructional events and then in several teaching models. The sequence for Chapter 7 is visualized in Figure 7.1.

FIGURE 7.1.
Visual Sequence for Chapter 7.

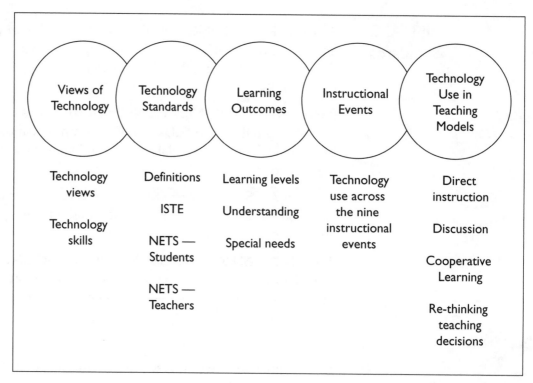

Views of Technology

Technology Standards

Learning Outcomes

Instructional Events

Technology Use in Teaching Models

Technology views

Technology skills

Definitions

ISTE

NETS — Students

NETS — Teachers

Learning levels

Understanding

Special needs

Technology use across the nine instructional events

Direct instruction

Discussion

Cooperative Learning

Re-thinking teaching decisions

TEACHER DECISION CYCLE: QUESTION 4

In the previous chapters of Section III, we asked these questions in the Teaching Decision Cycle:

- Chapter 4: Determining Learning Outcomes: *What is to be learned?*
- Chapter 5: Exploring Assessment Options: *How do you know if your students learned these outcomes?*
- Chapter 6: Exploring Teaching Options: *How will you assist students to learn?*

This chapter explores technology options (Figure 7.2) and asks two questions: "How can media and technology help students to learn?" and "How can media and technology decisions help you reexamine your previous decisions?"

FIGURE 7.2.
Teacher Decision Cycle: Technology Question.

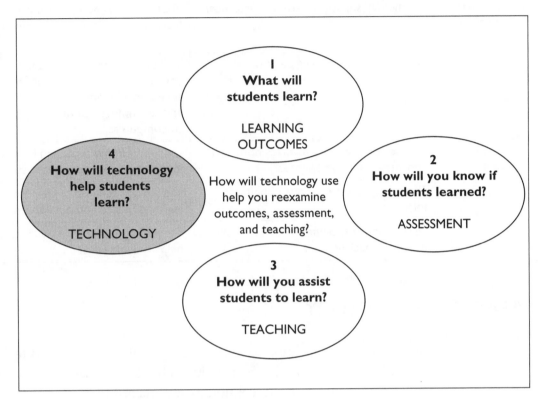

How will technology help students to learn?

This chapter is based on several important ideas:

- **IDEA 1:** The purpose of media and technology is to help students learn. The choice of media and technology must support learning outcomes.
- **IDEA 2:** Media and technology choices are teaching decisions. This means that your choice of media and technology must assist you in your teaching.
- **IDEA 3:** Instructional technology literacy involves both computer skills and curriculum integration skills.
- **IDEA 4:** Media and technology provide learning experiences that otherwise might not be possible. This idea suggests that you should look to media and technology for opportunities to create new learning environments that previously have not existed.
- **IDEA 5:** Reviewing new technologies helps you rethink the previous teaching decisions.

Implications of these ideas are summarized in Figure 7.3.

FIGURE 7.3.
Rationale and
Implications of
Technology Use.

Rationale for Using Technology	Implications
Technology supports learning outcomes.	Your technology choices must be based on learning outcomes for curriculum, units, and lessons.
Technology is a teaching decision.	Technology use is not an add-on feature in your teaching, nor should it be implemented based on administrative directives. Media and technology options range from chalk to computers.
Technological literacy involves both skills and integration experiences.	One must know tools and how to use tools in the classroom to support student learning.
Technology creates unique conditions for learning.	Technology can create new "environments for learning" inside and outside the classroom.
Technology possibilities merit reexamination of teaching.	Technology can change your teaching to help students learn.

VIEWS OF TECHNOLOGY

Your views about technology influence your attitudes toward technology and motivation to use it. As in the previous chapters on assessment and teaching, consider your views about technology and record them on paper.

Views of Technology

Task Rationale The first step in considering technology in your classroom is to examine your views on media and technology.

Task Guidelines Please respond in writing to the following questions:

1. Describe a memorable student experience you had with instructional technology.
2. Describe technology use in your teaching. If none, describe what you have observed in your cooperating teacher or in the school where you are working.
3. What are your reactions to the use of media and technology in the classroom, and what are these reactions based on?
4. How does (did) your teacher education program model media and technology use?

Reflectivity This entire Design Activity is a reflective exercise, so here is one more reflective question: What have you learned about yourself as a teacher from thinking about technology use?

TECHNOLOGY SKILLS

As the term *literacy* is increasingly seen as more than the ability to read and write, instructional technology (IT) literacy is more than knowing how to use computer software. How to use a software tool is a first step (tool use), but the more important competency is knowing how to use the software tool to help students learn (integration). Much of teachers' professional development in instructional technology is learning how to use the tool. For many teachers, this is a place to start; however, less support is given to teachers on how to use these tools in teaching.

A first step in becoming IT literate requires self-assessing what you already know. The following Design Activity prompts you to self-assess your knowledge, skills, and experiences in technology in two ways: (1) curriculum integration skills, or how you have used media and technology in the classroom, and (2) specific skills with technology tools.

Technology Skills

Task Rationale
Developing IT literacy requires first acknowledging what you know about media and technology for educational use. This is the curriculum integration experience you have. A second type of technology skills is tool use.

Task Guidelines
Use the chart to record your skill experience and areas you'd like to learn more about.

Curriculum Integration Skills	Technology Tool Use
What experiences have you had in usingmedia and technology in your teaching?	What media and technology tools do you use? Characterize your expertise level (novice, intermediate, expert)
What curriculum integration skills would you like to develop?	What tools would you like to know how to use and why?

Reflectivity
What challenges did you experience in completing this activity—particularly, the differences in the two categories of technology skills?

MEDIA AND TECHNOLOGY DEFINITIONS

Instructional media and technology

Media and technology become *instructional* media and *instructional* technology when they carry messages with an instructional purpose (Smaldino, Russell, Heinich, & Moldenda, 2005). In practice, computers, specialized software, personal digital assistants (PDAs), and the Internet are viewed as instructional technologies. When educators use the term *technology*, they mean instructional technology and, more narrowly, the use of computers and the Internet. Media and technologies that have successfully been used in schools are usually left undiscussed. Examples include chalk and blackboard, physical objects, maps, books, construction paper, and 35-mm slides. The overhead transparency, for example, is probably one of the most reliable "instructional technologies" developed.

Educational technology and instructional technology

Educational technology and *instructional technology* are terms used interchangeably in educational circles (Seels & Richey, 1994). The American Educational Communications and Technology (AECT) organization conducts an ongoing process to define the field and these differences. The term *educational technology* is viewed as the broader term encompassing technological systems, such as accounting, grade reporting, databases, and communication technologies. Instructional technology is viewed as a subset of educational technology. The 1994 definition of *instructional technology* is "the theory and practice of design, development, utilization, management and evaluation of processes and resources for learning." Consult the AECT website (www.aect.org) periodically for an update on this definition.

ISTE STANDARDS

The International Society for Technology in Education (ISTE) focuses on the use of technology in K–12 education and teacher education. ISTE sponsors a conference for public schools in instructional technology, the National Educational Computing Conference (NECC). Along with educators, education associations, businesses, and private foundations, ISTE developed the National Educational Technology Standards (NETS) for students, teachers, and administrators (ISTE, 2002). An initial set of Technology Foundation Standards for Students in prekindergarten through twelfth grade has been released, and additional standards will be released over time (see www.iste.org). Most of the state departments of education in the United States have adopted, adapted, or referenced the NETS standards.

NETS standards for students

The NETS standards for students include six categories that address technology competencies. Specific learning outcomes are listed for each category in Figure 7.4. For example, one learning outcome under Standard 3, Technology Productivity Tools, has students using "technology tools to enhance learning, increase productivity, and promote creativity." This learning outcome could conceivably cover many learning activities, but the goal provides a means to document student learning, productivity, and/or creativity.

NETS Standards for Students
1. Basic operations and concepts   • Students demonstrate a sound understanding of technology systems.   • Students are proficient in the use of technology.
2. Social, ethical, and human issues   • Students understand the ethical, cultural, and societal issues related to technology.   • Students practice responsible use of technology systems, information, and software.   • Students develop positive attitudes toward technology uses that support lifelong learning, collaboration, personal pursuits, and productivity.
3. Technology productivity tools   • Students use technology tools to enhance learning, increase productivity, and promote creativity.   • Students use productivity tools to collaborate in constructing technology-enhanced models, prepare publications, and produce other creative works.
4. Technology communications tools   • Students use telecommunications to collaborate, publish, and interact with peers, experts, and other audiences.   • Students use a variety of media and formats to communicate information and ideas effectively to multiple audiences.
5. Technology research tools   • Students use technology to locate, evaluate, and collect information from a variety of sources.   • Students use technology tools to process data and report results.   • Students evaluate and select new information resources and technological innovations based on the appropriateness for specific tasks.
6. Technology problem-solving and decision-making tools   • Students use technology resources for solving problems and making informed decisions.   • Students employ technology in the development of strategies for solving problems in the real world.

FIGURE 7.4. NETS Standards for Students (ISTE, 2002).

The second learning outcome in Standard 3 has students using "productivity tools to collaborate in constructing technology-enhanced models, prepare publications, and produce other creative works." Storybooks might be constructed out of stories written by students across a county school system, a state, or several countries. Online-posted stories with hyperlinks to pictures, email, and resources are student works that could not have been constructed without hypermedia and the Internet.

Guidelines for using NETS for students

ISTE's NETS initiative is grounded in the idea that the focus of technology is not technology integration but *curriculum integration* using technology. "The purpose of the learning activities is to focus the technology use on curriculum—discipline-specific, content-area curriculum—using technology as a tool to foster higher level outcomes" (http://cnets.iste.org/students/s_integration.html).

The NETS standards have been identified for grades PreK–2, 3–5, 6–8, and 9–12. The ISTE website should be consulted for the most up-to-date version of these standards (see http://cnets.iste.org). These standards include performance indicators for tool use, ethical issues, and learning use. Learning activities for different content areas and grade levels are also available. Activities have been developed for English language arts, foreign language, mathematics, science, social studies, and multidisciplinary topics.

NETS standards for teachers (this is you!)

The NETS initiative by ISTE also developed technology standards for all teachers. The specific performance indicators (Figure 7.5) can be useful for professional development or school or countywide implementation. Note that the first standard addresses tool skills, while standards 2 through 6 address curriculum integration skills. NETS standards for teachers include technology-rich activities in teacher education courses, including foundations courses, English language arts education, mathematics education, science education, and social studies education. Activities for foundations, early childhood programs, elementary education programs, middle school education programs, and secondary education programs can be found on the NETS site (see http://cnets.iste.org/teachers/t_book.html). The NETS website includes sample rubrics to help teacher education faculty assess technology use in lessons and units. Guidelines for software and website evaluation are also available. New teachers might also find this information useful.

NETS Standards for Teachers
I. Technology operations and concepts
• Demonstrate introductory knowledge, skills, and understanding of concepts related to technology (NETS standards for students).
• Demonstrate continual growth in technology knowledge and skills to stay abreast of current and emerging technologies.
2. Planning and designing learning environments and experiences
• Design developmentally appropriate learning opportunities that apply technology-enhanced instructional strategies to support the diverse needs of learners.
• Apply current research on teaching and learning with technology when planning learning environments and experiences.
• Identify and locate technology resources and evaluate them for accuracy and suitability.
• Plan for the management of technology resources within the context of learning activities.
• Plan strategies to manage student learning in a technology-enhanced environment.
3. Teaching, learning, and the curriculum
• Facilitate technology-enhanced experiences that address content standards and student technology standards.
• Use technology to support learner-centered strategies that address the diverse needs of students.
• Apply technology to develop students' higher-order skills and creativity.
• Manage student learning activities in a technology-enhanced environment.

FIGURE 7.5. NETS Standards for Teachers.

TECHNOLOGY ACROSS LEARNING OUTCOMES

In this section, we show how technology can address different learning levels using Gagné's taxonomy. Then we describe how technology can be used to foster student understanding. Finally, we introduce assistive technology for special needs students.

Technology for learning levels

Gagné's taxonomy combined cognitive, affective, and psychomotor capabilities into one framework (Gagné, Wager, Golas, & Keller, 2005). In this taxonomy,

NETS Standards for Teachers
4. Assessment and evaluation
• Apply technology in assessing student learning of subject matter using a variety of assessment techniques.
• Use technology resources to collect and analyze data, interpret results, and communicate findings to improve instructional practice and maximize student learning.
• Apply multiple methods of evaluation to determine students' appropriate use of technology resources for learning, communication, and productivity.
5. Productivity and professional practice
• Use technology resources to engage in ongoing professional development and lifelong learning.
• Continually evaluate and reflect on professional practice to make informed decisions regarding the use of technology in support of student learning.
• Apply technology to increase productivity.
• Use technology to communicate and collaborate with peers, parents, and the larger community in order to nurture student learning.
6. Social, ethical, legal, and human issues
• Model and teach legal and ethical practice related to technology use.
• Apply technology resources to enable and empower learners with diverse backgrounds, characteristics, and abilities.
• Identify and use technology resources that affirm diversity.
• Promote safe and healthy use of technology resources.
• Facilitate equitable access to technology resources for all students.

FIGURE 7.5. NETS Standards for Teachers (*continued*)

intellectual skills include concepts, procedures, and principles. A fundamental idea is presented first. More detailed ideas, which elaborate on the fundamental concept, procedure, or principle, are added (Reigeluth, 1999). All three use simple-to-complex sequencing in instruction.

Intellectual skills: Concepts

Concept learning is sequenced by the relationships between the concepts, moving from generalized concepts down to specific concepts. The idea here is to present the easiest, most familiar organizing concepts first (Novak & Gowin, 1984). Students can draw by hand concept maps in which they identify concepts and label the connections between the concepts (Figure 7.6). Thus, concept maps reveal what students know. Concept-mapping software can help students to encode and store conceptual relationships.

FIGURE 7.6.
Partial Concept
Map.

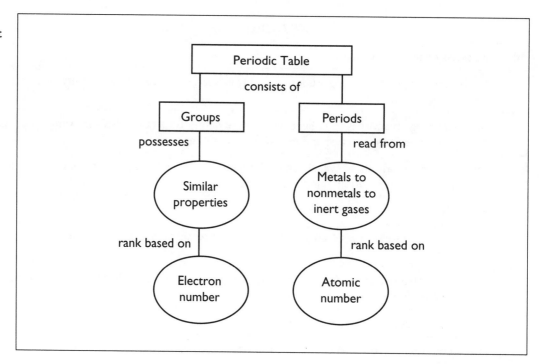

Another technology tool for conceptual learning is hyperlinking. Hyperlinking enables a user to move between locations in digital files or websites. Hyperlinking is also a feature in electronic books, where stories provide background on settings or characters or annotations from the author. Some electronic stories use hyperlinking to provide the reader with alternative story lines. Hyperlinking capabilities in web pages or electronic books help students discover more about a topic, communicate with others, or solve a problem. Another use could have students establish their own hyperlinks in word processing software, presentation software, or web pages to "map" their understanding between ideas, concepts, and resources. Concept maps, electronic books, or web pages give teachers and students thinking tools to organize knowledge, so that this knowledge can be meaningfully stored, retrieved, and used to enhance their existing human abilities (Figure 7.7).

FIGURE 7.7.
Teaching Options for Intellectual Skills: Concepts.

Teaching Strategy	Physical or Digital
Concept map	Hand-developed or software
Web pages	Hyperlinking to resources and experts
Hypertext	Hyperlinking to reveal connections between ideas
E-books	Multiple forms of media, annotation

Intellectual skills: Procedures

When students are to learn a process or a skill, the sequence of learning addresses the steps required to complete the task. Teaching approaches for *procedural* learning include observation, demonstration, role play, simulations, and field trips. Teaching may involve acting or actually performing the task as students observe the teacher's behavior. Specific procedures or subcomponents of the task can be demonstrated. Role play helps students directly experience and follow prescribed procedures. As the learning task becomes more complex and approaches a real-world task, field trips and lab activities prove effective. Field trips are near-authentic learning activities, where students directly experience the outside world. Laboratory activities also approximate real experience. However, field trips and labs require attention to logistics, safety, and cost issues. Simulation, such as students running their own business in a classroom, can partially substitute for real experience, but simulation requires significant planning and time on the teacher's part.

Instructional technologies useful for teaching procedures include microworlds and simulation software (Figure 7.8). Microworlds are computer-based environments where students accomplish a set of tasks, such as writing a story with student-created animated objects. More sophisticated microworlds enable students to develop an environment, such as an island, city, or ant colony, for the purpose of learning not only procedures but also conceptual and social knowledge about how the world works. Some microworld computer packages present already-built worlds for students to participate in, while others allow students to enhance or develop entirely unique objects. These "construction kits" require more support by the teacher, but rich learning may result from activities in which students are immersed in meaningful activity.

FIGURE 7.8.
Teaching Options for Intellectual Skills: Procedures.

Teaching Strategy	Physical or Digital
Demonstration	Live or remote location
Role play	Live or online role in web chat, conferencing
Lab	Live or digital lab simulation
Simulation	Live (student store), games, digital simulation construction kits
Microworlds	Digital to showcase detail and provide immersion
Field trips	Live or virtual

Related to microworlds, simulations frequently involve specific learning outcomes, such as reacting to a change in the environment. In the adult world, flying simulators give pilots near-authentic experience to quickly adapt to changes in airplane performance or weather conditions. Simulation packages in school help students drive an automobile, identify organisms or rock specimens (object identification programs), understand chemical reactions (digital lab environments), and make decisions (expert systems software).

Intellectual skills: Principles

For students to learn the "why" of concepts and procedures, a teaching strategy is to move from basic and observable *principles* to more detailed and complex principles. Instructional technologies for teaching principles include searching tools and digital reference works (Figure 7.9). Researching for information or expertise today involves Internet browsing skills. CD-based or online versions of reference works or specialized websites tap the power of hypermedia to include hyperlinks to text, visuals, audio, and video elements. Visualization tools help students understand the "why" of knowledge by translating text-explained principles into visually oriented principles. Visuals help the student understand concepts, procedures, and principles. Visuals can also be used to help the student represent or uniquely encode knowledge (Shambaugh, 1995). Mathematics understanding benefits from visualizing mathematics concepts (e.g., fractions, sets, integration, geometric proofs). Science education uses visualization to chart global geographical characteristics and changes, biogeochemical cycles, and chemical models, among other applications.

FIGURE 7.9.
Teaching Options for Intellectual Skills: Principles.

Teaching Strategy	Physical or Digital
Searching tools **Reference works** **Hypermedia** **Visualization**	Search engines Reference books or digital reference works Hyperlinking between reference entries Understanding "why" of knowledge

Cognitive strategies

Another level of learning is helping students become aware of their thinking strategies. These strategies contribute to the development of intellectual skills. Teaching may range from verbal reminders to explicit instruction on study skills strategies, such as the use of semantic maps, concept maps, or other diagrams (see Novak & Gowin, 1984). Instructional time may be required to introduce students to new strategies, along with guided practice and opportunities to test these new skills. Teaching cognitive skills as a separate course may not produce immediate results. These skills are more likely to transfer when they are taught and used in the context of actual learning of academic content. This implies that teaching time must be found within content areas to promote student development of thinking skills unique to that area (Figure 7.10).

Instructional technology applications may have a future in providing metacognitive assistance, such as study skills strategies related to a particular

FIGURE 7.10.
Teaching Options for Cognitive Strategies.

Teaching Options for Cognitive Strategies
• Separate courses dedicated to study skills strategies • Introduce study strategies in context with academic content • Teacher-provided strategies and student exploration of personal preferences

content topic. Computer tools, such as word processing or concept-mapping software, might include reflective prompts to help students think about their thinking in the context of the content area learning. Although textbooks may use reflective questions, such as those found in this text, their use in the actual context of learning would prove more useful. Such software would support reflective thinking, perhaps in addition to the experiential thinking (Norman, 1993) found in many activities, such as computer games. Microworld or simulation software, using reflective prompts, might be useful in helping students think about their decisions and the implications of their decisions.

Verbal information

Teaching for verbal information differs, based on whether the information is a name or label, individual facts, or organized information (Gagné, Wager, Golas, & Keller, 2005). Learning *names* or *labels* gives students meaningful ways of encoding and storing information, which are themselves cognitive strategies. *Facts*, meanwhile, require encoding based on their relationships to other pieces of knowledge. *Organized information* also benefits from encoding and personalized memory structures across a large base of knowledge.

Teaching strategies for learning verbal information may involve textbooks and other supporting media materials, such as maps, encyclopedias, other texts, and reference works (Figure 7.11). Encoding verbal information by using visuals can help students connect verbal information with visual representations. Connecting facts, in terms of conceptual relationships, can be the basis of organizers as teaching strategies, which are frequently found in teacher-led presentations.

FIGURE 7.11. Verbal Information Types and Media/ Technology Options.

Verbal Type	Characterized by	Technology Option
Label	Encoding and storage	Pictures
Facts	Relate information to other knowledge	Media, references, searching, e-books, visuals
Organizing information	Networks of knowledge	Organizers, concept maps

Sources of verbal information can be found in digital versions of encyclopedias and electronic books, which can be digitally annotated with hyperlinks. Search engines in software programs and websites also support learning new information. Concept-mapping programs could potentially provide visually meaningful advance organizers of conceptual information, as well as verbal information.

Affective learning

Aspects of the affective domain are inherent in learning intellectual skills, so learning outcomes that involve critical thinking and problem solving must consider outcomes of attention, appreciation, and valuing (Figure 7.12). Developing a positive attitude toward a skill, for example, is dependent on success in learning the skill. One way is to model appropriate attitudes by teachers or peers. Like cognitive strategies, development of this learning domain occurs over time. Other teaching strategies for promoting affective outcomes include role play, conflict resolution strategies, jurisprudential teaching, and cooperative groups. Role play allows students to directly experience human activity but in a systematic way in which students evaluate and discuss behavior. Role play creates a learning environment in which students can relate the classroom situation to the outside world (Joyce, Weil, & Calhoun, 2004).

FIGURE 7.12. Teaching Strategies for Affective Learning.

Teaching Strategies for Affective Learning
• Modeling of teacher or role model's behavior
• Role play
• Conflict resolution
• Jurisprudential approach to controversial issues
• Cooperative groups

More sophisticated role play involves conflict resolution and jurisprudential teaching. Conflict resolution uses student emotions toward current events, student behavior, and academic content to engage students in identifying reasons, feelings, and facts behind different views and to evaluate different courses of action (Gunter, Estes, & Schwab, 2003). Jurisprudential teaching examines differences in views and values on controversial issues. This strategy is typically used in middle and secondary courses, when students understand societal values and current issues. This approach has student groups taking positions on an issue, exploring positions, and qualifying their positions on examination of assumptions and implications (Joyce, et al., 2004).

Finally, group activity involves many formats, but in our discussion of promoting affective learning, students learn how to function as a group of individuals with a common purpose. Students learn that they contribute as individuals and also to the overall success of the group.

Multimedia programs, microworlds, and simulation can contribute to a rich learning experience. Students experience some features of the real world, such as the feelings and emotions of experiencing the world. Communication technologies, such as email and audio or video conferencing, enable students to see and hear what students are saying and feeling. Appreciation for cultural differences benefits from direct communication with those cultures. A major attribute for technology at the affective level of learning is to improve student motivation as technological tools and rich activities connect to student interests. Using these instructional technologies, along with structured learning tasks with clear expectations and instructions, teachers can offer students an active role in their learning.

Motor skills

Depending on the complexity of the skill, teaching psychomotor skills involves the mastery of a subskill, followed by the overall executive skill. Some physical coordination skills require a combination of skills. Teaching physical coordination skills usually involves observation of expert performance in addition to direct coaching of the skill. Continual practice, observation, and assistance of the development of skilled performance are hallmarks of coaching.

The use of instructional technology to assist psychomotor skills is relatively new and generally not available in schools. Specialized university programs may provide diagnostic resources of imaging and modeling to study complex physical coordination. A new form of technology to assist physically challenged individuals is called assistive technology (AT). AT tools help students perform school tasks such as seeing, listening, speaking, writing, and computing.

Summary

Figure 7.13 summarizes different teaching strategies and technology options for different levels of learning. Note that the taxonomy is a tool to think about

Learning Level	Teaching Strategies	Technology Assistance
Intellectual skills		
• Concepts	Textbooks, maps, pictures	Conceptual learning using concept mapping, hyperlinking
• Procedures	Field trips, role play, guest speakers	Microworlds, simulation, expert systems software
• Principles	Direct instruction, textbooks, inquiry, presentation, crayons	Searching, hypermedia, draw and paint programs, visualization,
Cognitive strategies	Note-taking strategies, writing, organizers, presentations	Computer-based note-taking, concept-mapping, or reflective writing software; presentation software
Verbal information	Visuals, organizers, textbooks, maps, encyclopedias, reference works	Draw and paint programs, concept mapping programs, searching, digital encyclopedias, electronic books
Affective	Role play, conflict resolution, jurisprudential, approach, groups	Multimedia, conferencing, microworlds
Motor skills	Modeling, coaching	Diagnostic tools, assistive technology

FIGURE 7.13. Teaching and Technology by Learning Level.

the complexity of learning and that your learning outcomes may include more than one learning level. The taxonomy idea helps us think about what we are asking students to know, appreciate, and do.

Technology for understanding

Instructors in teacher education programs caution about the overuse of learning objectives that begin with "Students will understand. . . ." The implication of the warning is to be clear about what student understanding means. Rather than avoiding the use of this term, Wiggins and McTighe (1998) provide some assistance in the educational use of understanding, based on what they call the "six facets of understanding" (Figure 7.14).

FIGURE 7.14.
Facets of
Understanding.

Facets of Understanding	
Can *explain*	Can *interpret*
Can *apply*	Have *perspective*
Can *empathize*	Have *self-knowledge*

From *Understanding by Design* by Grant Wiggins & Jay McTighe (1998). Copyright © by the Association for Supervision and Curriculum Development, 1703 N. Beauregard St., Alexandria, Va. Reprinted with permission.

Can explain

Explanation is one facet of understanding in which students are asked to explain what facts mean. Media and technology tools can be used to gather evidence to support explanations (Figure 7.15). Search engines and search strategies in CD products and web browsers can be used to search for information that students must then organize to support their explanations. Multimedia, presentation, and word processing software enable students to develop explanatory products that demonstrate their understanding.

Can interpret

Interpretation enhances student understanding beyond "explanation." Most information is not value-free. Not all people will see information in the same way. Media and technologies that help students read and tell stories are useful for understanding. Traditional printed media still play a major role in activities. Examine new media formats, such as e-books, animations, and story construction kits, which "give life to text." Students spend a lot of academic time reading. Why not give them the opportunity to not only write and read but also create their own works? Paint and graphics programs support text and visualization of narrative, as well as recording that narrative within multimedia products.

Facet	Technology Possibilities	Teaching and Assessment
Explanation	Multimedia and online searching uncover supporting evidence of ideas, feelings, events Multimedia development tools, presentation, and word processing tools to create products	Around themes, issues, or problems, students produce products that demonstrate how things work and why events happened Clear explanations of activities are needed with clear assessment
Interpretation	Multimedia, e-books, and hyperlinks to prompts and different avenues of thought Paint, audio, animation, and narrative construction (story) software Online discussion boards Using email to interview distant sources	Making sense of events by constructing unique representations, visuals, metaphors, and testimonials in stories, reports, and personal experiences Range of performance assessed through a rubric Teacher feedback necessary Guidelines for diversity and tolerance needed.
Application	Multimedia and online searching to obtain information Specialized tools (spreadsheets, databases) to make sense of data	Problem solving with diverse situations of relevance to students Instructional time may need to be given to tool learning and additional time for student activity Student choice and some freedom necessary to maintain motivation and innovative solutions
Perspective	Multimedia authoring and presentation software tools to present points of view Email, audio, or video conferencing for discussion Television and other media for sources of perspective	Students develop or explore cases, position statements, presentations, or stories that demonstrate points of view Tolerance for diversity and difference needs to be modeled by teacher and students Clear instructions, use of guiding questions, and performance standards needed
Empathy	Audio, video, email, and web boards provide additional direct experience	Communication with humans Strong emotional reactions will result from confronting new situations.
Self-knowledge	Digital diaries, and portfolios to develop reflectivity	Students develop products demonstrating personal growth Allow freedom for personal expression Takes time to develop

FIGURE 7.15. Examples of Using Technology in Teaching for Student Understanding.

Can apply

Media and instructional technology enable students to apply what they know. Drawing tools, calculators, maps, encyclopedias, and models have often been used. Some tools are devoted to particular tasks, such as geometry programs and weather instruments; others, such as GPSs (geographic positioning systems) and spreadsheets are general-purpose tools. Students use these tools to gather information to solve problems. In teaching and assessing understanding, teachers need to budget teaching time. More time may be needed to learn the software. Clear task explanations and assessment criteria must be developed. Rubrics that characterize the types of performance and ranges of performance across each type will probably be needed.

Have perspective

Technology tools can help students develop the capacity to see different points of view. Email, audio, and video conferencing give students a chance to directly experience different perspectives and realize that not all humans are alike. Different forms of popular media, including music, newspapers, magazines, advertising, radio, television, sculpture, dance, and new media (e.g., interactive stories, graphic books), enhance opportunities for students to experience different viewpoints.

Can empathize

Empathy is the ability to understand someone's situation, feelings, point of view, and motives. Instructional technology and media bring distant perspectives of other cultures into the classroom through direct communication via email, web boards, and conferencing.

Have self-knowledge

Giving students time to reflect and take action on their thinking can be important in assessing student understanding. Encouraging this reflectivity builds habits of reflection about one's thinking and work, all of which can be archived in personalized portfolios. Media can be used to visualize and represent student work. Digital tools extend human thinking, and the resultant new media provide students with new tools for personal expression.

Technology for special needs

Another aspect of technology in public schools is use of technology for students with special needs.

Assistive technology

Assistive technologies are any tools or strategies that assist human learning. Assistive technology (AT) includes a wide range of low-tech and high-tech tools to help students. One type of AT involves access technologies, which help students with disabilities gain access to existing curriculum materials. These technologies may include remote switch devices, specialized keyboards, and even household objects. Adaptive technologies, by contrast, are specially designed devices or systems to help students communicate, move, and control their surroundings. The tools differ, depending on the unique needs of a student, but are usually associated with the human senses of sight, sound, and touch. Examples can include phone systems, specialized software, and video enlargers. These AT tools help students see and read, hear and speak, and respond with physical movements. The purpose behind AT devices is to help individual students gain access to the existing curriculum.

Schools are required under law to provide assistive technology to students with disabilities if it supports students' access to an appropriate public education. This service must be provided by the school district at no cost to the family. Such devices are likely to be specified in each individual education plan (IEP). Specific guidelines can be consulted at the website of the Office of Special Education and Rehabilitative Services (see the Resources section at the end of this chapter).

Universal design for learning

The idea of AT is based on using the existing curriculum and supplying tools for individuals to access that curriculum. A larger perspective is universal design for learning (UDL). Universal design takes the stance that the human world, such as our homes, cities, objects, and schools, should be designed to cover the broadest population possible, including those with special needs, the elderly, children, and small adults. Four assumptions about teaching and learning characterize universal design for learning (CAST, 2003). The first premise is that students with disabilities should be characterized as falling along a "continuum of learner differences" rather than being a separate category of students. A second premise of UDL is that teachers make adjustments for all students. A third premise is that the teacher should consider a variety of curriculum materials and not focus on a single textbook. A fourth premise is that curriculum should be designed so that it is flexible and can accommodate these learner differences.

Digital media provide flexibility with content representation, control, and student engagement. Specialized AT tools provide additional access to digital media. Another attribute for UDL is a reminder of the diversity of students. The next Design Activity is provided to help you think through some of the principles of UDL.

24 Universal Design for Learning (UDL)

Task Rationale   This checklist is designed to evaluate your teaching strategies and materials using UDL principles (Burgstahler, 2002).

Task Guidelines   Comment on the degree in which your teaching setting is responsive to UDL principles.

Universal Design Principle for Instruction	Comments
Inclusiveness. In what ways does your classroom respect diversity?	
Physical access. How are labs, classroom, and field work accessible to all students?	
Delivery methods. What are the different types of instructional delivery methods and materials?	
Information access. To what extent are information and media accessible to everyone?	
Interaction. What are the different ways in which students interact with you and each other?	
Feedback. Describe the types of prompting and feedback given to students and their work.	
Demonstration of knowledge. Describe different ways in which students can demonstrate what they have learned.	

From Burgstahler, S. (2002). *Universal Design of Instruction.* Seattle: Do-IT, University of Washington, pp. 2–3. Available www.washington.edu/doit/Brochures/Academics/instruction.html

Reflectivity   How might your teaching strategies and materials change based on this self-assessment of your classroom?

- Based on what you wrote, what changes need to be made to ensure a UDL classroom?
- How might your teaching strategies and materials change based on this self-assessment of your classroom?

Flexibility in curriculum includes multiple ways for students to meet curriculum goals, and it ensures that the curriculum is accessible and appropriate for all learners. The first step for teachers is to continually learn about individual differences and to stay current on literature that disseminates new knowledge on learner differences. A second step is to think about flexible activity and assessment options for these different learners. See Resources at the end of this chapter for assistance.

TECHNOLOGY ACROSS TEACHING

Now we shift your decision making to how technology can be applied to different teaching approaches. First, we look at how technology might be used generically across most teaching, as characterized by Gagné's instructional events.

Technology for instructional events

Gagné (1985) defined *instruction* as those events designed to support internal learning, such as attending, learning, remembering, appreciating, physically coordinating, and problem solving. Gagné identified characteristics of all instruction (external conditions) that can assist the development of these mental processes (internal conditions). How technology might help teachers implement teaching in terms of these nine instructional events is summarized visually in Figure 7.16.

FIGURE 7.16. Examples Using Technology Across Instructional Events.

Instructional Event	Learning Activity with Technology
Gaining attention	Media presentation of example, incident, activity
Informing learner of the objective	Presentation tool depicting advance organizer
Stimulating recall of prior learning or learning that is needed	Digital review module, examples
Presenting the new "content"	Digital concept maps, presentations, hypermedia
Providing learning guidance	Simulated tasks, examples, authentic tasks, tutorials
Prompting student performance	Student activity involving communication, research, problem solving
Providing feedback on performance	Web boards for feedback
Assessing performance	Digital rubric, online self-scoring
Enhancing retention of learning	Student activity involving communication, research, problem solving across diverse settings

Gaining attention

"Gaining attention" is about shifting students' interests to the learning of the moment, which can be done in a number of ways. Instructional media are typically rich sources for gaining student attention. For example, with a learning outcome that addresses "appreciation of cultural differences," a teacher might think of online resources that connect students with students in other countries. Frequently, we look past our own neighborhoods or local cultures to gain appreciation of differences. Showing a video clip of an interview with several local residents, for example, or an audio recording, is likely to showcase many aspects of local diversity. Such a use of media quickly gains student attention, particularly if you pose a question such as "Who do you think this is?" The short media clip can initiate a class discussion of cultural difference. The clip can also point to student performance options, in which groups of students prepare their own interviews or stories from local residents. The idea here is that an opening activity can be the basis for an entire lesson, rather than merely acting as an attention getter. The effort you invest in a strong lesson opener can maintain student attention throughout the lesson.

Informing learner of the objective

A second readying event informs the learner of the objective of the instruction. These choices also include decisions about which strategies to use and time requirements. Frequently, the first and second instructional events are the same teacher behavior. For example, if you walk into the classroom and record the lesson agenda on the board, as well as key ideas, students become conditioned to the rules of classroom behavior and begin to record the notes you write on the board. Thus, you have gained student attention and informed students of what is to be learned today. Presentation software lends itself to not only visually informing students of the lesson or activity agenda but also acting as an organizer, a cognitive strategy in which new concepts to be learned are related to larger, organizing conceptual frameworks.

Stimulating recall

The third readying event activates prior knowledge, recalls what was learned previously, and relates this to what might be useful in today's instruction. An organizer identifies previously learned concepts. A digital presentation may include in the text of the organizer a hyperlink to a review activity, text, or visual that captures the major ideas of prior learning. Recall can also be used as a means to gain attention, the first instructional event. A strong opening activity can thus combine the first and third events: gain attention and stimulate recall. Other uses for this instructional event are to summarize student work, address general student difficulties, and report the range of student performance, depending on the prior learning and type of learning activity.

Presenting new "content"

The exact presentation of new material or new activities depends on the nature of the content and the teaching strategy used to present new learning. New content may be a continuation of a previous lesson or another activity in a thematic unit. The stimulus material could be case studies, examples, situations, simulations, a lecture, a guest speaker, a hands-on activity, a stimulating key question, or a demonstration. A whole variety of methods exist to present new material. Many of these options can be delivered using digital media. Guest speakers are a good example; the Internet can provide a recorded presentation or a live conversation. Provide providing as much direct experience as possible, through field trips on school grounds or in the community. Instructional media and technology provide resources to the classroom that may not have been possible before.

Providing learning guidance

The teacher assists the learner in various ways, from modeling behavior to questioning to reinforcing to the use of organizers. This instructional event parallels one of the central features of direct instruction, the use of guided practice, which can cover learner guidance and the next two instructional events. Technology approaches here can help students learn new knowledge and skills. For example, programmed learning strategies have been used where students must master new material before moving on. Hyperlinked products and online materials can "point" students to guidance, based on the teacher's use of tutorials, examples, and resources.

Prompting student performance

This event requires active participation by the student, demonstrating learning through performance, whether the performance is recall, synthesis, attitudinal change, physical skill improvement, or some other learning improvement. Instructional technology excels in this instructional event, as rich learning tasks benefit from digital tools to communicate, research, and solve problems (Harris, 2001). Learning outcomes that address student "understanding" necessitate student performance in some way, and digital tools increase students' capacity to research, represent, and communicate what they know.

Providing feedback

Next, teachers respond to student performance. This response may take the form of a spoken or written communication of some sort. This event frequently overlaps with the next one, assessing performance. Web boards, email, and video conferencing provide delayed or real-time feedback to students.

Assessing performance

This event determines a level of student performance keyed to the objectives of the activity. Digital rubrics, included within the digital learning task (e.g., CD-ROM, website), can help the student self-score performance and give the teacher the ability to communicate student performance.

Enhancing retention

Students need additional opportunities to bridge school learning and the real-life use of knowledge and skills. Digital technologies contribute to learning retention by presenting near-authentic activities in which students have to gather information, solve a problem, or propose a solution to a complicated issue.

Trying out technology in instructional events

Before we see how instructional events are addressed in different teaching models, see how instructional events can be used to evaluate one of your lessons on the use of technology.

25 Technology in Instructional Events

Task Rationale See how technology is used in a lesson activity organized by instructional events.

Task Guidelines
1. Identify a learning activity in one of your lessons.
2. Use the following chart to record how your activity could address each instructional event using instructional technology options.

Instructional Event	Learning Activity with Technology
Gaining attention	
Informing learner of the objective	
Stimulating recall of prior learning or learning that is needed	
Presenting the new "content"	
Providing learning guidance	
Prompting student performance	
Providing feedback on performance	
Assessing performance	
Enhancing retention of learning	

Reflectivity In what ways did this activity help you identify new options for teaching this lesson?

Technology use in teaching models

We now discuss how technology supports three teaching models discussed in Chapter 6: direct instruction, discussion, and cooperative learning.

Technology in direct instruction

Direct instruction is a behavioral model suitable for teaching basic skills and information. Teaching is broken down into manageable segments, and students are given suitable practice opportunities while teachers observe behavior and provide feedback until mastery is achieved. Direct instruction is efficient and is chosen partly because instructional time is limited or when a skill needs to be taught in a particular way. In Figure 7.17, the procedure for using direct instruction is matched with the instructional events and possible uses of technology.

FIGURE 7.17. Direct instruction, Instructional Events, and Technology Options.

Direct Instruction Steps	Instructional Event	Possible Instructor Action with Technology
	1. Gaining attention	Demonstration
1. Review	3. Stimulating recall of prerequisite learning	Teacher summary of prior content (media) or student work (presentation software); student questions
2. Inform	2. Informing the learner of the objective	Writing on board, verbal, handout, or presentation software
3. Present	4. Presenting the stimulus material	Teacher presentation using media and technology (presentation, multimedia, simulations, Internet)
4. Guided practice	5. Providing learning guidance	Teacher provides digitally archived examples, media-based or online activities with teacher support
4. Guided practice	6. Eliciting the performance	Class suggestions, individual prompting, email or web board suggestions
4. Guided practice	7. Providing feedback about performance correctness	Class examples, lab activities, homework, verbal comments on work using digital annotations or email feedback, web board comments
5. Independent practice	8. Assessing the performance	Comments, grading provided online or attached to digital products
6. Review and feedback	9. Enhancing retention	Repeating in subsequent lessons, additional diverse examples

The direct instruction model can also incorporate other teaching models or strategies at step 3, the presentation step. At this event, a lecture can be blended with the use of an organizer and presentation. Guided practice could also incorporate other teaching strategies, such as role play or cooperative learning.

Presenting new material involves the organization of content by arranging material into smaller parts, focusing on important points, presenting from general to specific, and taking into consideration the ages, styles, and abilities of students. The actual presenting of material can take many forms, from lectures to demonstrations and then observing the reactions and behavior of students to what is being said, presented, shown, or demonstrated. Here technology helps the teacher organize the delivery of new knowledge or skills, such as with the use of presentation software, concept maps, media-based modules, or hyperlinking to online sites for research.

Direct instruction provides numerous opportunities for assessment and media use. Assessing the performance, event 8, can include informal as well as formal assessment, such as when grades are needed. Media are typically introduced to present the stimulus material, but some forms of media, such as interactive technologies, may incorporate all of these events.

Technology in discussion

The major feature of discussion is a dialogue that generates questions and increases the teacher's ability to engage students in higher level thinking. The key to discussion is developing thoughtful questions and follow-up questions. In Figure 7.18, the syntax or teaching procedure of classroom discussion is listed alongside the appropriate instructional events. A web chat is used to approximate a digital version of a discussion.

The first two steps of the discussion model require teachers to read the material and develop factual, interpretive, and evaluative questions. This enables asking more thought-provoking questions in the classroom (Gunter et al., 2003). The second step compares ideas, reactions, and questions with a cooperating teacher and clusters broad, basic questions that raise an issue. Follow-up questions develop the ideas behind the basic question.

The third step is to assign the reading, some of which could be done in class. Ask students to prepare questions for discussion and give them adequate time to reread material before discussion. Technology use here might involve having students conduct additional research. Another option might be to have students pool their ideas from the reading and do so through email or a web board that has a conference area devoted to the discussion.

Both classroom discussions and web chats require an explanation of how the discussion model works and procedures for behavior. With web chats, the organizing and follow-up questions help to structure student dialogue. Conducting an effective discussion requires a nondirective role, particularly evaluating the weight given to questions that in your view are more correct than others. However, with web chats, the structure and policies will probably need to be different from those used in classroom discussion.

Instructional media may assume a major role in presenting the stimulus material, another instructional event. A movie or video clip may be shown in class to introduce students to new material or relate to prior instruction. Media can also be used to promote learning transfer by asking students to respond to questions about these new media-based examples.

FIGURE 7.18.
Classroom
Discussion,
Instructional
Events, and
Web Chats.

Discussion Steps	Instructional Event	Possible Instructor Actions with Technology: Web Chats
1. Prepare questions		
2. Cluster questions		
	1. Gaining attention	Start time established for a chat session and taking role
3. Introduce model and assign reading	2. Informing the learner of the objective	Brief students to procedures and behavior and to assigned reading and/or research
	3. Stimulating recall of prerequisite learning	Textual background to chat's purpose
4. Conduct discussion	4. Presenting the stimulus material	Establishing a protocol for who speaks, organized by groups or assigned
4. Use questions	5. Providing learning guidance	Organizing chat with a key question and limiting chat time
4. Use follow-up questions	6. Eliciting the performance	Allowing time for student responses
5. Review the process	7. Providing feedback about performance correctness	Review what students have discussed
5. Summarize student observations	8. Assessing the performance	Summarize student points; record participation
	9. Enhancing retention	Ask for student feedback on web chat activity and improvements; refer to web chat in subsequent lessons

Technology in cooperative learning

Cooperative learning aims to create a positive environment where people learn to work together to achieve their objectives. This aim should be kept in mind when using cooperative learning at a distance with instructional technology. Sometimes the activity is in real time (synchronous mode) with audio or video conferencing, but this requires that classrooms have the facilities and computers to handle the technical requirements. More often than not, in cooperative learning at a distance, people are not interacting at the same time (asynchronous mode). Distance learning can still use cooperative learning to create a positive working environment and develop cooperation and understanding of others. The major social features are listed in Figure 7.19.

As with classroom use of cooperative learning, *interdependence* in a cooperative work group requires a clear, mutual goal to be communicated and

FIGURE 7.19.
Cooperative
Learning
Requirements.

Criteria for Performance in Cooperative Learning
Interdependence: *Sink or swim together* **One-to-one interaction:** *Students help each other* **Individual accountability:** *Individual performance assessed and shared* **Social skills:** *Groups need social skills to function* **Group processing:** *Group reflects on what and how they are doing*

From Johnson, D. W., Johnson, R. T., & Smith, K. A. (1991). *Active learning: Cooperation in the college classroom.*
Reproduced by permission of Interaction Book Company. 7208 Cornelia Dr., Edina, MN 55435.

understood by members of the group. Resources must be shared, and tasks must be divided, with complementary roles assigned. The group should be encouraged to establish its own identity and competition with other groups. All of these features can be accomplished by using instructional technology, whether through the use of audio or video conferencing or by email or web boards.

One-to-one interaction in cooperative groups encourages students to support and help each other, willingly exchange resources so that everyone has access to the information of others, provide feedback, and give opportunities for individuals to challenge each other's conclusions. Such interaction can be accomplished when roles are clear.

Individual accountability within the group can be designed into cooperative work groups. Assessment can include observations of individual and group performance, individual tests, or dialogue. Using instructional technology, the teacher may or may not "see" the student but assesses student performance on the basis of what the students say to each other, individual contributions, and overall group performance.

The *social skills* aspect of working together "at a distance" requires teaching time. Social skills are not intuitive and must be taught. Students must be given opportunities to experience social interaction. Social skills can be assessed by using a rubric to categorize differences in performance and ranges of performances across these categories. In this case, the characteristics of cooperative learning can be used as the major categories in your rubric development.

TEACHING AND TECHNOLOGY OPTIONS

In the next Design Activity, examine your lessons and see how they can be improved through the use of media and technology. Ask yourself the question. "How does the use of media and technology support student learning? How does this use give me options I did not have before?"

Teaching and Technology Options in Your Lessons

Task Rationale   Examine possibilities for media and technology in your lessons.

Task Guidelines   Identify a lesson and one or more activities. Use the following table to record your media and/or technology choices.

Student learning?	Media and technology options	What does the option give me that I did not have before?

Reflectivity   What concerns do you have in using technology in your teaching?

USING TECHNOLOGY TO RETHINK TEACHING DECISIONS

- *What will students learn?*
- *How will you know if students learned anything?*
- *How will you support student learning?*
- *How might media and technology support your teaching and help students learn?*

Now we ask a fifth question (Figure 7.20)! Because the new instructional technologies enable radically new learning environments, looking to the possibilities of technology prompts this question:

- *How does the use of technology influence your previous decisions of learning outcomes, assessment, and teaching?*

Answering this fifth question brings us full circle in the Teaching Decision Cycle. This cycle was presented to help you systematically think through the teaching decisions of an effective teacher.

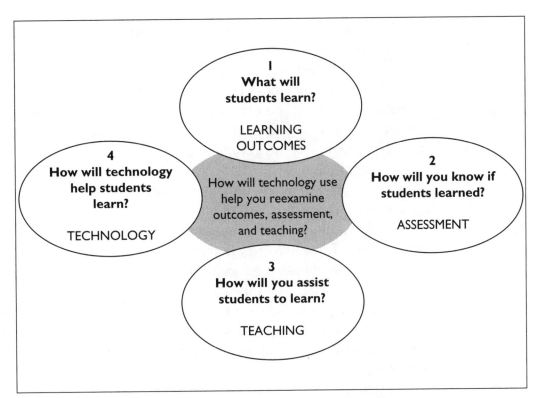

FIGURE 7.20.
Teacher
Decision Cycle:
Technology
Questions.

1
What will students learn?
LEARNING OUTCOMES

4
How will technology help students learn?
TECHNOLOGY

How will technology use help you reexamine outcomes, assessment, and teaching?

2
How will you know if students learned?
ASSESSMENT

3
How will you assist students to learn?
TEACHING

An Idea Worth Thinking About

"I think we're moving from the information age to the age of collaboration."
(Robert Greenburg, multimedia designer, in Carbone, 1999, p. 39).

It is likely that your students will live and work in a society where collaborating will be essential to community and global survival. How will you help today's students collaborate in person and at a distance?

Reflective Teaching

"If You Don't Understand How to Run This Computer Program, Ask One of the Seven-Year-Olds in Your Classroom to Explain It to You."

Many teachers look at the technology standards with fear and dread. They figure that because we live in such a technological age that their students will pick up the needed technological skills somewhere else—as long as it's not in their classroom. Many teachers are fearful of technology because they haven't had adequate training in using technology in the classroom. In many cases, the type of technology training that many teachers have experienced is more of an add-on approach to their instructional day that they do not appreciate. For example, in some schools, teachers are required to take their classes to the computer lab for a certain block of time each week. However, the teacher may have had little or no training on what to do with the students once they get to the computer lab. Simply taking students to the computer lab does not mean that a school has adequately incorporated technology into the curriculum. True technology integration means that the technology used enhances the instruction—not takes the place of instruction. Many teachers are simply not trained on how to merge technology into high-quality instruction.

This situation provides the perfect opportunity for teacher teaming and collaboration. Teachers who are less proficient in technology can work with teachers who are more proficient to create lessons that incorporate technology in a meaningful way. With this type of collaborative relationship, the less proficient teacher might actually experience technological successes that will enable further growth in this area. The students will also benefit because they are experiencing high-quality instruction that is enhanced by unique technological experiences.

Teacher Inquiry

- What aspects of technology use would you like to study in an action research or teacher research study?
- Is there a research study in which you could involve a peer in studying technology's use in the classroom?

REFERENCES

Burgstahler, S. (2002). *Universal design of instruction*. Seattle: DO-IT, University of Washington. Retrieved March 19, 2005, from www.washington.edu/doit/Brochures/Academics/instruction.html

Carbone, K. (1999). *The virtuoso: Face to face with 40 extraordinary talents*. New York: Steward, Tabori, & Chang.

CAST. (2003). *Universal Design for learning*. Retrieved March 19, 2005, from www.cast.org.

Gagné, R. M. (1985). *The conditions of learning* (4th ed.). New York: Holt, Rinehart, & Winston.

Gagné, R. M., Wager, W. W., Golas, K. C., & Keller, J. M. (2005). *Principles of instructional design* (5th ed.). Belmont, CA: Wadsworth/Thomson.

Gunter, A. A., Estes, T. H., & Schwab, J. H. (2003). *Instruction: A models approach* (3rd ed.). Boston: Allyn and Bacon.

Harris, J. (2001). *Design tools for the Internet-supported classroom*. Upper Saddle River, NJ: Merrill.

ISTE. (2002). *NETS-T: Preparing teachers to use technology*. Eugene, OR: International Society for Technology in Education.

Johnson, D. W., Johnson, R. T., & Smith, K. A. (1991). *Active learning: Cooperation in the college classroom*. Edina, MN: Interaction Book.

Joyce, B., Weil, M., & Calhoun, E. (2004). *Models of teaching* (7th ed.). Boston: Allyn and Bacon.

Norman, D. A. (1993). *Things that make us smart: Defending human attributes in the age of the machine*. Reading, MA: Addison-Wesley.

Novak, J. D., & Gowin, D. B. (1984). *Learning how to learn*. New York: Cambridge University Press.

Reigeluth, C. M. (1999). The elaboration theory: Guidance for scope and sequence decisions. In C. M. Reigeluth (Ed.), *Instructional-design theories and models: A new paradigm of instructional theory: Volume II* (pp. 435–453). Mahwah, NJ: Erlbaum.

Seels, B. B., & Richey, R. C. (1994). *Instructional technology: The definition and domains of the field*. Bloomington, IN: Association for Educational Communications and Technology.

Shambaugh, R. N. (1995). The cognitive potentials of visual constructions. *Journal of Visual Literacy, 15* (1), 7–24.

Smaldino, S. E., Russell, J. D., Heinich, R., & Moldenda, M. (2005) *Instructional technology and media for learning* (8th ed.). Upper Saddle River, NJ: Merrill–Prentice-Hall

Wiggins, G., & McTighe, J. (1998). *Understanding by design*. Upper Saddle River, NJ: Merrill.

RESOURCES

Print Resources

Belson, S. I. (2003). *Technology for exceptional learners: Choosing instructional tools to meet students' needs*. Boston: Houghton Mifflin.

How technological tools can assist different student needs.

Grabe, M., & Grabe, C. (2004). *Integrating technology for meaningful learning* (4th ed.). Boston: Houghton Mifflin.

A textbook that uses the activity-based model of technology use.

Harris, J. (2001). *Design tools for the Internet-supported classroom*. Upper Saddle River, NJ: Merrill.

Eighteen activity structures and guidelines on telecollaborative projects.

Howell, J. H., & Dunnivant, S. W. (2000). *Technology for teachers: Mastering new media and portfolio development*. Boston: McGraw-Hill.

A student portfolio workbook and CD-ROM. Links to articles and connected to activities.

Jonassen, D. H. (2000). *Computers as mindtools for schools: Engaging critical thinking* (2nd ed.). Upper Saddle River, NJ: Merrill.

Identifies different thinking tools or "mindtools" for different aspects of integrated thinking, including content thinking, critical thinking, and creative thinking.

Jonassen, D. H. (2003). *Handbook of research on educational communications and technology* (2nd ed.). Mahwah, NJ: Erlbaum.

Research foundations sponsored by AECT, the international IDT organization.

Roblyer, M. D. (2004). *Integrating educational technology into teaching* (3rd ed.). Upper Saddle River, NJ: Merrill.

Integrating technology into different content areas.

Valmont, W. J. (2003). *Technology for literacy teaching and learning*. Boston: Houghton Mifflin.

Literacy is a field that has embraced technology as a major form of assistance. This text looks at technology's role in promoting various forms of literacy, including reading and thinking strategies, word recognition and vocabulary, writing, listening and speaking, and graphic and visual. It has a chapter on using technology with children's literature.

Wepner, S. B., Valmont, W. J., & Thurlow, R. (2000). *Linking literacy and technology: A guide for K-8 classrooms*. Newark, DE: International Reading Association .

This book would make a great source to use for a class for teachers who are just beginning to incorporate technology into their classrooms. Provides actual examples of how other teachers effectively used technology in their classrooms. This book might give beginning teachers the confidence needed to create their own lessons and activities that feature a technology component. Lesson plans included.

Willis, J. W., Stephens, E. C., & Matthew, K. I. (1996). *Technology, reading, and language arts.* Boston: Allyn and Bacon.

Use of technology for different forms of teaching (social constructivist, cognitive constructivist, and direct instruction). A section on microteaching.

Web-Based Resources

Apple Learning Interchange
  http://ali.apple.com

Examples of technology use in classrooms.

AECT: Association for Educational Communications and Technology
  www.aect.org

The professional organization for the instructional technology field, sometimes referred to as IDT (instructional design and technology).

Children and Computers
  www.childrenandcomputers.com

Developmentally appropriate tools and website evaluation tools.

Edutopia
  www.edutopia.org

Educational site sponsored by the George Lucas Educational Foundation.

For Teachers
  http://4teachers.org

Tools to help teachers including creating web pages, posters, and rubrics.

International Society for Technology in Education (ISTE)
  www.iste.org

This professional organization focuses on technology use in pre-K–12 settings and has released standards for student and teacher use.

  http://cnets.iste.org/

ISTE's NETS standards for use of technology, aligned with most of the states'

departments of education standards; NETS standards exist for students, teachers, and administrators.

  http://cnets.iste.org/search/s_search.html

A searchable database of lessons or units containing technology-based activities by grade level and content area.

  http://caret.iste.org/

Center for Applied Research in Educational Technology (CARET). Research-based answers to questions concerning technology use.

  http://cnets.iste.org/teachers/t_book.html

National Educational Technology Standards (NETS) for Teachers: Preparing teachers to use technology.

  http://cnets.iste.org/students/s_book.html

National Educational Technology Standards (NETS) for Students: Connecting curriculum and technology.

Kids and Computers
  www.hcibib.org/kids/

A collection of resources for designers, producers, researchers, and practitioners of interactive media for children and adolescents.

Special Needs

CAST: The Center for Applied Special Technology.
  www.cast.org

An online resource for UDL.

Division for Early Childhood (DEC) of the Council for Exceptional Children
  www.dec-sped.org

Resources for young children with disabilities.

Office of Special Education and Rehabilitative Services (OSERS)
  www.ed.gov/about/offices/list/OSERS/ NIDRR/index.html?src-mr

Information on the policies of AT in the schools.

Orkwis, R. (1999). *Curriculum access and universal design for learning.* ERIC Clearinghouse on Disabilities and Gifted Education (Document No. E586). Retrieved from www.ericec.org/digests/e586.html

Rose, D., & Meyer, A. (2002). *Teaching every student in the digital age: Universal design for learning.* Alexandria, VA: Association for Supervision & Curriculum Development. Retrieved from http://ascd.org/publications/books/2002rose/

ed IT-integration projects.

Teaching Strategies

www.edhelper.com/

Source for 1,100 web quests in all content areas.

http://webquest.sdsu.edu/

The major source of information on webquests, as posted by its originator, Bernie Dodge.

www.ncrel.org/tech/

From the North Central Regional Educational Laboratory: many resources, including rubrics and webquests, on the use of technology, including a framework for effective technology use, found at http://www.ncrel.org/engauge/

www.gmu.edu/facstaff/part-time/strategy.html

Use of discussion and technology in the classroom.

www.fno.org/webdesign.html

"From Now On" is an electronic journal. This topic provides resources for designing school websites.

www.sitesalive.com

Examples of student inquiry around the world.

www.nectas.unc.edu/topics/atech/atech.asp

From the National Early Childhood Technical Assistance Center: AT resources, funding, and legislation.

http://jamaica.u.arizona.edu/ic/edtech/strategy.html

Numerous links to teaching and learning and methods strategies, including classroom management.

U. S. Department of Education

www.pt3.org/

Home page for the PT3 (Preparing Tomorrow's Teachers to Use Technology) project, a set of federally fund

Completing Your Lessons

**Section II:
Discovering
More About
Your Classroom**

Section II described what you can learn about your classroom, in terms of three categories of information:

- The full range of *content* to be learned by students
- Who your *students* are
- The nature and reality of the *learning setting*

**Section III:
Developing
Lessons**

Section III prompted you to respond to the five questions of the Teacher Decision Cycle:

- What are the *learning outcomes?*
- How will you *assess* student learning in the lesson?
- What *teaching strategies* will you use to support student learning?
- How can *instructional media and technology* be incorporated into the lesson to help students learn?
- How can *technology* help you reexamine your teaching decisions?

This WRAPUP section reviews the suggested lesson plan format and includes a Design Activity that asks you to complete one or more lessons.

Design Activities

DA 27: Revised Lesson Plans

The following visual connects these questions to the components of the lesson plan format.

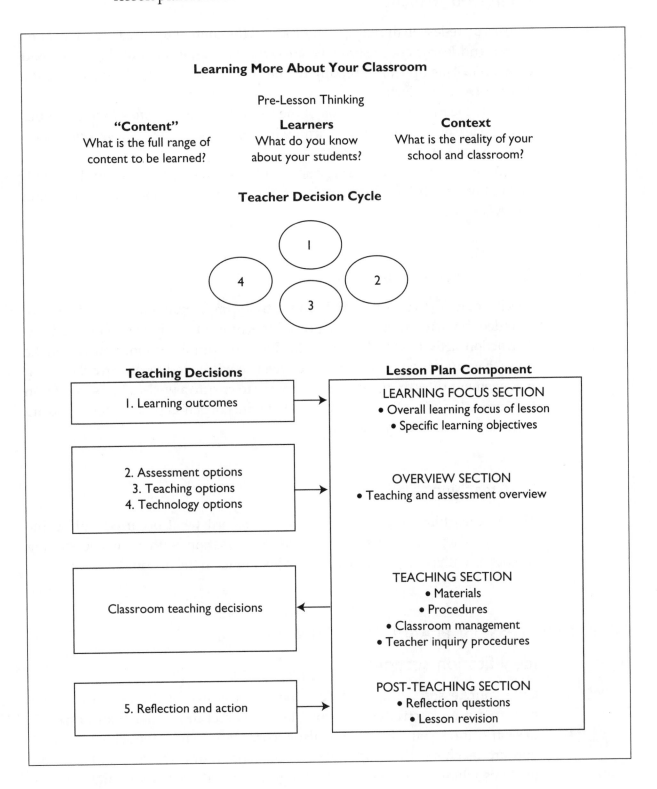

Learning More About Your Classroom

Pre-Lesson Thinking

"Content"	**Learners**	**Context**
What is the full range of content to be learned?	What do you know about your students?	What is the reality of your school and classroom?

Teacher Decision Cycle

1
4   2
3

Teaching Decisions

| 1. Learning outcomes |

| 2. Assessment options
3. Teaching options
4. Technology options |

| Classroom teaching decisions |

| 5. Reflection and action |

Lesson Plan Component

LEARNING FOCUS SECTION
• Overall learning focus of lesson
• Specific learning objectives

OVERVIEW SECTION
• Teaching and assessment overview

TEACHING SECTION
• Materials
• Procedures
• Classroom management
• Teacher inquiry procedures

POST-TEACHING SECTION
• Reflection questions
• Lesson revision

SYSTEMATIC DECISION MAKING

Pre-lesson thinking

One uses pre-lesson thinking to think about the content to be learned, what one knows and learns about students, and what one knows about the school and classroom. This up-front thinking readies you for subsequent decisions in the Teacher Decision Cycle.

In the learning focus section of the lesson plan, the *learning focus* identifies how the lesson contributes to learning in a broad sense. Specific *learning objectives* are used to identify learning.

Actual decisions in your lesson about assessment, teaching, and technology options are briefly summarized in the overview section under "Teaching and Assessment overview."

Classroom teaching

Specific details such as materials and activity implementation procedures are recorded in the teaching section. Procedures typically include opening activity, instruction activities, and closure. In this procedural section, you can make notes to yourself about transitions between activities and record any classroom management rules or procedures necessary to ensure a well-run lesson. Within the "procedures" section, we have added data collection procedures if you are conducting a teacher inquiry project.

Post-teaching

The post-teaching section reminds you to record what occurred during the teaching. These reflections, as well as conversation with your cooperating teacher or with peers, should lead to adjustments in the lesson.

REVISITING LESSON PLAN COMPONENTS

Identification section

Give your lesson a title that describes the essence of the lesson in terms of learning and activity. Title your lesson something other than Lesson 1, Lesson 2, and so on. This section also records your name, the school in which you are teaching, the grade level, your cooperating teacher, and the date or dates when the lesson will be taught. The date helps you archive your lesson plans.

Learning focus section

This is the most important section of the lesson plan. Merely recording a topic or activity name does not communicate the purpose of the topic or activity. For example, writing "food pyramid" as the lesson does not communicate its purpose. Instead write, "Healthy eating habits: Organizing food groups." A *learning focus* description may depict the sequence or flow of teaching across topics, themes, and activities but within an overall learning intent. Record how this lesson fits into an overall set of lessons or a unit. Estimate the time to teach the lesson.

Overview section

The teaching and assessment overview summarizes the different teaching strategies to be used in the lesson. For example, you might record that you are using a blend of direct instruction and cooperative learning. Assessment could be of student performance on homework at the beginning and an observation checklist for student behavior and performance in cooperative work groups. A "materials" list can be included here to remind you of materials you will need.

Teaching section

The teaching section lists implementation procedures. Procedures may include a numbered list of activities keyed by what you do as the teacher and what students do in activities. These procedures may also be directly keyed to the procedural steps of different teaching strategies, such as direct instruction, discussion, and cooperative learning, which were described in Chapter 7.

Another possible procedural template would be to use Gagné's instructional events, ranging from "gaining attention" to "transfer." In the suggested lesson plan, we suggest an introductory activity. Next is teaching new knowledge, which may include direct instruction, presentations, or activities. A closure activity is recommended to focus student attention on a summary of what they have learned, leaving them with a question to think about or assigning practice or homework.

New teachers report awkwardness in transitioning from one set of teaching activities to another. Your lesson plan might include prompts to yourself on how to move from an opening activity to the main lesson to the closing activity. Any specific rules or procedures for students to follow should be recorded. In this way, you connect the general rules and procedures of your classroom management plan to specific behavior required in the lesson.

Another suggestion for the teaching section is to include prompts to collect data for any action research or teacher inquiry project. This serves to include data collection as just another teaching procedure and provides a reminder to collect data such as observational checklists, notes, rubric assessments, or student work.

Post-teaching section

A good lesson becomes an even better lesson when the post-teaching section becomes a habit. Here, record brief comments on reflective questions, which are provided in our suggested lesson plan format to get you used to thinking about important issues. Over time, replace these questions with your own. A revised lesson plan puts "reflectivity into action" rather than recording what went right or what went poorly. In full-time teaching, you will be hard pressed to record detailed lesson plans or significant reflective comments. These suggestions are directed to new teachers in their initial teaching. If your lessons are to be shared, other teachers will welcome whatever details, guidelines, and caveats you can provide.

The next Design Activity provides an official prompt to draft and revise lessons to be taught. The format of the lesson plan organizes your plan, alerts you to materials you will need, and records procedures to refer to when teachng. In the long run, this format provides a template to archive and document your growing set of lessons. Such documentation will come in handy if you choose to seek National Board Certification®.

DESIGN ACTIVITY
27
Revised Lesson Plans

Task Rationale   Complete your draft lessons.

Title of Lesson

IDENTIFICATION SECTION

    Teacher Candidate:

    School: **Grade level:**   **Date(s):**

    Cooperating teacher:

LEARNING FOCUS SECTION

    Subject Unit: **Time Estimate:**

    LEARNING FOCUS:

OVERVIEW SECTION

    Materials:

    Objectives:

- What will students learn in lesson?
- Match with appropriate state standards, if applicable

    Teaching and Assessment Overview:

- Briefly statement on teaching strategies and how assess learning

TEACHING SECTION

    Procedures:

- Introduction or opening activity or review
- Instruction/activities
- Transitions
- Closure: review, assignments
- Classroom management rules or procedures
- Teacher inquiry procedures

POST-TEACHING SECTION

    Lesson plan reflective questions:

- What did the students learn during your lesson, and how do you know?
- What would you do differently the next time you teach this lesson and why?
- What went well during this lesson, and how do you know?
- What did you learn about teaching?
- What did your cooperating teacher say about your teaching?
- How well did you incorporate issues of diversity, special needs, and technology?

    Modifications or reteach strategies:

TEACHING YOUR FIRST LESSONS

Preparing for teaching

- Your lesson plan is just a plan. A lesson plan should record clear intent (learning focus) and key details to implement the lesson.
- Lesson planning contributes to confidence.
- Lessons do not record all that you do as a teacher. Allow students to ask questions, think through new topics, and complete activities.
- Share your draft lesson with others and strive to make improvements.
- If you adopt any features of someone else's lesson, make sure you acknowledge the source.

Teaching

- Be familiar with the lesson plan, but avoid using it as a "script."
- The lesson plan provides a mental rehearsal to teaching and keeps you on track.
- New teachers will experience tension in moving through a lesson plan and reacting to students' reactions and performance.
- As you teach, you are conducting ongoing analysis or needs assessment—a form of "during lesson" thinking, as opposed to pre-lesson or pre-unit thinking. Here you learn about your students and what they know.
- Make adjustments in your lessons as you formatively assess student learning. Reteaching may be necessary for some aspects of the lesson and with some students.
- Consider student learning that might be occurring outside your learning outcomes.

Reflection

- Record your impressions and reflections as soon as you can. Record them by hand and transcribe later. Your memory may not help you with important details if you wait "until the weekend." This habit takes discipline but will improve your daily teaching.
- Move beyond "what works and what doesn't work" to "what does it mean for my students to learn the content?"

Action

- Make notes on your lesson plan for revisions or guidelines.
- Update your lesson plans for use in the future, such as future teaching, use in portfolios, job searches, and sharing with others.

Developing Units

8 Designing and Teaching Units

Main Idea of This Chapter
Units organize what students will learn in ways that help them learn.

INTASC Standards Addressed in This Chapter

Principle 3 LEARNER DIFFERENCES: The teacher understands how students differ in their approaches to learning and creates instructional opportunities that are adapted to diverse learners.

Principle 4 TEACHING REPERTOIRE: The teacher understands and uses a variety of instructional strategies to encourage students' development of critical thinking, problem-solving, and performance skills.

Principle 5 LEARNING ENVIRONMENTS: The teacher uses an understanding of individual and group motivation and behavior to create a learning environment that encourages positive social interaction, active engagement in learning, and self-motivation.

Principle 7 PRE-UNIT THINKING: The teacher plans instruction based on knowledge of subject matter, students, the community, and curriculum goals.

Principle 8 REFLECTIVE PROFESSIONAL: The teacher understands and uses formal and informal assessment strategies to evaluate and ensure the continuous intellectual, social, and physical development of the learner.

Focus Questions

- What kinds of major decisions do you make in developing units?
- What can you learn from pre-unit thinking?
- What does a unit look like?

Design Activities

DA 28: Unit Intent Statement
DA 29: Pre-Unit Thinking
DA 30: Unit Overview

BUILDING A UNIT

For many teachers, developing units provides the basis for lessons. Units are frequently constructed around a theme, which supports a teacher's overall goal for the school year. Units also cover a large range of state standards, as units address a bigger learning picture than the lesson level. Units also help to address county and school initiatives and agendas. So why not start at the unit level with developing instruction? Within the teaching of lessons, important issues of student learning, assessment, and teaching come into play.

What this chapter is about

Unit development begins with determining the scope, learning focus, and sequence for the unit (Figure 8.1). We suggest a format for organizing units and then revisit needs assessment again as "Pre-Unit Thinking." The Teacher Decision Cycle is reviewed. Considerations for integrative units are discussed, followed by an elementary level unit and a secondary level unit. We end the chapter by asking you to provide an overview of your unit, which you may be developing. A wrapup section, "Completing Your Unit," follows this chapter and includes a Design Activity to document your designed unit.

FIGURE 8.1.
Visual Sequence for Chapter 8.

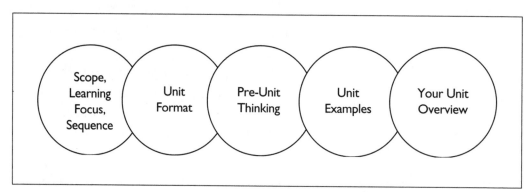

TEACHER DECISION CYCLE IN UNITS

The same cycle of decisions introduced in Section III, Developing Lessons, is used to develop units (Figure 8.2). In your unit plan, answer these questions.

Teacher Questions	Teacher Decisions
What will students learn?	Learning outcomes
How will you know if they learned anything?	Assessment purpose and tools
How will you support student learning?	Teaching options
How will technology help students learn?	Technology options
How will technology help me reexamine my teaching decisions?	Learning outcomes, assessment, teaching

FIGURE 8.2.
Teacher Decision Cycle: Unit Questions.

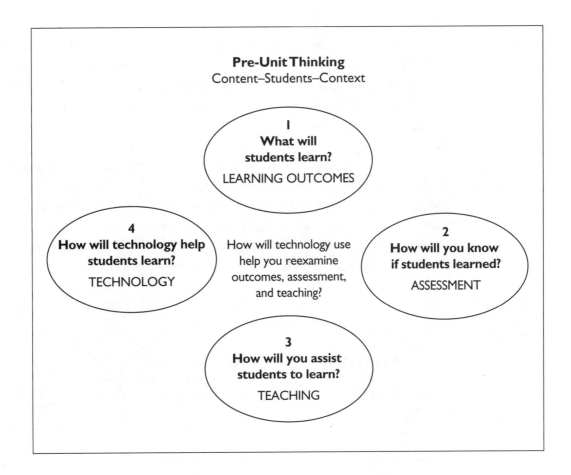

DETERMINING SCOPE–LEARNING FOCUS–SEQUENCE

The terms *scope* and *sequence* are frequently used to characterize the process by which you design a unit (Figure 8.3). The scope of a unit involves the range of learning to be accomplished, whether it involves combinations of knowledge, skills, or appreciation. In an overall sense, scope involves determining what is to be learned across a school year. Units help to partition the school year into manageable chunks of teaching organized along some rationale.

FIGURE 8.3.
Traditional
Scope and
Sequence.

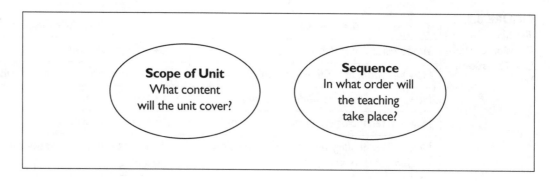

This rationale for the organization of the unit provides the sequence part of "scope and sequence." *Sequence* decisions specify the order in which the content is to be taught, usually across some conceptual or skill level and from simple to complex. These units and lessons within units can be expressed by using themes to illuminate the nature of the learning. Descriptive titles help students understand what the unit and lessons are about.

Gunter, Estes, and Schwab (2003) remind us that *focus* on learning should be inserted within "scope" and "sequence" (Figure 8.4). They recommend using a visual of descriptive topics to see the sequence of learning. We extend this idea of "focus" across lessons in terms of a *learning focus,* as the lessons must support the unit's learning goal(s). Identifying an overall focus for the unit helps you maintain this learning focus within each lesson.

FIGURE 8.4.
Scope, Learning
Focus, and
Sequence.

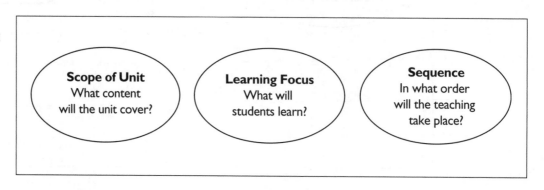

The following Design Activity records your first ideas on choosing a unit using "scope–learning focus–sequence" as a thinking tool. These written ideas can then be examined through pre-unit thinking.

DESIGN ACTIVITY 28

Unit Intent Statement

Task Rationale   This Design Activity records your choice of a unit and describes your initial intent to help students learn. What you write in this Design Activity can be inserted into Section 1.0 of your unit plan, described later in this chapter.

Task Guidelines   Your unit should involve the following information:

Scope   1. **Unit Title.** Provide a descriptive title that captures the learning intent for this unit.
2. **Content area and grade level.** Identify the subject areas and grade level(s) for this unit.
3. **Unit Need.** Why is the unit needed, and what is your motivation for selecting this unit topic?

Learning Focus   4. **Learners.** Who are your students?
5. **Learning outcomes.** List the specific learning objectives.

Sequence   6. **Time length.** How many lessons and/or days will this unit require? Provide descriptive titles for each of the proposed lessons to reflect the sequence of learning and activities.

Reflectivity   • What experiences have you had in developing and/or teaching units?
• How does your cooperating teacher develop and teach units?

USING A UNIT FORMAT

The unit format provides categories to document your instructional intent (Figure 8.5). The overview section provides brief descriptions of why the unit is needed, learning outcomes, school and classroom context, overview of teaching and assessment strategies, evaluation criteria, and references. The lessons section includes the lesson plan details.

FIGURE 8.5.
Suggested Unit
Format.

Cover: Unit Title, Grade Level, Content Area(s), Your Name

Table of Contents

Overview Section

1. **Unit Description**

   • Unit description, rationale for choosing, learning outcomes, major teaching strategies
   • Mission statement of learning beliefs

2. **Pre-Unit Thinking**

   • School profile
   • Learner differences issues—differences in how students learn the "content"
   • How content has been taught previously
   • New options for teaching (including media and technology possibilities)
   • Resources and constraints
   • Teacher inquiry questions
   • Summary of findings—What did I learn?

3. **Overview of Unit and Lessons**

   • Unit sequence: identify learning outcomes and major activities in each lesson
   • Summary of major teaching strategies
   • Summary of assessment tools used
   • Summary of instructional media and technology used

4. **Unit Evaluation**

   • List criteria you will use to evaluate the unit's success

5. **References**

   • List of references, websites
   • List of people consulted or interviewed

Lessons Section

6. **Lesson Plans** (for each lesson include the following):

   • Descriptive title
   • Overall learning focus
   • Specific learning objectives
   • Materials, instructional media, and technology
   • Teaching and assessment used in this lesson
   • Teaching procedures
   • Teacher guidelines (transitions, classroom management rules and procedures)
   • Samples of handouts, worksheets, materials, visuals, web pages, and the like
   • Teacher inquiry procedures (e.g., gathering data and using it to adjust future teaching)
   • Reflective comments from any field testing or concerns for actual teaching
   • Changes made following teaching

1.0 Unit description

This section communicates why the unit is needed. The mission statement is included here, as your views of teaching and learning provide the basis for your teaching decisions. The overall purpose of this section is to provide enough information for another teacher to know what this unit was about and to interest the teacher to read more.

2.0 Pre-unit thinking

School profile

Describe the local community, county school system, and the individual school. Grade levels, enrollment, and faculty numbers are useful, but try to go beyond the numbers. If you were to describe the school to an acquaintance, what would you say about the school? Describe the overall philosophy of the school and policies that may pertain to this unit, such as inclusion, technology, and parental involvement.

How content has been taught

Describe the classroom setting in which this unit has been taught. Describe how this unit has been taught before by you, a peer, or your cooperating teacher. If the unit is new with no prior teaching history, describe how students have previously learned the content.

How content could be taught

You have three options on deciding how your unit's content can be taught. First, how you teach the content may be based on how your cooperating teacher or colleague has taught it. Second, you teach the content in terms of how you believe it can be taught. Your judgments are based on your experience with teaching the content (i.e., *pedagogical content knowledge*).

A third option is to find out more about teaching options from consulting experts, peers, and other teachers; doing some reading and research; and incorporating some of the suggestions or ideas. Tap the vast experience of other teachers, which may be found online, published in books, journals, or periodicals, or found just down the hall from your classroom. In the unit plan outline, we urge you to research three different teaching strategies that could be used.

Learner differences

Summarize the teaching adjustments you may need to make for the range of students in your classroom. These issues constitute matters of learning preferences, cognitive styles, special needs, cultural differences, and diversity. However, it is constructive to think of differences across all learners and to make adjustments in content and teaching. This is the idea behind the universal design for learning, discussed in Chapter 7.

Media and technology

Identify media and technology possibilities. Consider new options you may not have had before. You should write about how the use of media and technology will help students achieve learning outcomes.

Resources and constraints

What critical resources do you need for this unit? Knowing this information simplifies how much supporting development (e.g., handouts and activities), time, and coordination (e.g., assistance, equipment) will be needed. What issues, such as time and resources, limit the implementation of the unit?

Teacher inquiry questions

If you are conducting systematic inquiry into your teaching, record any procedures to remind you to collect "data," such as notes on your teaching and samples of student work.

Summary of pre-unit thinking: What did you learn?

What did you learn from pre-unit thinking that needs to be incorporated in the unit? Summarizing what you learned is probably the most important section in pre-unit thinking. The next Design Activity organizes pre-unit thinking as thinking prior to developing a unit.

Pre-Unit Thinking

Task Rationale This task readies your thinking to make teaching decisions for a unit. This Design Activity documents Section 2.0 pre-unit thinking in the unit plan format.

Task Guidelines Briefly describe the following by citing your experiences, other teachers, and outside sources. These sources should be identified in what you write and cited in a references list.

1. School profile.
2. Classroom setting and how content has previously been taught.
3. Document three outside sources that report on alternative teaching strategies.
4. Learner differences.
5. Instructional media and technology.
6. Resources and constraints.
7. Teacher inquiry questions and procedures.
8. Summary of findings: What did you learn?

Reflectivity How did this pre-unit thinking help you make unit decisions?

3.0 Overview of unit and lessons

This section introduces the unit. In your first paragraph, write about the overall *learning focus* for the unit and how the individual lessons support these outcomes. Briefly describe the purpose of each lesson, major teaching activities, assessment, and the media and technology you plan to use.

In a second paragraph, summarize the major *teaching strategies* used across the unit. Your lessons may follow a predictable pattern, with certain teaching strategies used in each lesson. If so, describe this pattern. In some lessons, quite different strategies may be used. The purpose of this section is to reveal that you can clearly identify different teaching strategies and why they are used. How you use instructional media and technology could also be included here.

In a third paragraph, summarize how you *assess* student learning. Remember from Chapter 5 that assessment has many purposes. You should identify the tools you are using and the purpose for the assessment, whether that purpose is *diagnostic* (determining what students know), *formative* (how students are learning), or *summative* (where grades are recorded). Keep in mind that formative assessment may be embedded in your teaching strategies.

4.0 Unit evaluation

This section records how you will determine if your unit is a success. List the questions you will ask yourself or others that might evaluate the unit. These questions define what you mean by a "successful" unit. At the very minimum, you should ask: "Were the learning outcomes met?" Other questions could involve teaching strategies, technology use, and learning more about your students. Record how students reacted and what you learned from them.

5.0 References

List the printed material and websites you consulted. Acknowledge any use of lesson and unit materials. List the individuals you may have talked with.

6.0 Lesson plans

The heart of the unit is a set of related teaching lessons. These lessons should include the components identified in Chapter 4.

DEVELOPING INTEGRATED UNITS

Multidisciplinary teaching is sometimes used to address the full range of academic knowledge and real-world experience. Involving a range of learning outcomes across content areas is sometimes referred to as integrated units. Teaching at the elementary and middle grades provides many opportunities to focus on thematic-based activities. Elementary teachers who are responsible for most of the content learning for their students have control over how multidisciplinary teaching can be implemented.

In the middle grades, students are faced with more formal content areas, but guidelines by the National Middle School Association (1995) recommend that a carefully thought out curriculum is essential for the development of adolescents. Students in the middle grades need a curriculum that helps them learn about the world into which they are entering and in ways that are related to their immediate interests.

Secondary curriculum tends to be discipline-structured, with the greatest challenge to connecting different content areas. The ISTE-NETS database (see Resources at the end of Chapter 7) provides unit activities to implement multidisciplinary approaches. Each activity in the database includes content standards from two or more subject areas and incorporates the NETS standards for students.

Integrated lessons, units, and curriculums must be knowledgeable, efficient, and well orchestrated, yet also maintain flexibility within broad goals (Krogh, 1995). The unit plan can be situated within an overall plan for the school year. Careful planning at the beginning of the school year will help to ensure that the range of learning outcomes, stretched across many categories of state standards, is addressed over the school year.

There are numerous forms of integrated instruction. One of the most commonly practiced is nested curriculum, in which multiple skills are targeted within each subject area. Another format involves subjects that are taught separately but each features similar themes (Fogarty, 1991). Two forms of integrated units (and curriculums) can be used: the project approach and curriculum webs.

Project approach

The project approach can be considered an example of immersion, in which students are immersed in a topic and discover connections across different content areas (Katz & Chard, 1989). Students are typically involved in the planning, and projects may span several days to several weeks. Projects, although keyed to broad classroom or school goals, are based on student interests and can be pursued by individuals or groups.

FIGURE 8.6.
Example of
Curriculum Web.

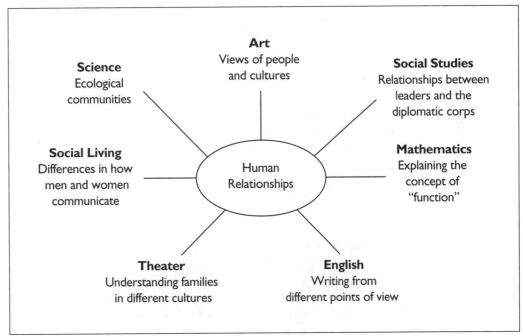

Unit webs

In a webbed approach, a theme is connected to different content areas. As a result, accountability of content area standards is easily documented. Probably the most common example of webs is the units developed for holidays in the elementary grades. The notion of "human relationships" could be the focus for a webbed set of units for almost any grade level and would be appropriate as a schoolyear theme. For example, in Figure 8.6 a simple web identifies how the idea of "human relationships" could be addressed across different content areas in a secondary school.

EXAMINING AN ELEMENTARY LEVEL UNIT

The following section describes a health unit written by two fourth-year teacher education students in an undergraduate instructional design course. Figure 8.7 outlines a unit called "Nutrition for Second Graders," which has fifteen lessons. The topic is integrative by nature, as the learning covers

FIGURE 8.7.
Elementary Unit
Contents.

Nutrition for Second Graders
1.0 Unit description • Unit description and learning outcomes • Mission statement
2.0 Unit pre-unit thinking • School profile • Classroom environment • How content has been taught and assessed • Special education, diversity, and individual differences
3.0. Teaching and assessment overview • Teaching approaches • Assessment tools • Media and technology • Classroom management
4.0 Lesson sequence overview • Sequence of lessons and learning outcomes for each lesson
5.0 Unit evaluation
6.0 Lesson plans • Lesson 1 included here as an example • Lessons 2–15 not included for reasons of space

Adapted from Annie Ripley and Abbie McCarty. Used with permission.

knowledge, decision making, and affective learning. However, this unit was keyed to a state's learning standards specifically addressing health. The example includes pre-unit thinking and one lesson.

1.0 Unit description

The unit description (Figure 8.8) provides an overview of the educational purpose for the unit, the educational level, and what students will learn. The number of lessons is specified across a length of time. The teaching features and what students do are also described. The mission statement for both teachers is included. This section also describes the content area, educational level, and overall learning outcomes for the unit. This section should be descriptive enough to give a reader an idea of what the unit is about, what learning is to be achieved, and major features of the teaching.

FIGURE 8.8.
Elementary Unit
Description.

Unit Description: Nutrition for Second Graders
Unit Description and Learning Outcomes
This health unit will teach second graders to use good eating habits. It is our goal to inform students about different types of foods that they can choose to eat that will help them stay healthy. During this unit we will apply all lessons to the real world, in hopes that students will carry the information that they gain with them. This unit is comprised of 15 lessons and it will spread over a three-week period, having one lesson per day. The lessons range in time from 45 minutes to 90 minutes. The lessons contain hands-on activities, demonstrations, read-alouds, class projects, and classroom discussion. The unit will conclude with student presentations and a luncheon based on the entire unit.
Mission Statement of Our Learning Beliefs
As a teacher, my mission is to meet the needs of all students by creating a positive environment, providing empathy, and incorporating various types of learning strategies into my classroom. My students will be provided with a rich curriculum and various opportunities to apply their knowledge both in and out of the classroom. As a teacher, I hope to continually assess my students, as well as share this information with the parents and the student. In addition, I will repeatedly evaluate myself as a teacher and make the necessary changes in order to maximize my learning, as well as the students' learning. I will strive to create a classroom that helps to boost self-esteem, encourages students to continue trying, and allows everyone to succeed no matter what level they are at. (Annie)
My mission is for my students to enjoy and embrace learning. I strive to intrinsically motivate my students to learn more about themselves and the world around them. I want to know what interests my students and what helps them learn to their highest potentials. I care about my students and expect respect from them. I have high expectations of my students because I want them to achieve great things. I will encourage interaction among the students and a positive environment in my classroom. I will also strongly encourage and model the helping of others. My top priority is to make a difference in the lives of my students so that they will then make a difference in the lives of the people they meet. (Abigail)

2.0 Pre-unit thinking

The term *pre-unit thinking* is structured to help you to think about "content," learners, and context *before* designing a unit (Figure 8.9).

Pre-Unit Thinking

School Profile

School W: The school where this unit will be administered is positioned in a nearby county. The school ranges in grades from kindergarten to fourth grade. There are 202 children enrolled at my school, a school with a 15.5:1 student to teacher ratio. Thirty percent of the students enrolled at the school receive free or reduced lunch. There is little racial diversity, with nearly 100% Caucasian. (Annie)

School J: My school contains grades preschool to fifth. Its population is 565 students. In terms of ethnicity, the school is made up of 1% African American and 99% Caucasian students. Twenty-two percent of the students receive a free or reduced price lunch. There is a 17.7:1 ratio of students to teachers. (Abigail)

Classroom Environment

In a regular second grade environment, students are inquisitive and are excited about learning and moving around. They enjoy working with their classmates, because they love to share their ideas. At this point in their lives, second graders are beginning to slow down a little bit and begin to reason and concentrate. According to the American School Counselor Association, a second grader may express a lack in confidence; therefore, we will do our best to foster a positive environment and promote high self-esteem. Their language skills are really developing, and they need the time to communicate with their peers and the teacher. www.myschoolonline.com/content_gallery/0,3138,41714-141817-44-23700,00.html

How Content Has Been Taught and Assessed

During a specific nutrition lesson that was taught in a second grade classroom at School W, the students are asked to sort real or plastic foods by size, color, shape, etc. They also discuss where foods come from, such as milk and meat coming from animals. The students are introduced to a book called *The Edible Pyramid* by Loreen Leedy. The students then make a pyramid rhyme book by selecting two words, a word from a food group and a word that rhymes with that word. A class book is then created from this.

At School J, nutrition is rarely taught except during the physical education/health time period. The only time nutrition is addressed in the classroom is if an issue is brought to the attention of the teacher.

Special Education, Diversity, and Individual Differences

In terms of the visual learner, there are many demonstrations and activities that allow the students to visualize certain concepts. This is shown in the water activity, various books that are read, the hungry caterpillar activity, and many research activities. Visual learning is included in every lesson. The food pyramid guide poster is utilized at the front of the classroom for each lesson.

For the auditory learner, a story is read aloud during most lessons. Directions are also given to students verbally. There is a class discussion in every lesson to allow students to develop their communication and listening skills. There are numerous kinesthetic learning opportunities in this unit. The students have many opportunities to work hands-on activities. For example, students create a menu, a newsletter, a song, and an art activity, which includes nutritional concepts.

Students work with a partner or group in various activities to stay on task. This promotes cooperative learning and establishes a community of learners. Students that need more attention from the teacher will receive this when the teacher is walking around monitoring the class activities. If a student needs extra time to complete an assignment due to limitations, then the extra time will be provided.

FIGURE 8.9. Elementary Pre-Unit Thinking.

School profile

Both student teachers rely on numbers to "tell the story" of the schools they are teaching in. Information on enrollment, student-to-teacher ratio, and location is useful, but a sense of the school culture is missing. If you were to ask someone to "tell me about the school you are teaching in," you would also be interested in the school climate, approach to teaching and assessment, and student characteristics.

Classroom environment

The overall characteristics of second-grade students are useful, particularly when supported by a source. A more detailed description would be valuable and include the climate for learning and approaches to classroom management, a common interest of new teachers.

How content has been taught and assessed

Both teachers describe the differences in nutrition-as-content in the two schools. At School W, one lesson was described; little seems to have been taught in School J. Clearly, there is a need for instruction in School J. Both teachers can learn from each other in the development and teaching of this unit.

Special education, diversity, and individual differences

The two teachers describes how the unit addressed learner styles, in terms of visual, auditory, and kinesthetic preferences, but did not describe actual student differences, as they were unfamiliar with the individual students. This section also identifies the use of partner groups and the availability of the teacher to provide individual attention. When these first lessons are taught, the "lessons learned" can be reflected in this section.

3.0 Teaching and assessment overview

The teachers identify the major teaching strategies as direct instruction, hands-on activity, demonstrations, discussion, peer learning, and modeling (Figure 8.10). Student projects comprise the primary assessment. Other assessment tools include observation, determination of prior knowledge, discussion, student answers on dry erase boards, and teachers' reflections. Media are central to this unit, with the use of children's books. The computer is used to gather information from the Internet, and posters, encyclopedias, games, dry erase boards, and an overhead projector are also used.

Major Teaching Strategies

Direct instruction, hands-on activities, demonstrations, class discussion, peer learning, and modeling.

Major Assessments Used

The major assessments used for this unit are the projects that the students create. This projects include a newsletter, a song, a menu, a food guide pyramid worksheet, a meat and poultry group worksheet, the classification of a combination food, recipes written by students, a research question worksheet, stories written by students, a crossword puzzle, and a presentation. Other assessments include observation, determination of prior knowledge, class discussion, reflection on lesson plans, and answers on individual dry erase boards.

How Instructional Media and Technology Is Used

There are many uses of instructional media and technology in this unit, which include a food guide pyramid poster, children's books, the computers, the Internet, encyclopedias, various games, dry erase boards, an overhead projector, and the use of a nurse for information.

Specific Classroom Management Rules, Procedures, Routines

Individual Students:

- Listen while others talk.
- Don't interrupt while someone else is talking.
- Respect other's ideas and projects.
- Directly talk to one another during classroom discussion to maintain thoughtful dialogue.
- Use a toilet paper tube that is green on one half to show that you are fine.
- Use a toilet paper tube that is red on one half to show that you need help.
- Raise your hand when you want to talk or ask a question.
- Keep your hands, feet, and objects to yourself.
- Follow directions.

Group Guidelines:

- Everyone should participate.
- Help members of your group.
- Work nicely together and be respectful.
- Use inside voices.

Teacher Routines:

- Use a clipboard for classroom discussions and group activities.
- Always have the instructional sheet available for working on computers.

FIGURE 8.10. Elementary Unit Teaching and Assessment Overview.

4.0 Lesson sequence overview

The overall learning focus for the unit is helping second-grade students develop healthy eating habits. Figure 8.11 lists the sequence of the unit's fifteen lessons, including learning outcomes, student activities, and a time estimate for each lesson. Included here is the rationale as to why lesson 1 precedes lesson 2. Is there some conceptual learning that needs to occur first in lesson 1? Or is the topic choice based on some other reason? A visual representation of lessons 1 through 15 would help the reader gain a sense of how the lessons developed across three weeks. This visual representation could include a descriptive title, learning, and activity, as shown next.

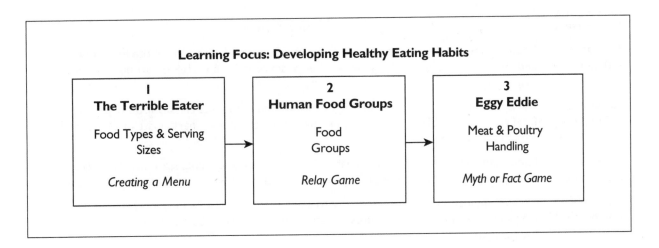

Another strategy is to summarize the lessons into broad categories, as shown next. This approach works well with a unit with many lessons. According to the list of lessons in Figure 8.11, the first two lessons increase students' awareness of food types and how they are arranged in a food pyramid. Lessons 3 through 9 examine different food groups. Lessons 10 through 13 feature specialized topics, and Lessons 14 and 15 use a student presentation to demonstrate healthy eating practices. Lesson 14 covers the development of a presentation, and Lesson 15 allows students to showcase these presentations.

Depicting Lesson Sequence by Categories	
Lessons 1–2	Food pyramid and food groups
Lessons 3–9	Different food groups
Lessons 10–13	Nutrition topics: water, serving sizes, food labels, good manners
Lessons 14–15	Student presentation on healthy eating habits

5.0 Unit evaluation

Figure 8.12 lists questions used to evaluate the success of the unit. At the very minimum, these questions should include the extent to which students learned.

Other questions could address the use of teaching strategies, such as literature to gain student attention and relate eating habits to their own families. The use of games as a supplementary strategy could also form the basis for a question. Another question could ask: "What teaching strategies help second-grade students learn good eating habits?"

Lesson Sequence Overview	
Learning Focus for Unit Staying healthy by using good eating habits.	
Lesson Learning *(time estimate)*	**Major Activity**
Lesson 1 (60 minutes)	Food groups and the number of servings per group, classify foods from the food pyramid, and create a menu including all the number of servings from each food group in a day. The major activity is creating a menu.
Lesson 2 (45 minutes)	Draw pictures that represent an assigned food group. Students classify food objects into food groups while playing a relay game. The major activity is to participate in a food guide pyramid relay game.
Lesson 3 (60 minutes)	Foods and daily servings for the meat and poultry group. Students learn how to handle meat properly. The activity is playing a myth or fact game with the meat and poultry group.
Lesson 4 (60 minutes)	What combination foods are and how to place them into the various food groups. The activity is a relay race that requires the students to place combination foods in their food groups.
Lesson 5 (60 minutes)	Eating foods from the fats, oils, and sweets group is a bad habit. The activity is making a recipe for a fun and healthy snack.
Lesson 6 (70 minutes)	The dairy group and the number of servings a day in this group. The activity is researching the dairy group and creating a story about the facts they found.
Lesson 7 (70 minutes)	Gain information about the fruit group and learn about the number of daily servings. The major activity is to research the fruit group and create a crossword puzzle.
Lesson 8 (70 minutes)	Foods in the vegetable group and the number of daily servings for this group. The activity is researching the vegetable group and answering a research question worksheet.
Lesson 9 (60 minutes)	The bread and grains group and daily servings through class discussion. The activity is creating a food rhyme book.
Lesson 10 (60 minutes)	Importance of water through a demonstration and class discussion. The major activity for this lesson is creating a newsletter about the importance of water.
Lesson 11 (75 minutes)	Accurate serving sizes by reading a book, class discussion, and an informational worksheet. Activities include creating a "Very Hungry Caterpillar" and a song about serving sizes.
Lesson 12 (60 minutes)	How to read food labels through class discussion. Activity is creating an advertisement based on information and facts from a food label.
Lesson 13 (60 minutes)	How to use good manners using a handout, a discussion, and an Internet search. The activity is distinguishing between good manners and bad manners.
Lesson 14 (90 minutes)	Healthy eating. The major activity is preparing a presentation of a previous lesson. Students choose the format.
Lesson 15 (90 minutes)	Promote healthy eating using a presentation. Examples will be discussed in class. The activities include the presentation and discussion.

FIGURE 8.11. Elementary Unit Lesson Sequence.

Questions could be asked about transitions between parts of the lesson. What new classroom management rules or procedures need to be implemented? Were the media materials designed appropriately, and what changes need to be made in the use of time?

Yet another question would address the transfer question, "What strategies could be used to help second-grade students apply what they learned in school to how they eat at home?" The answer to this question could be the basis for lesson revisions for future teaching of the unit.

Unit Evaluation
Questions to evaluate the unit's success in terms of student learning
• Were the students able to identify all food groups? • Can the students list foods from each food group? • Are the students able to read food labels? • Can the children tell why water is important? • Do the children know the correct daily serving number for each food group? • Are the students able to plan a healthy menu? • Are the students able to create a presentation about a nutritional concept?

6.0 Lesson example

Figure 8.13 records the first lesson of the fifteen originally designed for this unit. Here in a sample lesson, you can sense how teaching is helping second-grade students learn nutrition information and appropriate eating habits. If literature was used in each lesson, the lesson title might use the story's title as the title for the lesson. An important feature of the lesson plan is writing out the *learning focus*, which communicates to the teacher the learning purpose of the lesson. Note that the *learning focus* describes what students learn, not merely student activity. Many teacher lessons might just record "Food Pyramid" as the learning focus. Most experienced teachers know the learning purpose of the lesson, but for new teachers, recording a *learning focus* gets them in the habit of focusing on student learning, not merely student activity.

You will note in Figure 8.13 that this lesson includes many details. For new teachers, it is typical to record detailed reminders in the procedure section. This serves three purposes. First, the list helps to visualize and record a logical procedure. Second, the list provides a ready reference. Third, upon reflection and revision, changes can be easily made and archived for future use.

Lesson One: The Terrible Eater

IDENTIFICATION SECTION

Teacher Candidate: Abigail McCarty and Annie Ripley

School: **Grade level:** 2   **Date(s):**

Supervising teacher:

LEARNING FOCUS SECTION

Subject: Introduction to the Food Pyramid   **Time Estimate:** 60 minutes

LEARNING FOCUS for LESSON: Maintain a healthy lifestyle: Knowing foods can be classified into groups and arranged in a pyramid by serving size.

OVERVIEW SECTION

Materials:

- *Gregory, The Terrible Eater* by Mitchell Sharmat
- Food pyramid worksheets for each student
- Picture of food pyramid
- Paper and pencil
- Pre-made menu template for each student

Objectives:

What will students learn in lesson:

- Food groups and daily servings per group.
- Classify foods into a food pyramid.
- Create a menu for a day using the number of daily servings for each food group.

Match with appropriate state standards, if applicable.

HE.2.6.2 record eating and exercise habits and discuss positive and negative health behaviors.
HE.2.6.3 work with a family member to plan a family meal.

Teaching and Assessment Overview:

- Share their ideas with the class.
- Peer learning.
- Group discussion.
- Listen while classmates share answers.
- Direct instruction, using guided practice, individual practice, modeling.

TEACHING SECTION

Teacher Preparation:

- Gather all materials.
- Put poster up in room.

Procedures:

- Introduction or opening activity or review (10 minutes)

    1. Ask students to name some of their favorite foods and why.
    2. Ask students what makes something a "favorite food."
    3. Explain to students that we will be talking a lot about foods for the next few weeks.
    4. Tell students that we are going to read a book about food to start our unit.

FIGURE 8.13. Elementary Unit Lesson One.

- **Instruction/Activities (35 minutes)**

1. Read *Gregory, The Terrible Eater* by Mitchell Sharmatt.

   - Generate class discussion about story and why Gregory was such a terrible eater.
   - Ask students what they do when their parents give them something to eat that they do not like.
   - Ask students if they are willing to try new foods.

2. Ask students what the food pyramid is. Allow time for students to discuss.
3. Explain to them that the food guide pyramid is something that is shaped like a pyramid and shows how many servings of each food group we should have each day.
4. Show students a picture of the food pyramid.
5. Ask students to name each food group.
6. Ask students why the food pyramid is shaped like a pyramid.

   - Explain to them that the largest group is on the bottom and it is the bread and grains group, and this is the one that has the most servings.
   - The one at the top is the smallest, and it is the fats, oils, and sweets group. We should have the least servings from this group.
   - The group with the least servings is on the top, and the group with the most servings is on the bottom.

7. Ask the students if they know the number of servings for each group. Allow students to volunteer answers and generate class discussion.

   - The top of the pyramid is the fats, oils, and sweets group. We should eat very little from this group.
   - Daily servings for the dairy and meat groups are 2–3 servings.
   - Daily servings for the vegetable group are 3–5 servings.
   - Daily servings for the fruit group are 2–4 servings.
   - Daily servings for the bread group are 6–11 servings.

8. Explain to students that it is very important to have a variety of foods from each one of the food groups.
9. Ask students what types of foods they do not like. Once a list is generated, tell students that they should try foods from all of the food groups, even some of the foods that they do not like.
10. Encourage students to help their parents in the kitchen. Children are more interested in eating foods that they prepare.
11. Encourage children to go shopping with their parents and help to pick out new foods.
12. Tell students that it is important to eat the right number of servings for each food group each day. These foods give us many nutrients that help our body to grow and stay strong.
13. Have the students share in a class discussion where their favorite foods are located in the food pyramid.
14. Tell students that they will be filling out a food pyramid. Model what you want students to do by showing them a blank food guide pyramid and explain the following procedure, using the blank pyramid as an aid.
15. Tell students that they need to put different kinds of foods from each food group on their blank pyramid. Students may draw the picture or write the name of the food. Encourage students to think about the foods that Gregory ate, the picture of the food guide pyramid that they saw at the beginning of the lesson, the foods that people said they did not like, and the foods that their classmates did like.

FIGURE 8.13. *(continued)*

16. Have students add the number of servings in each group on the side of their pyramid.
17. Pass out the food pyramids to each student and allow time to finish. As students work, walk around the room and offer assistance where needed.

- **Closure: Review, assignments (15 minutes)**

1. Discuss some of the answers on the food pyramids.
2. Answer any questions that the students may have.
3. Explain to students that they will be creating a menu for one day.

   - Should include breakfast, lunch, dinner, and snacks.
   - The menu must contain all the servings from each food group.
   - Fats, oils, and sweets should be used sparingly.

4. Hand out the menu template and complete.
5. As students work on their menus, remind them to refer to the picture of the food guide pyramid that they saw at the beginning of the lesson. Remind them about the food guide pyramid that they just created to be sure that they have the correct number of servings for each group included in their menu.
6. Encourage students to talk to their families about the food pyramid and how important it is to eat the number of servings for each group every day.

- **Media, materials, or technology used**

  - Fiction book
  - Internet

- **Teacher research procedures**

  - Collect all papers and evaluate.
  - Note and reflect on the responses during the class discussion.
  - Through observations and student work decide whether this material needs to be retaught.

- **References used**

www.nal.usda.gov/ fnic/Fpyr/pyramid.gif
Sharmat, M. (1980). *Gregory, The Terrible Eater.* New York: Simon and Schuster.
http://home.att.net~teaching/health/pyramid.pdf

FIGURE 8.13. Elementary Unit Lesson One (*continued*)

EXAMINING A SECONDARY LEVEL UNIT

The following section describes a unit written by a fourth-year teacher education student in an undergraduate instructional design course. Figure 8.14 outlines a unit called "Changing Ecosystems," four lessons designed for a tenth-grade honors science class. Lesson 1 was featured in Chapter 4, Determining Learning Outcomes.

1.0 Unit description

The mission statement provides an overview of how students view their role in education (Figure 8.15). This section also describes the content area, educational

FIGURE 8.14.
Contents of
Secondary Unit
Example.

Changing Ecosystems
1.0 Unit description
• Mission statement • Unit goals (unit description and learning outcomes) • Reason for choosing unit
2.0. Unit needs assessment
• Content • Learners • Context
3.0 Teaching and assessment overview
• Teaching approaches • Assessment tools
4.0. Lesson sequence overview
• Sequence of lessons • Learning outcomes for each lesson
5.0. Lesson plans
Lesson 1
• Lesson plan • Presentation • Activity
Lesson 2
• Lesson plan • Presentation • Activity
Lesson 3
• Lesson plan • Presentation • Activity
Lesson 4
• Lesson Plan • Presentation • Activity

Adapted from Whitney Hatcher (2002). Reprinted with permission.

level, and overall learning outcomes for the unit. In addition, here this student explains her rationale for choosing this unit.

2.0 Pre-unit thinking

Content

The teacher candidate identifies that students should already understand conceptual knowledge of ecosystems (Figure 8.16). One suggestion here would

FIGURE 8.15.
Secondary Unit
Description.

Unit Description

My Mission

My mission is to provide an environment conducive to student learning where I respect the students, provide them with constructive criticism, and show them the importance of the subject matter they are learning. I wish to ensure that everyone in my classroom is treated equally and that I provide several ways that the students can learn the information provided. I want to be patient and kind with my students, yet I want them to have respect for me as their teacher.

Unit Description and Learning Outcomes

This unit is about balanced and unbalanced ecosystems. It is designed to teach students about four main themes: interactions among organisms, cycles in ecosystems, population growth, and ecosystem change. The unit was developed around chapters five and six of *Science Interactions* by Glencoe/McGraw-Hill. The unit was developed for an honors science ten class, but it can be modified to fit the curriculum of another science class.

After the unit has been completed, students should be able to:

- Describe the components of an organism's habitat and niche.
- Relate feeding relationships of organisms to the flow of energy in ecosystems.
- Identify the different trophic levels in an ecosystem.
- Compare and contrast the ways carbon, water, and nitrogen cycle through ecosystems.
- Compare and contrast linear growth and exponential growth.
- Describe how environmental factors place limits on population growth.
- Recognize how species' interactions regulate population size.
- Sequence the events that occur in ecological succession.
- Describe some effects of human activity on ecosystems.

Reason for Choosing this Unit

I chose to do this unit because it is one that I know I will have to teach when I do my student teaching. I have already taught two of the lessons from this unit, so I had a place to start.

be to preassess the students' level of conceptual knowledge. Another purpose for assessment is to learn what students know. The teacher candidate also identifies that the unit will be taught during her full-semester internship and that she hopes to conduct action research on the use of different forms of testing.

Learners

It is not uncommon in a first unit to find little written about the students. This section requires some work to find out more about learner differences in a classroom. This information can be obtained most efficiently by talking with a cooperating teacher or colleagues. Developmental characteristics of students could also be discussed here. In classrooms where "no diversity" seems to exist, look deeper to see the range of differences in students.

Context

Another suggestion would recommend expanding the description of the school and classroom culture. Describe how the content has previously been taught. Students may or may not have experience with new teaching strategies. The teaching approaches used in this example include direct instruction, cooperative learning, and discovery learning. The pre-unit thinking aims to discover to what extent students have experienced these approaches. Comment on room resources and technology availability. In addition to school and classroom culture, this section prompts one to think about essential needs and how to deal with limited resources.

FIGURE 8.16.
Secondary Unit
Pre-Unit
Thinking.

Pre-Unit Thinking

Content

This unit is designed to teach students about interactions and changes in ecosystems. The students should already have a base knowledge about the concepts that are taught in this unit because they should have already been introduced to the theme of ecosystems.

The classroom that this unit was designed for consisted of twenty-two honors students. The students' tables were arranged in a U-shape around the room. The High School is located in a semi-urban area and is made up of a population of predominantly white, middle-class students.

This unit was designed to use computer-based presentations to give the students notes. Therefore, the teacher needs to be knowledgeable about computers and presentation software. This unit also enables students to build their own experiments.

This unit will be used during my upcoming semester of student teaching. I am considering doing my action research project on different assessment methods. I want to see if students learn more from authentic tests or from traditional tests. This unit provides several opportunities for me to try out both forms of testing in the classroom. I can use traditional tests and quizzes for each chapter and I can use such authentic tests as lab reports, carrying out an experiment correctly, and reporting research data in the form of a class presentation.

Learners

This unit was designed for an tenth-grade honors science class at a local high school. The class consisted of twenty-two students. There is not much diversity. It consists mainly of white, middle-class students. There were no special needs students in the classroom.

Context

This unit requires the use of a video projector and computer. The two projects can be very time consuming and take up classroom space. The teacher can come up with different activities or possibly just have students carry out only one of the projects during the unit to save time and space.

3.0 Teaching and assessment overview

The teacher candidate identified direct instruction, cooperative learning, and discovery learning as her three major teaching strategies (Figure 8.17). Direct instruction used computer-based presentations as a delivery mechanism, but the use of presentations is itself a teaching strategy that is frequently equated with direct instruction. In this example, direct instruction is viewed as a lecture strategy, while direct instruction can involve guided and individual practice. Presentation is a cognitive teaching strategy in which concepts are structured based on their conceptual relationships. See Joyce, Weil, and Calhoun (2004) for a discussion on learning from presentations, as well as direct instruction (Gunter et al., 2003).

The teacher candidate uses an appropriate mix of assessments, including activity questions, text review questions, and student activity. One suggestion would be to provide more detail on student activity performance expectations, using observation checklists, performance checklists, and rubrics.

FIGURE 8.17. Secondary Unit Teaching and Assessment Overview.

Teaching and Assessment Overview
Teaching Approaches
• Direct instruction was used several times throughout the unit during the computer-based presentations in which students are taught the material out of the book. Direct instruction was used because it was the best way to present the material in the textbook.
• Cooperative learning was used during most of the activities. Students tend to like to work together in groups, especially on projects. Students often learn more from each other than working independently.
• Discovery learning was used during several of the activities. Most students enjoy discovering for themselves why something happens.
Assessment Tools
The forms of assessment that I have built into this unit are questions about activities, questions about each section in the book, and lab reports. I used the types of assessment that I did because they are good ways to review the material that has been taught. These forms of assessment are also indicators to the teacher as to what the students have mastered and what they have not mastered.

4.0 Lesson sequence overview

Figure 8.18 lists the sequence of the unit's four lessons, including lesson outcomes and lesson procedures. The first lesson was featured in Chapter 4.

As this unit helps students learn four themes of ecosystems, each of the four lessons could communicate this more clearly with a descriptive label. The first lesson could be labeled as: "Lesson One: Interactions

FIGURE 8.18.
Secondary Unit
Example Lesson
Sequence.

Lesson Sequence Overview

Lesson One Outcomes:

- Describe the components of an organism's habitat and niche.
- Relate feeding relationships of organisms to the flow of energy in ecosystems.
- Identify the different trophic levels in an ecosystem.

Lesson One Procedures:

- Computer-based lecture on the interactions among organisms. Ask the students for examples of organisms that fit the vocabulary words. (15 minutes)
- "Web" Your Appetite activity. (35 minutes)
- Summation questions from the activity. (20 minutes)
- Questions at the end of section 5.1 in the book. (15 minutes)
- Discuss answers to both sets of questions. (15 minutes)

Lesson Two Outcomes:

- Compare and contrast linear growth and exponential growth.
- Describe how environmental factors place limits on population growth.
- Recognize how species' interactions regulate population size.

Lesson Two Procedures:

- Water cycle activity. (25 minutes for set up and 5 minutes at the end of each class period to observe the set-up and record results)
- Computer-based lecture. (20 minutes)
- Section 6.2 review questions. (20 minutes)
- Go over the review questions. (10 minutes)
- At the end of the unit students will write up their results from the activity. (25 minutes)

Lesson Three Outcomes:

- Compare and contrast the ways carbon, water, and nitrogen cycle through ecosystems.

Lesson Three Procedures:

- Introduce lesson and give directions for the game. (10 minutes)
- Students play game and record data. (40 minutes) Complete game summary questions for homework if they did not get to them in class.
- Go over game summary questions. (10 minutes)
- Computer-based presentation on section 6.1. (20 minutes)
- Students answer questions end of section 6.1, go over questions as class. (20 minutes)

Lesson Four Outcomes:

- Sequence the events that occur in ecological succession.
- Describe some effects of human activity on ecosystems.

Lesson Four Procedures:

- Ecological succession in pond water cultures activity. (25 minutes for set-up and 20 minutes every two days for two weeks for observations and recording results)
- Computer-based lecture. (20 minutes).
- Section 6.2 review questions. (20 minutes)
- Go over review questions. (10 minutes)

Among Organisms." This labeling signals a clear sequence of flow of the lessons across the learning focus of the unit. Possible labeling could consist of the following:

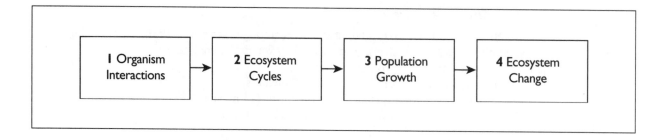

5.0 Lesson plans

Lesson 1 can be found in Chapter 4. The conceptual content of ecosystem interactions is structured around a textbook. Lessons generally include a mix of teacher activity (computer-based lecture), student activity (web activity, game, water culture, review questions), and class activity (discuss review questions). Teaching strategies involve direct instruction using computer-based presentations and a blend of cooperative learning and discovery learning using a web-based activity, water cycle activity, a game, and a pond cultures activity. Discovery is a central feature in Lesson 3, using a game on predator–prey relationships. Students discover what happens to the population of two species in a predator–prey relationship. This activity leads to a classroom discussion of students' responses and then to a list of game summary questions. The discussion then leads to a presentation on unbalanced ecosystems. Student review is accomplished through text review questions.

Assessment involves individual responses to activity questions and text review questions and then classroom discussion of these responses. Assessment also is embedded in the student activities. For example, in Lesson 2, students complete a water cycle page in a weather journal (developed from a previous unit) by labeling evaporation, condensation, and precipitation processes. Another example is a formal lab report required of students in the culminating pond cultures activity.

Roughly ninety minutes appears dedicated to each lesson in this honors science ten class. Lesson 4 involves a pond water cultures activity to demonstrate ecological succession. This activity requires some time to complete. In addition to the activities spent on the first day, this lesson involves thirty minutes spent every two days for two weeks for observations and recording of results. Figure 8.19 visualizes the sequence or "flow" of activity within the lesson.

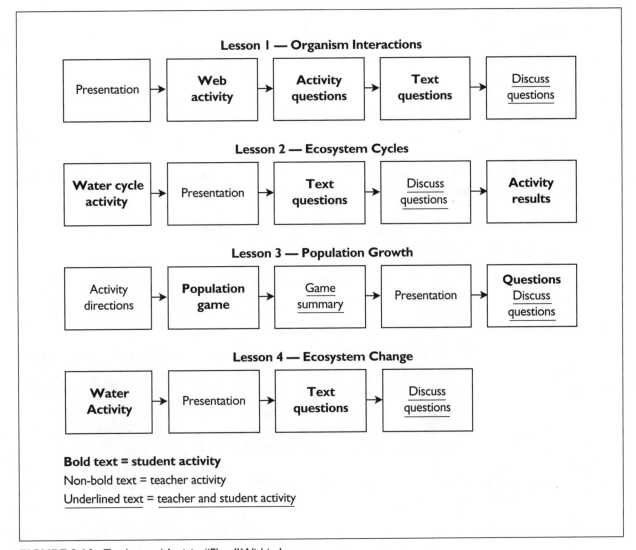

FIGURE 8.19. Teacher and Activity "Flow" Within Lessons.

SUMMARIZING YOUR UNIT

The following Design Activity prompts you to record the flow of your lessons, learning outcomes, teaching, assessment, and technology decisions.

DESIGN ACTIVITY

30

Unit Overview

Task Rationale   This Design Activity provides an overview of your unit and supporting lessons. Insert it into your unit document.

Task Guidelines   Briefly record descriptions of the following:

1. **Unit sequence.** How are lessons used to support unit learning goals? Write out each lesson title, and explain what occurs in each lesson and what student learning is to be achieved.
2. **Teaching strategies.** Name and summarize the major teaching approaches used.
3. **Assessment strategies.** What forms of assessment are you using to assess student learning? What will you know as a result? How will you use this information?
4. **Instructional media and technology.** Summarize what media and technology are being used in the unit and explain why you are using them. Mention any critical considerations on their use.

Reflectivity   How do you appraise the prospects of your unit, based on what you wrote in this Design Activity?

SUMMARY

Understanding what goes into a good lesson will pay off in your development of units. Unit development allows teachers to make more strategic teaching decisions that will benefit students across the school year. These unit decisions should be made while keeping in mind the events that occur during the school year, such as holidays, interruptions, and typical peaks and valleys. Units are fun to develop, as they leverage your knowledge, experience, and creativity. Students can be the best sources of effective units, if you listen to what they have to say and how they react to your teaching. The wrapup for Section IV prompts you to complete and evaluate your unit.

School life is structured "to the max," and children discover this quickly. Finding unstructured time to get to know your students can pay off during teaching time. For example, teachers can discover the child who is lost in a big

"Provide unstructured time for teacher–student relationships."
(Wood, 1998, A Time to Learn, p. 85)

school in unstructured time, when different forms of contact exist. George Wood suggests that lunchtime can be a time for communication rather than a time for control. Sometimes this unstructured time, he says, needs to "find its own structure," depending on your school. The same idea might apply to teachers' professional development. In other words, give teachers professional time to talk together without an agenda. In such opportunities, the workshop flyer should identify a time of the day that is labeled: "No Agenda."

Reflective Teaching

"Unit-Lite"

Veteran teachers may steer clear of developing units because units seem so time consuming to plan and put together. Beginning teachers may shy away from developing units because they *know* they're time consuming to plan and put together! The trade-off may be to engage in a sort of "unit-lite." Unit-lites are the units that you can find in many teacher magazines and on the Internet. These units are centered on a random topic. They often contain a book list of literature to use, and they include numerous student activities, worksheets, and games. Although these units may indeed be focused on interesting and thought-provoking topics and they may contain high-quality student activities and literature suggestions, these units are missing a crucial element: *Your students!* These prepared units do not address the needs of your specific class or the learning goals you have established for the year. Use these unit-lites as a resource for meaningful units that you develop. When you take the responsibility to develop a unit yourself, you can be certain that the needs of your students and what you want them to learn will always be at the forefront of the units that you create.

Teacher Inquiry

- How might you conduct inquiry with a peer in your school or at a different school in terms of addressing the same themes? The different ways in which each of you address important themes in different settings might prove to be a useful study.

REFERENCES

Fogarty, R. (1991). *The mindful school: How to integrate the curricula*. Palatine, IL: IRI/Skylight.

Gunter, M. A., Estes, T. H., & Schwab, J. (2003). *Instruction: A models approach* (4th ed.). Boston: Allyn and Bacon.

Joyce, B., Weil, M., & Calhoun, E. (2004). *Models of teaching* (7th ed.). Boston: Allyn and Bacon.

Katz, L., & Chard, S. (1989). *Engaging children's minds: The project approach*. Norwood, NJ: Ablex.

Krogh, S. L. (1995). *The integrated early childhood curriculum* (2nd ed). Boston: McGraw Hill.

National Middle School Association. (1995). *This we believe: Developmentally responsive middle level schools*. Columbus, OH: Author.

Wood, G. H. (1998). *A time to learn*. New York: Plume Penguin.

RESOURCES

Print Resources

Krogh, S. L. (1995). *The integrated early childhood curriculum* (2nd ed.). Boston: McGraw Hill.

> Helpful introductions on the social-emotional-cognitive-physical development of the whole child. Examples of web-based curriculum for language, mathematics, science, social studies, art, and music and movement. Two chapters on using web curriculums in the preprimary class and the primary grades.

Roberts, D., & Kellough, B. (2000). *A guide for developing interdisciplinary thematic units*. Dubuque, IA: Kendall Hunt.

Tanner, D. (1989). A brief historical perspective of the struggle for an integrative curriculum. *Educational Horizons, 65* (1), 7–11.

> Integrated curriculum implementation has been a difficult "sell" in some schools.

Wiggins, G., & McTighe, J. (2001). *Understanding by design*. ASCD/Merrill.

> See Chapter 8, "Applying Student Understanding to Unit Design."

Wolfinger, D. M., & Stockard, Jr., J. W. (1997). *Elementary methods: An integrated curriculum*. New York: Longman.

> Part II describes integrated curriculum development through different disciplines, language and literature, themes, and issues. Also, sections on planning, teaching, and assessment.

Web-Based Resources

www.coollessons.org/coolunits.htm

> A source of lessons and units, along with rubrics, research help, problem-based learning, and many webquests.

www.eduref.org/Virtual/Lessons

> Lesson plans in the Educator's Reference Desk database are organized by grade level and subject, including arts, computer science, foreign language, health, information literacy, interdisciplinary, language arts, mathematics, philosophy, physical education, science, social studies, and vocational education. The site also welcomes contributions!

http://ipr.ues.gseis.ucla.edu/classroom/units.

> This site includes units in which K–12 students use primary resources in their learning activities.

www.teachingheart.net/

> A site developed by Colleen Gallagher for primary teachers.

www.csun.edu/~hcedu013/

> Lessons, units, and resources for teaching social studies.

www.d.umn.edu/~lmillerc/TeachingEnglish-HomePage/TeachingUnits/units.htm

> An archive of English units from students.

Completing Your Unit

Principle 1 PEDAGOGICAL CONTENT KNOWLEDGE: The teacher understands the central concepts, tools of inquiry, and structures of the discipline(s) he or she teaches and can create learning experiences that make these aspects of subject matter meaningful for students.

Principle 2 DEVELOPMENTALLY APPROPRIATE TEACHING: The teacher understands how children learn and develop, and can provide learning opportunities that support their intellectual, social and personal development.

Principle 3 LEARNER DIFFERENCES: The teacher understands how students differ in their approaches to learning and creates instructional opportunities that are adapted to diverse learners.

Principle 4 TEACHING REPERTOIRE: The teacher understands and uses a variety of instructional strategies to encourage students' development of critical thinking, problem solving, and performance skills.

Principle 5 LEARNING ENVIRONMENTS: The teacher uses an understanding of individual and group motivation and behavior to create a learning environment that encourages positive social interaction, active engagement in learning, and self-motivation.

Principle 6 COMMUNICATION: The teacher uses knowledge of effective verbal, nonverbal, and media communication techniques to foster active inquiry, collaboration, and supportive instruction in the classroom.

Principle 7 PRE-UNIT THNKING: The teacher plans instruction based upon knowledge of subject matter, students, the community, and curriculum goals.

Principle 8 ASSESSMENT: The teacher understands and uses formal and informal assessment strategies to evaluate and ensure the continuous intellectual, social, and physical development of the learner.

Principle 9 REFLECTIVE PROFESSIONAL: The teacher is a reflective practitioner who continually evaluates the effects of his/her choices and actions on others and who actively seeks out opportunities to grow professionally.

- What have you learned about your classroom by using pre-unit thinking?
- What is the learning focus for your unit?
- What assessment tools support student learning in your unit?
- What major teaching strategies will you use in your unit?
- How might instructional media and technology be featured in the unit?
- How will you know if your unit implementation is successful?

DOCUMENTING TEACHER DECISIONS IN YOUR UNIT

Developing units involves the following three levels of thinking and decision making:

Levels of Thinking in Unit Development	
LEVEL 1	
Scope	What "content" does the unit cover?
Learning Focus	What will students learn?
Sequence	What is the order of lessons and why?
LEVEL 2	
Pre-Unit Thinking	What do you know about the "content," your students, and the reality of the learning setting, including school and classroom environment?
LEVEL 3	
	Teacher Decision Cycle
	1. What will students learn?
	2. How do you know students have learned?
	3. How will teaching help students learn?
	4. How will technology help students learn?
	5. How will technology reframe decisions 1 through 4?
Lessons	Overall learning focus, specific learning objectives, teaching strategies, assessment, and media/technology use.

Level 1: Scope–learning focus–sequence

The idea of scope–learning focus–sequence helps you think through the broad decisions on unit development. "Scope" requires you to decide what content the unit will cover. "Focus" requires you next to decide what the principal student learning outcomes will be. If you are developing a health unit on nutrition, then your learning focus might be: "Develop healthy eating habits." This overall learning focus is represented within *each* lesson of the unit, and one lesson might include the following learning focus: "Healthy Eating Habits: Understanding Food Groups." Finally, "sequence" requires you to decide on the chronological order of teaching. What teaching will occur in lesson 1, lesson 2, lesson 3, and so forth? In Chapter 8 we visually sequenced, as seen here, the descriptive titles for the student teacher's four lesson themes in a four-lesson ecosystems unit.

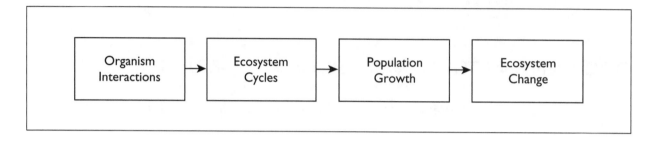

Level 2: Pre-unit thinking

After making decisions on scope, learning focus, and sequence, conduct a *pre-unit thinking* review of the full range of content to be learned, who your students are, and the reality of the classroom setting. The *pre-unit thinking* contributes to better decisions in individual lessons. We used *pre-lesson thinking* in Chapter 3 as you were developing your first lessons. In developing units, however, it is not necessary to conduct this review for all lessons, just in advance of making unit decisions.

Based on what you learn from *pre-unit thinking*, you may need to adjust your original decisions for scope, learning focus, and sequence. These changes can then be incorporated into lesson details.

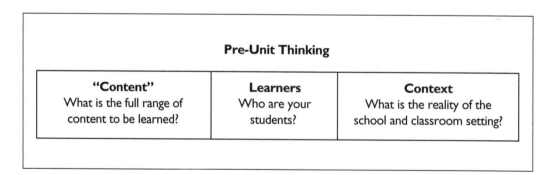

Level 3: Lessons

The third level of decision making in unit developments involves lessons and uses the Teacher Decision Cycle to systematically organize your decision making on learning outcomes, assessment, teaching, and technology. The following graphic visually summarizes the unit development process and the teaching decisions you make before and after teaching.

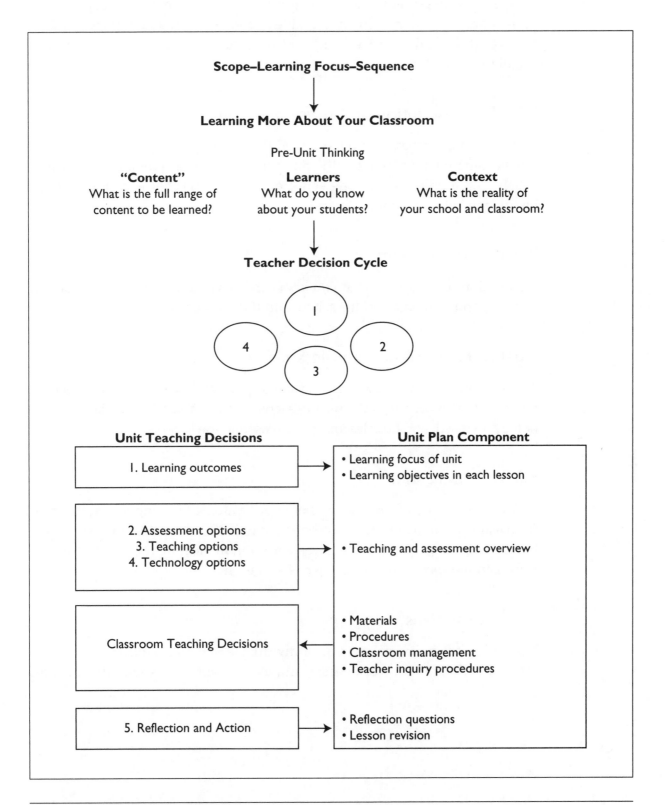

REVISITING UNIT COMPONENTS

1.0 Cover and references

A cover, incorporating the unit title, grade level, and content areas, presents a professional appearance. Include a table of contents with either page numbers or tabs. At the end of the unit, a list of references and media sources may be useful to the reader.

2.0 Unit description and mission statement

This section describes the unit and student learning outcomes. Your rationale for choosing the unit, along with your personal mission statement of learning beliefs, communicates a strong sense of you as a teacher and how you see instruction helping students learn.

3.0 Pre-unit thinking

This section summarizes what you know and what you learned about content, learners, and the context of the school and the classroom.

4.0 Overview of unit and lessons

This section describes how each lesson supports the overall learning focus of the unit. It also describes the major teaching strategies, how media and technology are used, and how learning is assessed in the lessons.

5.0 Unit evaluation

Reflective questions were used to help you evaluate teaching lessons. A more formal approach to reflection is needed for units. The key question here is asking the question: "How effective was your unit in meeting the overall learning focus and the specific learning objectives of each lesson?"

6.0 Lesson plans

The bulk of the unit consists of the individual lesson plans. Examples of teaching materials, student work sheets, and assessment tools should be included with each lesson.

Unit Outline and Checklist

Task Rationale   Use this outline to document your teaching decisions for a unit.

Cover: Unit Title, Grade Level, Content Area(s), Your Name

- A cover can include a visual or a visual indicative of your unit.

Table of Contents

- Use either a page numbering or tab system.

1.0   Unit Description

- Unit description and learning focus
- Rationale for choosing unit
- Mission statement of learning beliefs
- School mission statement (optional)

2.0   Pre-Unit Thinking

- School profile
- How content has been taught previously
- How content could be taught
- Learner differences issues
- Media and technology possibilities
- Resources and constraints
- Teacher inquiry questions
- Summary of findings: what did I learn, and what will I include in the unit as a result?

3.0   Overview of Unit and Lessons

- Unit sequence: what students learn and major activities in each lesson
- Summary of major teaching strategies
- Summary of instructional media and technology
- Summary of assessment

4.0   Unit Evaluation

- List criteria to evaluate the unit's success

5.0   References

- List of references, websites
- List of people consulted or interviewed

6.0   Lesson Plans. For each lesson, include the following:

- Descriptive title
- Learning focus of lesson
- Specific student learning

(continued)

- Time estimate
- Teaching and assessment
- Learner differences
- Materials, instructional media, and technology
- Procedures (opening, teaching, closure)
- Samples of handouts, worksheets, materials, visuals, web pages, and so on
- Teacher inquiry procedures (e.g., gathering data and using it to adjust future teaching)
- Classroom management rules and procedures
- Reflective comments from any field testing or concerns for actual teaching

EVALUATING YOUR UNIT

To evaluate your first unit, ask yourself three questions: *What* will you evaluate? *Who* does the evaluation? *When* does one evaluate?

What to evaluate?

To evaluate the success of your unit, you have to define what success means. We suggest organizing the "what you will evaluate?" question in terms of three categories: how *effective* your unit was, how *efficient* the design and implementation of the unit were, and how *appealing* the unit was to your students.

Effective units are those in which student learning occurred, which is the purpose of teaching the units in the first place. Effective assessments provide teachers with this information.

Efficient units are those in which an appropriate amount of time was spent in developing and teaching them. Good ideas may require significant up-front time to develop, such as one's first lessons, integrative lessons, and the development of rubrics. This investment of time, however, may be worthwhile. Answering the "how efficient was my unit?" question will tell you that some aspect of materials development may need to be curtailed or alternative materials may need to be selected rather than developed by you.

Evaluating units with *appeal* is an important question, because effective and efficient units may not be all that attractive to students. Instruction with low student appeal most likely will affect how effective these units will be in the long run. Your lessons may be low in efficiency if you are spending time trying to motivate your students to become excited about a low-appeal activity. New teachers look for activities that stimulate student interest, but after using these high-appeal introductory activities, they resort to low-appeal instruction. Humans want to learn, and learning *is* hard work, but this work should be rewarding to students and teachers.

Who evaluates?

In formal instructional design activities, someone other than the designer or teacher usually evaluates the success of an implementation. This is the case in funded projects in which an external reviewer is required to evaluate the use of program funds. In classrooms, teachers become their own evaluators, although bringing in other teachers to provide feedback can be helpful, particularly with new ideas and strategies. Forgotten as evaluators are the students themselves, as good teachers continually assess student reactions to their teaching and ask them for suggestions. Depending on the age of students, you can ask for student reactions, observe student reactions, and solicit written comments.

When to evaluate?

In formal ID activities, projects are evaluated at different stages of their development and implementation. *Formative program evaluation* is conducted as a project is being developed and benchmark stages are selected. If a project is being field tested, it can be continually evaluated. *Summative program evaluation*, meanwhile, judges a project's success after a suitable trial period. Determining a sufficient trial is a question that needs to be answered in these formal instructional design and development activities.

Teachers conduct both formative and summative program evaluation, but not in the formal sense as writing reports. Formative evaluation of one's teaching goes on daily, and the amount of record keeping depends on one's time and personal disposition to reflect and record one's reactions. Summative activities usually take the form of looking at student performance during an official grading period or at the end of the school year. Another example where summative evaluation is used is evaluating a workshop you have attended or have delivered yourself. The following visual provides some examples of times when formative and summative evaluation are conducted.

Formative and Summative Evaluation	
Formative Evaluation	**Summative Evaluation**
• Prior to teaching	• Grading periods
• Daily teaching	• End of school year
• End of lesson, unit	• Workshop

To summarize program evaluation in terms of unit development, see Figure Unit-1 on the next page.

What, Who, and When of Unit Evaluation
What to evaluate?
1. **Effectiveness:** Were the unit's learning outcomes achieved, and how do you know? Were the teaching strategies appropriate, and what changes need to be made? Were your assessments appropriate to how you taught? Did they assess student performance? Overall, what did you learn about teaching the content?
2. **Efficiency:** How much time did you spend in developing this unit? How difficult was it to teach? What needs to be changed? What needs to be added or deleted?
3. **Appeal:** How did your students react to this unit? Did you ask them for feedback? What changes need to be made so that your lessons "connect" with your students?
Who evaluates?
• **Instructor:** Ongoing self-assessment of learning outcomes and learner performance.   • **Student:** Asking, observing, and written responses.   • **Peers:** Observations from fellow teachers, co-teaching   • **External reviewers:** Formal evaluation by outside experts.
When to evaluate?
• **During the school year:** ongoing self-assessment of teaching performance.   • **Unit completion:** evaluation of unit goals, actual teaching, and student/teacher performance.   • **End of school year:** student learning, teacher learning, adjustments for next year.

Unit evaluation

The following Design Activity uses the categories of effectiveness, efficiency, and appeal to help you evaluate your unit of instruction. This activity assumes that you have taught this unit, although formative evaluation can be conducted on the design for a unit that has not been taught to review its teaching decisions.

DESIGN ACTIVITY

32

Unit Evaluation

Task Rationale   Evaluate the teaching of your unit.

Task Guidelines   Respond to the following questions:

Effectiveness
1. Was the teaching approach appropriate to the desired learning?
2. Was the unit's learning focus achieved? Did students learn anything?
3. Did you have appropriate and sufficient assessment tools in place to determine the extent of student learning? For example, was your designed rubric, if used, accurate in accounting for differences in student learning?
4. Did media and technology help students learn?

Efficiency
5. How much time and resources were required to develop and implement this unit?
6. How much effort did teaching and assessment require?

Appeal
7. Did students enjoy the lesson overall, and were they engaged in learning?
8. Did you ask students for feedback on the unit?

Reflectivity
- What other issues should be included here to ensure an effective unit?
- What does a "successful" unit mean?

TEACHING YOUR UNIT

Here are some guidelines in teaching and learning from your first unit.

Preparing for teaching

- Determine the learning focus for your unit. Each lesson should support this learning focus in some way.
- Unit development can be fun and rewarding and give you confidence in teaching.

- Select a unit that can be taught in a week or two. Some units may require longer to implement, depending on the types of learning desired.
- Unit plans document how you as a teacher help students learn. What roles do you play, and what roles do students play?
- Share your draft unit with your cooperating teacher, peers, or colleagues.

Teaching

- Be familiar with your lesson plans, but avoid using them as a "script." Know that conditions will change and that you will need to make on-the-spot adjustments. Try to document these and revise your unit accordingly.
- Provide students adequate time to think through new topics and fully participate in activities.
- As you move through your lessons and react to students' reactions and performance, you may need more time in each lesson or more days to implement activities. Try to schedule some "slack" in your lesson and unit planning to accommodate these adjustments and reteaching.
- Ensure that the unit provides a clear description of how you will assess student learning. How will you use this information in your subsequent teaching?

Reflection

- Record impressions and reflections as soon as you reasonably can. Record them by hand and transcribe later. Your memory may not help you with important details if you wait "until the weekend." This habit takes discipline. Make notes on your lesson plans, particularly guidelines for future use of your unit.
- Use the sample reflective questions to guide you in reflecting on important issues. Comment on what seems particularly crucial for you.
- The unit evaluation provides a written documentation of the success of your unit. The questions you ask yourself define what you mean by "success." One criterion for success should always address the learning focus of the unit.
- Key learning for the teacher would be a greater understanding of what it means for students to learn the content.

Action

- The first level of action is to record your reflections and take action.
- Make notes on your lesson plan for revisions or guidelines.
- Update your lesson plans and units for future use. Documented, successful units can be used in portfolios, job searches, sharing with others, and your future teaching assignment. Others will be interested in a unit that has been taught and improved.

SECTION

V Growing as a Teacher

9 Developing Curriculum

Main Idea of This Chapter
Curriculum is about who decides what "content" gets taught in schools. Designing instruction on a curriculum level creates lessons and units that take into account these multiple influences.

INTASC Standards Addressed in This Chapter

Principle 7 PRE-UNIT THINKING: The teacher plans instruction based upon knowledge of subject matter, students, the community, and curriculum goals.

Principle 10 RELATIONSHIP-BUILDING: The teacher fosters relationships with school colleagues, parents, and agencies in the larger community to support students' learning and well-being.

Focus Questions

- What is meant by curriculum?
- Who influences curriculum decisions?
- What professional organizations influence curriculum decisions?
- In what ways can curriculum shape your school?
- What schoolwide curriculum initiatives would help your students?

Design Activities

DA 33: Content Area Standards Using an Integrated Curriculum
DA 34: School Themes

WHAT THIS CHAPTER IS ABOUT

Chapter 9 looks at curriculum in three ways. The first view examines several definitions of *curriculum*, including the school curriculum, the taught curriculum, the null curriculum, and the hidden curriculum. The second view describes major categories of external influences on curriculum, including national initiatives, state agencies, professional associations, educational publishers, and social critics. The third view of curriculum examines local influences, which include schools and school districts, teachers, students, communities, and parents.

The next section of this chapter discusses content area curriculum models, as suggested by professional organizations devoted to content areas, such as math and social studies. Also discussed are the use of integrative curriculum approaches to address multiple content areas.

The third section of this chapter describes three examples of curriculum models that characterize schools in very different ways. These examples include charter schools, the basic school, and universal design for learning (UDL). The sequence for this chapter is visualized in Figure 9.1.

FIGURE 9.1.
Visual Sequence for Chapter 9.

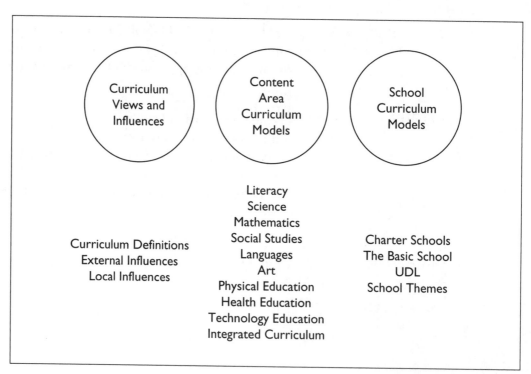

LESSONS, UNITS, AND CURRICULUM

In Chapters 4 through 7, we looked at developing *lessons* to focus on identifying learning outcomes and ways to help your students achieve those outcomes (Figure 9.2). Lessons include the procedural details of daily teaching based on a clear sense of student learning.

FIGURE 9.2.
Instructional
Levels and Book
Chapters.

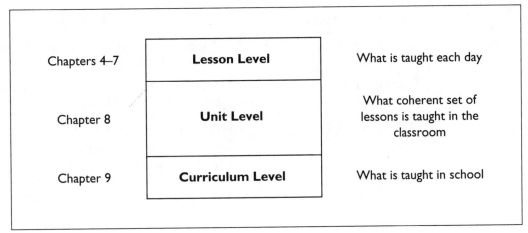

Chapters 4–7	**Lesson Level**	What is taught each day
Chapter 8	**Unit Level**	What coherent set of lessons is taught in the classroom
Chapter 9	**Curriculum Level**	What is taught in school

Designing lessons on a *unit level* allows teachers to connect lessons in a coherent fashion based on a clear sense of how a unit helps students achieve learning outcomes, standards, or objectives. Units help teachers address state standards in ways that are appropriate for their students. Units allow students to learn over time and involve them in a variety of meaningful solo and social structures. Units also provide multiple forms of assessment evidence that student learning is occurring and information to make revisions in teaching.

The challenge of translating "content" to teaching is influenced by a third level of instructional development—*curriculum*. At this level, decisions are made on what is taught in schools. Curriculum decisions remain, for the most part, local concerns of counties and school districts, but these decisions are increasingly influenced by state learning standards. Other influences can be found from an ongoing ebb and flow of national initiatives. Various professional content area organizations, which are highlighted later in this chapter, also provide a national influence on curriculum.

CURRICULUM VIEWS AND INFLUENCES

Definitional views

Curriculum is about *what* content gets taught (Figure 9.3). The official body of content to be taught is the *school curriculum*, which is written down and documented, and for which states, school boards, and parents hold the school accountable. Individual state standards comprise the learning outcomes required of students in that state, but school curriculum is what is supposed to be taught by teachers to achieve these learning outcomes.

Teachers face the task of translating state standards into a coherent curriculum across a range of learner differences. In addition, this task must be

FIGURE 9.3.
Definitional Views of Curriculum.

Curriculum Views	Definitions
School curriculum	What is officially taught in schools and accountable to external influences
Taught curriculum	What is really taught in schools, part of which may be aligned with external influences
Null curriculum	What is not taught in schools
Hidden curriculum	What is communicated to students as being valued by teachers and administrators

accomplished at different grade levels in unique schools. Thus, the *taught curriculum*, or operational curriculum (Arends, Winitzky, & Tannenbaum, 2001), becomes the norm for classrooms. Some of what actually gets taught may align with the school curriculum. Many of the outside, extracurricular activities, which are regarded as nonacademic areas, are in fact "content" learning opportunities for schools in which significant student learning occurs. This distinction is a matter of individual perspective, but extracurricular content is a major concern of students, particularly in middle and secondary schools.

Educators frequently cite two other terms that help us think about what is taught in schools. The terms address what is not taught and what is obliquely taught. The first term is the *null curriculum*, that which is not taught in schools, the content that is missing and perhaps should be there, such as health and nutrition. Schools that eliminate music and the arts, for example, have contributed to the null curriculum. Whether a subject should be taught is grist for discussion that usually centers on the issue of available funds but also reveals what people believe school should be about.

The second term is the *hidden curriculum*, content that is communicated but is not directly taught to students. Hidden curriculum involves the values, perceptions, and attitudes that educators have toward topics, events, and people. Educators communicate these values in some way, such as attitudes toward different students or academic subjects. Rules of behavior, one aspect of classroom management, may not be followed if rules of behavior assigned to playgrounds and extracurricular activities are different.

The influences on curriculum decisions can also be viewed as those coming from outside the school and those within and close to the school.

External curriculum influences

A number of external factors, such as national initiatives, state agencies, professional content area associations, educational publishers, and, to some extent, social critics, influence what schools teach (Arends et al., 2001). Figure 9.4 summarizes the external and local influences on deciding what content is taught in schools.

FIGURE 9.4.
External and Local Influences on Curriculum.

External Influences on Curriculum	Local Influences on Curriculum
National initiatives State agencies Professional associations Educational publishers Social critics	Schools and school districts Teaching and teacher histories Students Communities Parents

National initiatives

Published tests, such as the Iowa Test of Basic Skills and the Scholastic Aptitude Tests (SAT), have been a common feature in schools. In particular, the use of tests to secure admission to college, such as the SAT and Advanced Placement examinations, has prompted many teachers to direct their teaching in honors courses toward these tests.

The most significant contemporary federal legislation affecting all students, parents, teachers, and curriculum is the No Child Left Behind Act (NCLB). The major feature of this legislation for schools is requiring states to implement accountability covering all public schools and students. This accountability addresses reading and mathematics, annual testing for all students in grades 3 through 8, and annual statewide progress objectives ensuring that all groups of students reach proficiency within twelve years. School districts and schools that fail to make adequate yearly progress toward these proficiency goals will be subject to improvement, corrective action, and restructuring measures. Schools that meet or exceed adequate yearly progress are eligible for state academic achievement awards.

Another example of federal legislation, that has had a major impact on schools, parents, and children is the Individuals with Disabilities Education Act (IDEA). First signed in 1990, the amendments of 1997 strengthened academic expectations and accountability for the nation's estimated 5.8 million children with disabilities. The focus of IDEA changed from one that provided disabled children access to an education to one that improves results for all children in our education system. The amendments strengthened the role of parents in educational planning and decision making on behalf of their children. The updated legislation prioritized the student's educational planning process on promoting meaningful access to the general curriculum.

In addition to federal legislation, reports funded by the federal government have had an influence on curriculum decisions. One source of data is the National Research Council (NRC), which was organized by the National Academy of Sciences in 1916 to communicate to the science and technology community the academy's purposes of furthering knowledge and advising the federal government. The NRC's Division of Behavioral and Social Sciences and Education (DBASSE) applies what is known in the behavioral and social sciences to educational issues. The division's areas of expertise include anthropology, child development, demography, economics, education, history, law, gerontology, linguistics, political science, psychology, sociology, and statistics. One often-cited NRC report is *How People Learn: Brain, Mind, Experience, and School* (Bransford, Brown, & Cocking, 2000). The book pulls together current scientific knowledge about human learning and relates this knowledge to teachers and teaching. The perspective of this report toward curriculum is that the purpose of schools is to help "students make sense of their surroundings and ready them for the challenges of the technology-driven, internationally competitive world." A summary of what science has learned about learning is found in Chapter 1 of this book.

One example of a national report that has influenced curriculum decisions is *A Nation at Risk*, developed by the National Commission on Excellence in Education (1983). This report criticized the U.S. education system as substandard and recommended stiffer academic standards and more time in school. Its conclusions have been criticized as an incorrect picture of schools (see Berliner & Biddle, 1995). A second example affected the curriculum of teacher education programs. The report, *A Nation Prepared: Teachers for the Twenty-First Century* (Task Force on Teaching as a Profession, 1986), proposed that teacher education programs be designed as five-year graduate programs rather than undergraduate programs and led to the establishment of a national certification board.

State agencies

In the 1960s, the federal government became more involved in education. Federal money flowed to state educational departments. Local control of public schools, financed to a great degree by state revenue and local property taxes, became diffused with this new state money. State governments became further involved in establishing state standards, which necessitated testing to determine how students and schools were faring. In addition, states came to control the licensing and testing of teachers and the content topics that could be taught (Spring, 2002).

One organization that supports state educational officials who are responsible for elementary and secondary education in the United States is the Council of Chief State School Officers (CCSSO). According to this organization,

"Education policy is primarily the responsibility of the states," and states have a primary role in educating children and determining that its children learn.

A national organization with strong ties to states is the Interstate New Teacher Assessment and Support Consortium (INTASC). INTASC members include state teacher licensing and program approval officials, independent standards boards officials, and representatives from various national education organizations. In the preface to this book, we discussed the ten INTASC core principles, which describe teacher competencies across all grades and subjects. INTASC's various projects involve the reform of teacher preparation, licensing, and professional development.

Professional associations

A description of relevant national professional educational associations would be chapter in itself. Content area organizations will be briefly discussed in the next section of this chapter because they directly affect content area teaching. Curriculum decisions are being scrutinized and influenced from many directions, and one major category of influences is professional associations, some of which are listed in Figure 9.5.

FIGURE 9.5. Professional Content Area Organizations.

Professional Content Area Organizations
American Federation of Teachers (AFT)
Association for the Advancement of Science (AAS)
International Reading Association (IRA)
International Society for Technology in Education (ISTE)
National Assessment of Educational Progress (NAEP)
National Association for Sport and Physical Education (NASPE)
National Board for Professional Teaching Standards (NBPTS)
National Congress of Parents and Teachers (PTA)
National Council for the Accreditation of Teacher Education (NCATE)
National Council for the Social Studies (NCSS)
National Council of Teachers of English (NCTE)
National Council of Teachers of Mathematics (NCTM)
National Council on Education (NCE)
National Education Association (NEA)
National School Boards Association (NSBA)

Educational publishers

The publishers of textbooks still exert a significant influence on what is taught in public schools. The states that adopt book titles, as well as the professional educational associations that have supervised their development, further influence the publication of textbooks. In addition, states that represent significant sales to publishers may exert considerable influence on what titles are actually written and available to other states or other schools.

Individual critics and advocates

Individuals and their writings have had some influence on what is taught in classrooms and the experiences that teachers have in teaching the curriculum. An example is *Cultural Literacy: What Every American Needs to Know* (Hirsch, 1987), which advocated and listed foundational knowledge for all citizens. This title provides an example of the *null curriculum*—namely, that what is not listed is not important or, at the very least, "out of sight, out of mind."

Another influential book was *Savage Inequalities: Children in American Schools* (Kozol, 1991), which documented the funding differences between and within school districts. *A Place Called School* (Goodlad, 1984) used surveys to report the daily conditions teachers face in school. Another title, *Pedagogy of the Oppressed* (Freire, 1998), examined certain premises of education, such as the view of teacher and student as depositor and depositee. This view used the metaphor of banking, in which a student receives "deposits from the teacher." The alternative, according to Freire, is "problem posing" in which both teacher and student learn from each other through dialogue.

Local curriculum influences

What schools teach is also influenced by local factors, which are not always acknowledged but have been in existence since the beginning of organized education. These influences include school culture, teaching and teacher histories, evolving student characteristics, community traditions, and parental expectations. To ignore these influences in the determination of what schools teach is to lose many possibilities for building human relationships between students, between teachers and students, between teachers and parents, and between students and their parents. As states and the federal government have increased their influence and role on curriculum decisions, the actual implementation of requirements has been translated to a great extent by the following local influences.

Schools and school districts

No one school is alike. Each is a product of many influences, including the people, businesses, and institutions in the community. Schools take on a unique character from the teachers who teach in them, as well as from the students who attend the schools. School district administrators, in turn, supervise what goes on in individual schools, including the official school curriculum and to some extent the unique ways in which teachers implement the school curriculum and the performance of students against state learning standards.

For many years, national testing consisted of only once-a-year administration of a published test, such as the Iowa Test of Basic Skills. The results provided teachers and parents with one source of how students were performing.

Teachers, however, conducted the predominant form of evaluation in ways that made sense to them. The culture of school has evolved to include both local influences and the increasing demands of state and federal requirements.

Teaching

School culture is also a product of teachers, staff, and administrators. The experiences of teachers, whether those who stay for a short period of time or those who have been employed over many years, influence what content is taught and how it is taught. Schools include one or more groups or associations of educators who may collectively influence what is taught. Every school has a history in which teachers remain the key players. Learning this history can help a teacher understand why certain content is taught and other content is not.

New teachers quickly observe the differences in each school and classroom. They experience what it means to make teaching decisions in the classroom. New teachers add to what they have learned in teacher education courses with how experienced teachers address classroom management, content teaching, and the pressures of other responsibilities and the ever-changing classroom day. The individual culture of schools becomes a factor in how new teachers develop lessons and units.

Students

Teachers are keen observers of student behavior and how they react to instructional activities. Expert teachers come to understand the differences in students and how to adjust to these differences daily. The taught curriculum undergoes constant revision by informed teachers who, despite increasing responsibilities, remain primarily motivated to help their students.

Communities and parents

Communities also influence school culture and what is taught. Students become parents themselves, and the cycle of new students continues in many communities. This continuity of teachers and schools helps students extend their learning from the family back to the schools. Many school initiatives are formally recognizing the value of communities and parents. Parental involvement is seen as an important goal for schools.

Parents and citizens may sit on school boards or join local PTAs and have a direct influence on curriculum. Ad hoc or temporary formations of citizens may be involved in the promotion of school bond issues to construct new schools, as social policy becomes increasingly less directed to fight inequality of various kinds (Schorr, 1997). Community groups may raise funds or provide labor to build new playgrounds. Increasingly, schools are turning to local corporate support for financing computers, facilities, and other equipment.

CONTENT AREA CURRICULUM MODELS

Professional organizations have achieved agreement as to what constitutes student learning in their particular content areas. The overall thrust behind the standards movement is that a curriculum based on standards provides the basis for a clearly defined curriculum. In addition, it is believed that high standards, coupled with ongoing assessment to monitor the results, will result in high levels of student achievement (Delandshere & Arens, 2001). The sources for these content area standards are listed in Figure 9.6.

FIGURE 9.6. Sources for Content Area Curriculum Standards.

Sources for Content Area Curriculum Standards

Literacy
National Council of Teachers of English and International Reading Association. (1996). *Standards for the English Language Arts.* Urbana, IL.

Science
American Association for the Advancement of Science. (1993). *Benchmarks for Scientific Literacy.* Washington, DC.

Mathematics
National Council for the Teachers of Mathematics. (1989). *Curriculum and Evaluation Standards for School Mathematics.* Reston, VA.

Social Studies
National Council for the Social Sciences. (1994). *Expectations of Excellence: Curriculum Standards for Social Studies.* Washington, DC.

Languages
National K–12 Foreign Language Resource Center.
www.educ.iastate.edu, nflrc

Arts
National Committee for Standards in the Arts. (1994). *Dance, Music, Theatre, Visual Arts: National Standards for Arts Education.* Reston, VA.

Physical Education
National Association for Sport and Physical Education. (1999). *National Standards for Physical Education.*
www.aahperd.org/naspe/

Health Education
Joint Committee on National Health Education Standards. (1995). *National Health Education Standards.* Available from the American School Health Association (P.O. Box 708, 7263 State Route 43, Kent, OH 44240).

Association for the Advancement of Health Education, 1900 Association Drive, Reston, VA 22091

Technology Education
International Technology Education Association. (1996). *Technology for All Americans.*
www.iteawww.org/TAA/TAA.html

Literacy

The traditional definition of *literacy* is the ability to read and write. This definition has been enlarged to cover an ability to read, write, speak, listen, and communicate visually. Becoming literate can become an overarching goal for any content area or field of endeavor (Shambaugh, 2000). Viewing literacy as only reading and writing limits one's use of literacy in many forms of teaching. The ability to read, write, speak, listen, and communicate visually can apply to all subjects at all educational levels (Valmont, 2003).

Science

The idea of what it means to be scientifically literate forms the basis for science standards (American Association for the Advancement of Science, 1993). The combination of science, math, and technology is advocated by focusing on central ideas in these fields. These standards, clustered into grade levels, encourage questioning over answers alone and working together to discover answers and generate more questions, akin to what a working scientist does.

Mathematics

Traditionally, learning mathematics meant learning to solve mathematical problems rather than conceptual understanding. Mathematics standards now center on five broad goals: the ability of students to value mathematics, reason mathematically, communicate mathematics, solve problems, and have mathematical confidence (National Council for the Teachers of Mathematics, 1989).

Social Studies

The focus for teachers of social studies, according to recent standards, is the development of a responsible citizen. As this content area can draw on other content areas, new standards focus, not on memorization of dates, but on conceptual understanding of different themes, including culture, power and authority, production and consumption, and global connections (National Council for the Social Sciences).

Languages

As with literacy and language arts, foreign language (or "world languages," as one of our students advised) instruction addresses a student's ability to read, write, speak, and listen. In addition to these interrelated skills, foreign language instruction addresses cultural sensitivity. As the United States increasingly becomes more international, foreign language instruction at elementary grades is taking advantage of a child's ability to learn a new language. The National K–12 Foreign Language Resource Center at Iowa State University is funded by the U.S. Department of Education to improve student learning of foreign languages at the elementary and secondary school levels.

Arts

The arts have their own standards for dance, theater, music, and visual arts (National Committee for Standards in the Arts, 1994). The five basic standards include the ability to communicate on a basic level in all four areas, communicate proficiently in one area, and develop and present basic analyses of works of art. A student must have some informed acquaintance with exemplary works of art from different cultures and historical periods. Finally, students need to be able to relate different types of art knowledge within and across the four disciplines.

Physical education

Physical education and health education are frequently taught together, although significant content exists for both. The National Association for Sport and Physical Education published the *National Standards for Physical Education* (1999). These physical education standards call for a student to be able to appreciate the role of physical activity in one's health, perform a variety of physical activities, be physically fit, and participate regularly in physical activity.

Health education

Health education addresses topics of nutrition, anatomy, mental health, substance abuse, sexuality and family life, and disease prevention. The "content" of health education stresses the appreciation for these topics as a major component. To assist schools in developing and evaluating comprehensive health education programs, the Joint Committee for National School Health Education Standards (American School Health Association, 1995) developed guidelines for school health standards. The committee's goal emphasized the need for school health education and created a framework for local school boards to use in determining content for the health curriculum in their communities. There are seven broad standards that promote health literacy, which is the capacity of individuals to obtain, interpret, and understand basic health information and services and the competence to use such information and services in ways that enhance health. For each standard, there are performance indicators to help educators determine the knowledge and skills that students should possess by the end of grades 4, 8, and 11.

Technology education

Technology education has replaced what was known as industrial arts and broadens the scope of concern to more than workplace-related education. Technology education strongly embraces the notion of technological literacy. In 1996, the International Technology Education Association (ITEA) launched *Technology for All Americans* as a means to advance technological literacy for students. Technological literacy is far more than the ability to use technological tools; it is the ability to use, manage, understand, and assess technology. The standards were built around a cognitive base, as well as a doing/activity base, and they include assessment checkpoints at specific grade levels (K–2, 3–5, 6–8, and 9–12).

Integrated curriculum

The content-area standards provide a means to connect teaching to learning. The teacher can choose the best practices that fit whatever content or combination of content areas is being taught. For young children, teachers can combine standards with developmentally appropriate practice, as advocated by the National Association for the Education of Young Children (NAEYC).

One way in which standards from more than one content area can be combined is through an *integrated curriculum*—lessons and units that support standards from different content areas and typically use themes to organize their scope. Students directly experience multiple academic and other "content" through exploration, interpretation, and engagement. Rather than just talking about content, integrated approaches allow students and teacher to explore and work together. Students may be given some degree of choice in activities. Different teaching strategies are used rather than direct instruction alone. A blend of direct instruction, role play, discussion, and cooperative learning might be used within a single lesson.

Two forms of integrated curriculum teaching can be used (Neuharth-Pritchett, de Atiles, & Park, 2003). One form is the so-called project approach, in which students are immersed in the topic and discover connections across different content areas (Katz & Chard, 1989). Assessment is usually in the form of projects revealing student understanding. A second approach uses a concept maplike means to visualize the different content areas that emanate from one topic. This approach allows a teacher to more easily document what content area standards have been met.

Integrated approaches take time to plan and can be developed like units. The investment pays off in a number of ways, such as learning across different content areas, direct experience with the content, stronger student motivation, and individual and group learning. Time can be saved with integrated lessons, rather than teaching individual lessons for each content area. Integrated curriculums have been around for a long time, but the standards movement gives early childhood and elementary teachers an incentive to see how integrated curriculums can be used in daily teaching (Krogh, 1995).

The following Design Activity asks you to identify content standards across multiple subject areas.

DESIGN ACTIVITY 33

Content Area Standards Using an Integrated Curriculum

Task Rationale   This Design Activity gives you practice in designing an integrated curriculum.

Task Guidelines   You will be designing the major pieces of an integrated unit:

1. Choose an overall theme, idea, or topic, such as listening, as a topic for elementary use, or being the new kid, as a possible topic for secondary use, in which you might be looking at culture, history, and language.
2. Decide which integrated approach you will be using: either an *immersive project approach*, in which the topic, idea, or theme drives your decisions, or the *webbing approach*, where certain features of the theme are integrated into traditional content area lessons.
3. Record the overall purpose of the unit.
4. Sketch out a set of lessons over a particular time period, in which students explore the topic. Identify what is to be learned in each lesson, and identify relevant content area standards.
5. For each lesson, list what students do and what the instructor does.
6. For each lesson, describe the assessment evidence that learning will be achieved.

Reflectivity
- What form of integrated approach works best for you?
- What teaching challenges can you see in using an integrated curriculum?

SCHOOL CURRICULUM MODELS

Models of curriculum that address entire schools differ, based on how they view the purpose of school.

Charter schools

Charter schools are schools established to give parents a choice over public schools. Charter schools may provide specialized programs, assistance, and stricter accountability provisions in their curriculum. These schools run independently of the public school system, and they tend to tailor their programs to community needs. Not all states have charter school legislation. Where legislation exists, parents may opt to send their children to charter schools. Charter schools have autonomy in setting up their own accountability system. Those who sponsor a charter school must usually provide accountability information at three intervals: evaluation of applications, ongoing monitoring or oversight, and renewal of charters at the end of their term, which is usually three to five years. Charter schools have existed since the early 1990s, but evidence on their performance is mixed (see www.nea.org/charter/index.html). Given autonomy and freedom, concerned individuals involved with these programs face the same issues you face with curriculum: What is to be taught? Making decisions on this question is very often a difficult process.

The Basic School

The Basic School concept supports elementary education as a neighborhood for children to continue their learning from the neighborhood where they have spent their first years. Ernest Boyer established the Basic School Network in 1994. The network began as a twelve-school demonstration project engaged with the four priorities for school excellence identified by Boyer (1995) in *The Basic School: A Community for Learning*. The curricular idea for the basic school is not a new curriculum but a new way to think about the curriculum. The Basic School Network gives priority to literacy and language. Language includes reading, writing, and the languages of numbers and art. Four priorities frame all curricular decisions: the school as community, a curriculum with coherence, a climate for learning, and a commitment to character. The traditional content is fitted within eight integrative themes that are known as the core commonalities. Thus, the curricular model of the basic school can be regarded as integrative in nature. The core commonalities are viewed as "essential conditions of human existence that give meaning to our lives" (Boyer, 1995, p. 85). The eight commonalities are the life cycle, the use of symbols, membership in groups, a sense of time and space, response to the aesthetic, connections to nature, producing and consuming, and living with purpose.

Universal design for learning

The idea of universal design for learning (UDL) was introduced in Chapter 7, UDL goes beyond assistive technology and promotes whatever changes are needed in the curriculum that make learning accessible and achievable by all individuals. Flexible materials and activities provide alternatives for students of differing abilities, rather than students having to adapt to fit existing facilities and materials. For example, web-based materials are designed so blind students can access the content. Specific accommodations for students may still be necessary, but UDL may reduce the need for special accommodations. Design principles that embrace UDL principles (Burgstahler, 2002) are listed in Figure 9.7. (See also the Design Activity in Chapter 8.)

FIGURE 9.7.
Universal Design Principles.

Universal Design Principles	
Inclusiveness	Create a classroom environment that respects and values diversity
Physical access	Ensure that classroom equipment and materials are accessible to all students
Delivery methods	Teaching methods should address student abilities, interests, and previous experiences
Information access	Materials and websites should be accessible to everyone
Interaction	Encourage different ways for students to interact with all participants
Feedback	Provide prompting during and after an activity
Demonstration of knowledge	Provide options for students to demonstrate what they have learned

Burgstahler, S. (2002). *Universal design of instruction* (pp. 2–3). Seattle: DO-IT, University of Washington. Available at www.washington.edu/doit/Brochures/Academics/instruction.html

School themes

Educators sometimes decide to focus on a particular curricular priority, such as reading or mathematics. Collectively, teachers may develop a thematic focus to rally around when planning next year's instruction. School themes help to address school priorities in traditional content area lessons and units. School wide themes can be used to develop integrative instruction where more than one content area might be addressed in individual lessons. The following Design Activity gets you thinking about developing a rough sketch of what curriculum might look organized around one or more themes.

DESIGN ACTIVITY

34

School Themes

Task Rationale This Design Activity gives you an opportunity to design curriculum based on school themes.

Task Guidelines 1. Pick one of the core commonalities themes suggested by the basic school concept discussed earlier in this chapter.

> The Life Cycle
> Use of Symbols
> Membership in Groups
> A Sense of Time and Space
> Response to the Aesthetic
> Connections to Nature
> Producing and Consuming
> Living with Purpose

2. Use the school in which you have been teaching as the context for your response.
3. Outline a unit based on one of these themes, or choose a theme of your own choosing. The choice could be one that relates to the needs of the school in which you have taught.
4. Identify student learning for the unit. List related lessons and how each lesson, supports your thematic unit. Within each lesson, briefly describe instructor activity and student activity.
5. Describe how parents and the community might be involved.

Reflectivity • How did this activity help you think outside the box regarding teaching strategies?
• What is your reaction to the eight core commonalities of the basic school? Would these themes work for secondary education?

SUMMARY

• "What is taught?" is not a simple question, but teachers still have the responsibility of partly answering this question, as they translate school curriculum into the taught curriculum.

- Savvy teachers stay current on which way the wind is blowing, as much of their world revolves around the agendas from these influences.
- Professional organizations representing content areas have developed standards for student learning. Integrated curriculum becomes one approach to teach across multiple content area standards, particularly for elementary teachers, who must be competent to teach across multiple subjects.
- Curriculum can frame the daily activity of the whole school, depending on which program is being used. Well-thought-out programs usually result from teachers collectively investing in efforts for students and constantly improving on their work.

An Idea Worth Thinking About	How shall we spend our day?

Ask this question of yourself and your students. This idea was gleaned from George Wood's (1998) book, *A Time to Learn*. Wood left academia to become principal for a rural high school. This question of "How shall we spend our day?" was the strategy behind reorganizing the teacher day and the student day, so that all might have "time to learn." Following are recommendations chosen for their relevance to new teachers who are developing lessons and modified for both elementary and secondary classrooms.

- Reduce the daily number of shifts between content areas.
- Pair up teams of teachers with teams of kids.
- Provide each student with an adult point of contact.
- Provide unstructured time for teacher–student relationships.
- Begin with what you want students to do, and design the curriculum from there (i.e., the backward design approach of Wiggins & McTighe, 2001).
- Advance students in grade levels by demonstrating their proficiency in portfolios of student work.
- Shift roles to student-as-worker and teacher-as-coach.
- Teach fewer things better; less is more.
- Have every student do something significant for the school or community.

What were your reactions to these strategies? Were they liberating? Did they seem possible? Reluctance to consider these ideas, says Woods, is due to

---

tradition, lack of vision, lack of working models, and bureaucracy. His approach is not to bypass standards but to avoid standardization of schools and to design schools, the curriculum, and the school day on the basis of how these decisions affect teachers' ability to help students learn. He advises that your decisions should be based on what is good for students today, not on what worked years ago, and that you should learn from other models and try to *imagine* what your classroom can be like.

Reflective Teaching

From "Out of Your Hands" to "Right at Your Doorstep"

It is easy for veteran and beginning teachers alike to feel distanced from the curriculum that they are required to teach. Teachers commonly feel that curriculum decisions are out of their hands, because it seems that curriculum is developed by some "outer entity" within the state education system. However, with the issue of teacher accountability, curriculum issues are landing right on the doorstep of classroom teachers everywhere. In many cases, teachers are asked to document or prove how they are meeting the content standards established within the curriculum. Formal assessments are being developed that align with all of the content standards—not just the content standards that are interesting or fun to teach. As more and more teachers closely examine the content standards for which they are held accountable, many are surprised to discover the vast spectrum of just what they are required to teach *and* what they are required to make certain that students learn. Curriculum decisions suddenly become classroom decisions: *How do I address this particular content standard? Which content standards should have the highest priority? What is the best sequence to use to address these content standards?* It has now become the responsibility of the administrators to make certain that the teachers within the building are addressing the curriculum. It has become the responsibility of the classroom teacher to find the most efficient means for addressing the content standards and the curriculum in its entirety.

Teacher Inquiry

- This chapter should suggest many options for teacher research, such as integrated approaches. Is there a schoolwide curriculum initiative or school theme being proposed or implemented that you might use in your future teaching? How might your efforts be documented?
- How could you share this documentation with others?

- One caution is conducting teacher inquiry with other teachers in other schools because we have come to believe that one feature of research is that we have to compare something. Teachers express concern that the research will ultimately make a judgment that one school is better than another. The focus in teacher inquiry should be to look at how content is taught (taking into account the differences in schools and students) and how this teaching helped students learn.

REFERENCES

American Association for the Advancement of Science. (1993). *Benchmarks for Scientific Literacy*. Washington, DC: Author.

American School Health Association. (1995). *National health education standards*. Kent, OH: Author

Arends, R. I., Winitzky, N. E., & Tannenbaum, M. D. (2001). *Exploring teaching: An introduction to education* (2nd ed.). Boston: McGraw-Hill.

Berliner, D. C., & Biddle, B. J. (1995). *The manufactured crisis: Myths, fraud, and the attack on America's public schools*. Reading, MA: Addison-Wesley.

Boyer, E. L. (1995). *The basic school: A community for learning*. San Francisco: Jossey-Bass.

Bransford, J. D., Brown, A. L., & Cocking, R. R. (2000). *How people learn: Brain, mind, experience, and school* (expanded ed.) Washington, DC: National Academy Press.

Burgstahler, S. (2002). *Universal design for learning*. Wakefield, MA: Center for Applied Special Technology.

Delandshere, G., & Arens, S. A. (2001). Representations of teaching and standards-based reform: Are we closing the debate about teacher education? *Teaching and Teacher Education, 17,* 547–566.

Freire, P. (1998). *Pedagogy of the oppressed* (20th anniversary ed.). New York: Continuum.

Goodlad, J. I. (1984). *A place called school: Prospects for the future*. New York: McGraw-Hill.

Hirsch, E. D., Jr. (1987). *Cultural literacy: What every American needs to know*. Boston: Houghton Mifflin.

ITEA. (1996). *Technology for all Americans: A rationale and structure for the study of technology*. Reston, VA: International Technology Education Association

Katz, L., & Chard, S. (1989). *Engaging children's minds: The project approach*. Norwood, NJ: Ablex.

Kozol, J. (1991). *Savage inequalities: Children in America's schools*. New York: Crown.

Krogh, S. L. (1995). *The integrated early childhood curriculum* (2nd ed.). Boston: McGraw Hill.

National Association for Sport and Physical Education. (1999). *National standards for physical education*. Reston, VA: Author.

National Commission on Excellence in Education. (1983). *A nation at risk: The imperative for educational reform*. Washington, DC: U.S. Government Printing Office.

National Committee for Standards in the Arts. (1994a). *Dance, music, theatre, visual arts: National standards for arts education*. Reston, VA.

National Committee for Standards in the Arts. (1994b). *National standards for arts education: What every young American should know and be able to do in the arts*. Rowley, MA.

National Council for the Social Sciences. (1994). *Expectations of excellence: Curriculum standards for social studies*. Washington, DC: Author.

National Council for the Teachers of Mathematics. (1989). *Curriculum and evaluation standards for school mathematics*. Reston, VA: Author.

Neuharth-Pritchett, S., de Atiles, J. R., & Park, B. (2003). Using integrated curriculum to connect standards and developmentally appropriate practice. *Dimensions of Early Childhood, 31*(3), 13–17.

Schorr, L. B. (1997). *Common purpose: Strengthening families and neighborhoods to rebuild America.* New York: Doubleday.

Shambaugh, R. N. (2000, August). What does it mean to be x-literate? Literacy definitions as tools for growth. *Reading Online, 4*(2). Retrieved March 19, 2005, from www.readingonline.org/newliteracies/lit_index.asp?HREF =/newliteracies/shambaugh/index.html

Spring, J. (2002). *American education* (10th ed.). Boston: McGraw-Hill.

Task Force on Teaching as a Profession. (1986). *A nation prepared: Teachers for the twenty-first century.* New York: Carnegie Corporation of New York.

Valmont, W. J. (2003). *Technology for literacy teaching and learning.* Boston: Houghton Mifflin.

Wiggins, G., & McTighe, J. (2001). *Understanding by design.* Upper Saddle River, NJ: Prentice Hall.

Wood, G. H. (1998). *A time to learn.* New York: Plume Penguin.

RESOURCES

Print Resources

Eisner E. W. (1994). *The educational imagination: On the design and evaluation of school programs* (3rd ed.). New York: Macmillan.

Written at the curriculum level, this text discusses curriculum ideologies and the explicit, implicit, and null curriculums and has a chapter on the different purposes of evaluation.

Flinders, D. J., & Thornton, S. J. (1997). *The curriculum studies reader.* New York: Routledge.

Curriculum readings selected on the basis of their impact, perspectives, and current issues.

National Education Commission on Time and Learning. (1994). *Prisoners of time.* Washington, DC: U. S. Government Printing Office.

A report on how time was used in high school.

Senge, P., Cambron-McGabe, N., Lucas, T., Smith, B., Dutton, J., & Kleiner, A. (2000). *Schools that learn: A fifth discipline fieldbook for educators, parents, and everyone who cares about education.* New York: Doubleday.

New tools for thinking outside the box.

Wood, G. H. (1998). *A time to learn.* New York: Plume Penguin.

Rethinking the school day to make better use of the time teachers and students spend in school.

Web-Based Resources

American Alliance for Health, Physical Education, Recreation, and Dance
www.aahperd.org/

"AAHPERD is an alliance of six national associations and six district associations and provides members with resources, support, and programs to help practitioners improve their skills and so further the health and well-being of the American public."

The Basic School
www.jmu.edu/basicschool/INTRO.HTML
Basic School Network.

Charter Schools
www.uscharterschools.org/pub/uscs_docs/index.htm

U.S. Department of Education–funded website providing information on charter schools, including research on the effectiveness of the concept.

www.charterfriends.org/
Charter Friends National Network

www.ncsc.info/

National Charter School Clearinghouse, including links to individual states, lessons, and materials.

The Council of Chief State School Officers (CCSSO)
www.ccsso.org/

This organization supports the efforts of states to direct curriculum in schools.

IDEA: Individuals with Disabilities Education Act of 1997
www.ed.gov/offices/OSERS/Policy/IDEA/index.html

Online source for archived information on IDEA.

www.ap.buffalo.edu/~idea/

IDEA Center.

National Association for the Education of Young Children (NAEYC)
www.naeyc.org

The professional organization for early childhood educators.

National K–12 Foreign Language Resource Center
www.educ.iastate.edu/nflrc/

U.S. Department of Education–funded program.

National Research Council (NRC)
www.nationalacademies.org/nrc/

Source for more than 2,800 online reports, as well as news releases, e-newsletters, links to magazines and journals, and other online features.

No Child Left Behind Act (NCLB) (2002)
www.ed.gov/nclb/landing.jhtml

U.S. Department of Education site.

Universal Design for Learning
www.design.ncsu.edu/cud/

The Center for Universal Design.

www.cast.org/udl/

Center for Applied Special Technology (CAST).

www.washington.edu/doit/

DO-IT stands for Disabilities, Opportunities, Internetworking, and Technology. This program addresses individuals with disabilities in challenging academic programs.

www.w3.org/WAI/

Web Accessibility Initiative, World Wide Web Consortium.

www.usdoj.gov/crt/ada/statute.html

Americans with Disabilities Act of 1990

10 Reflecting on Your Learning

Main Idea of This Chapter
*Good teachers continually self-evaluate
their performance.*

INTASC
Standards
Addressed in
This Chapter

Principle 9 REFLECTIVE PRACTITIONER: The teacher is a reflective practitioner who continually evaluates the effects of his/her choices and actions on others and who actively seeks out opportunities to grow professionally.

Focus Questions

- What did you learn from this text?
- What did you learn about teaching from designing lessons and units and then teaching them?
- What is your lesson planning process?
- Do you want to become National Board Certified®?
- How do you want to improve in your use of technology skills?
- What is your professional development plan?

Design Activities

DA 35: Evaluate Your Learning
DA 36: Reevaluate Your View of Teaching
DA 37: Reevaluate Your Planning Process
DA 38: Choose a National Board Certification® Area
DA 39: Improve Your Technology Skills
DA 40: Develop a Professional Development Plan

WHAT THIS CHAPTER IS ABOUT

Self-evaluation can be regarded as a way to put *reflectivity* into action. In instructional design, this process is known as program evaluation, and its purpose is to evaluate the "success" of your program. In this case, your "program" is the lessons, units, and curriculum that you have designed and taught.

This chapter provides Design Activities to help you evaluate the unit that you have designed using this text. This chapter has you self-evaluate what you have learned from a course that uses this text, as well as actual teaching of the lessons and unit you developed. We ask you to take another look at how you view learners, learning, and your role in the educational process. We ask you to describe, elaborate, and visualize *your* planning process. Finally, we have you look to the future in terms of professional development. Figure 10.1 visualizes the main topics of Chapter 10.

FIGURE 10.1.
Visual Sequence for Chapter 10.

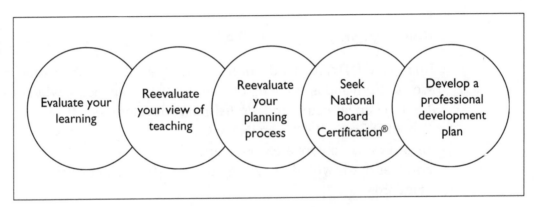

REFLECTING AND SELF-EVALUATION ARE GOOD

Reflecting and evaluation are necessary if we are to grow as people and teachers. Some of this evaluation will be formal, as teachers are being held accountable to states that license teachers. However, much of teacher evaluation consists of self-evaluation. If teachers are to be regarded as professionals, they must continue to set their own standards, above and beyond those imposed by others. Within instructional design, *evaluation* becomes a benchmark phase in which we self-evaluate our design decisions, reflect on what occurred in the classroom, and then make teaching adjustments for tomorrow or next year's teaching. We hope that you see yourself as a learner alongside your students, as one feature of good teaching is learning from students. As teaching is partly a moral activity and what we do has an impact on the lives of our students, we must commit ourselves to ongoing improvement of our teaching.

EVALUATE YOUR LEARNING

In Chapter 2, we summarized the benefits of instructional design for teachers. These benefits include ID as a pragmatic tool, one that helps you systematically *develop and reflect* on your lesson and unit development. Being prepared reduces anxiety in the classroom! We also cited ID as helping you understand who your learners are, the full range of the content for students to learn, and the reality of the school and classroom.

ID prompts you to think through different teaching options, including how technology supports learning. We cited ID's benefit in improving your accountability to students, the school, and parents. Its systematic features help to develop reflective habits. ID also matches up with the INTASC standards, which are used nationwide to assess competent teachers. These standards are used in the National Board Certification® discussed in this chapter. Next, we use these standards to help you self-evaluate your learning from this text.

Self-evaluation using INTASC standards

To review, INTASC stands for Interstate New Teacher Assessment and Support Consortium and is made up of state education agencies, which are responsible for teacher licensing and professional development (Council of Chief State School Officers, 1992). The INTASC model core standards apply to all teachers regardless of content area or expertise. In Figure 10.2 we again list the INTASC core standards with descriptive titles to help you understand the essence of the standards.

We use *pedagogical content knowledge* to characterize Principle 1, that teachers should understand their content areas but also to be able to teach the content. Principle 2, *developmentally appropriate teaching*, is borrowed from early childhood education. Understanding the developmental needs of all learners of all ages informs good teaching decisions. We characterize Principle 3 with the terms *teach across learner differences*. We have discussed diversity, multiculturalism, and special needs as variations of learner differences. Principle 4 we characterize as *teaching repertoire*, or being able to use a variety of teaching strategies. Increasing one's teaching skills in terms of multiple teaching strategies is one possible goal for all teachers' professional development.

Principle 5 is characterized as *learning environments*, and it is in this category that classroom management can be self-evaluated. Effective classroom management can be developed to support learning outcomes, and specific behavior becomes a part of the content to be learned. As a result, classroom management and appropriate student behavior can be designed into lessons, units, and curriculums.

Self-Assessment	INTASC Core Standards
1. Pedagogical content knowledge	**Principle 1:** The teacher understands the central concepts, tools of inquiry, and structures of the discipline(s) he or she teaches and can create learning experiences that make these aspects of subject matter meaningful for students.
2. Developmentally appropriate teaching	**Principle 2:** The teacher understands how children learn and develop, and can provide learning opportunities that support their intellectual, social and personal development.
3. Learner differences	**Principle 3:** The teacher understands how students differ in their approaches to learning and creates instructional opportunities that are adapted to diverse learners.
4. Teaching repertoire	**Principle 4:** The teacher understands and uses a variety of instructional strategies to encourage students' development of critical thinking, problem solving, and performance skills.
5. Learning environments	**Principle 5:** The teacher uses an understanding of individual and group motivation and behavior to create a learning environment that encourages positive social interaction, active engagement in learning, and self-motivation.
6. Communication	**Principle 6:** The teacher uses knowledge of effective verbal, nonverbal, and media communication techniques to foster active inquiry, collaboration, and supportive instruction in the classroom.
7. Pre-unit thinking	**Principle 7:** The teacher plans instruction based upon knowledge of subject matter, students, the community, and curriculum goals.
8. Assessment	**Principle 8:** The teacher understands and uses formal and informal assessment strategies to evaluate and ensure the continuous intellectual, social, and physical development of the learner.
9. Reflective professional	**Principle 9:** The teacher is a reflective practitioner who continually evaluates the effects of his/her choices and actions on others and who actively seeks out opportunities to grow professionally.
10. Relationship building	**Principle 10:** The teacher fosters relationships with school colleagues, parents, and agencies in the larger community to support students' learning and well-being.

FIGURE 10.2. INTASC Core Standards and Self-Assessment Categories (1992).
Used with permission by the Council of Chief State School Officers.

Principle 6 deals with the teacher's use of *communication* strategies to support learning environments. This principle suggests the need for teachers to attend to their own literacy development. This development includes writing, speaking, listening, and verbal literacy, as well as what it means to be literate in different content areas. Principles 4 through 6 could be considered instructional technology competencies. Principle 7 evaluates your knowledge of subject matter, students, community, and curriculum goals, collectively organized in this book around *pre-unit thinking* (i.e., needs assessment), where we prompted you to think about content, learners, and context.

Principle 8 addresses formal and informal *assessment*. Within this competency, teachers understand that assessment can take many forms, not just formal tests and grading, and that assessment is an ongoing teaching activity. Principle 9 acknowledges the *reflective professional* category and to what extent thinking about teaching translates into action. Finally, Principle 10 we label as *relationship building*. Teaching benefits from tapping student assistance outside the classroom, including other education professionals, parents, community leaders, and those from outside agencies.

In the next Design Activity, we use the ten INTASC core standards to help you self-evaluate your learning in using this text within a course of study, as well as your learning from actual classroom teaching.

Evaluate Your Learning

Task Rationale This Design Activity evaluates your learning using this text within a course, along with practicum teaching, organized by INTASC core standards.

Task Guidelines Summarize your teaching in terms of the ten INTASC standards.

Self-Assessment	What You Learned
1. Pedagogical content knowledge	
2. Developmentally appropriate teaching	
3. Learner differences	
4. Teaching repertoire	
5. Learning environments	
6. Communication	
7. Pre-unit thinking	
8. Assessment	
9. Reflective professional	
10. Relationship building	

Reflectivity What were your strengths and weaknesses? Identify areas for improvement.

REEVALUATE YOUR VIEW OF TEACHING

In Chapter 1, we used a Design Activity to record your views on learning and teaching. You drafted a mission statement that condensed these thoughts into an enduring statement that characterized you as a teacher. Next, we discuss four aspects of what goes into a mission statement.

Learning

The question *"What is learning?"* remains one of the hardest questions to answer. The response you drafted in Design Activity 1 is worth reexamining. Your answer to this question provides a window into what you will design in your lessons, units, and curriculums. Your personal views of learning should, however, be examined in light of what is known about learning. See, for example, *How People Learn* (Bransford, Brown, & Cocking, 2000) and related titles to stay up-to-date on the growing knowledge about human learning. The challenge here is twofold; first, to maintain a habit of reading up on new research and teaching practices and, second, to think about how this new knowledge might help your students to learn.

Teaching

The question *"What is teaching?"* usually produces a list of human attributes that we can generally agree constitutes a good teacher. These attributes tend to include "likes students," is "enthusiastic," and is "creative." However, good teaching must also include attributes such as "assesses student performance." We follow up the question *"What is teaching?"* with another question, *"What is Instruction?"* What are the elements of your instruction that contribute to student learning? Does your teaching frequently address, for example, Gagné's instructional events? Does effective instruction consist of these events, or are there others?

Learners

The question *"How do you view learners?"* provides another probing question. Your response illuminates how you plan, how you make adjustments in the classroom to learner differences, and how you assess learner performance. Note also the words you use. These words can reveal how you view students.

Your role and mission

The responses to the previous questions can be distilled and synthesized into an enduring statement, a paragraph, or even one sentence that crystallizes your thinking. By "enduring," we mean not one that is fixed but one that guides you through the school day, a statement that evolves over time to fit your self-identity and how you see yourself as an educator.

In the next Design Activity, use these four categories to self-evaluate your current views of teaching.

Reevaluate Your View of Teaching

Task Rationale This Design Activity records your current views of teaching, students, and learning.

Task Guidelines
1. **Learning:** How do you define learning?
2. **Teaching:** What is teaching? What is instruction?
3. **Learners:** How do you view students?
4. **Your Role:** How do you see yourself in the educational process?
5. **Mission:** Revise your mission statement from Chapter 1. Try to incorporate important ideas from the elements here into your mission statement. Refer to the INTASC core standards for ideas.

Reflectivity
- How did your mission statement change?
- How do you feel about yourself as a teacher based on what you wrote?

REEVALUATE YOUR PLANNING PROCESS

In Chapter 2, we asked you to critique several ID models. Think about your current process to plan lessons and units. What systematic features of these models make sense for you in planning lessons and units? Before we ask you to reflect on your lesson planning process, we will briefly discuss each question we will ask in the next Design Activity.

Steps in lesson development

Designing your first lessons may have been difficult. You may not have known where to begin. Your first step may have been in thinking up student activities. You may have adopted an approach from your cooperating teacher or colleague or adapted someone else's lesson. Earlier, we asked you to observe your cooperating teacher's planning habits or talk with peers. You probably noticed the differences in the formats and detail from what we have asked you to complete. Now that you have developed and taught some lessons, you can begin developing your own process.

Key issues in lesson development

The idea behind pre-lesson thinking and, later, pre-unit thinking was to organize your thoughts *before* choosing student activities. This level of thinking asked you to record what you knew about your students, what you knew about the content and teaching the content, and what you knew about the reality of the classroom setting. We urged you to investigate how other teachers have developed lessons and units to address the student learning in your teaching. This activity served to activate your existing teacher knowledge or suggested the need to do some research. What you write may also suggest opportunities for professional development.

Planning habits and routines

New teachers need to write out lesson plans in detail to record learning outcomes, teaching procedures, and other details. This detail can be studied prior to teaching, and the preparation helps to reduce anxiety. This level of detail does not need to be strictly adhered to, as teaching will never follow a script. This is why experienced teachers tend not to record detailed procedures. Their brief plans document their learning focus, activities, and personalized guidelines.

Improvements in lesson development

In the following Design Activity, identify what aspects of your planning process you want to improve.

Reevaluate Your Planning Process

Task Rationale This Design Activity documents your planning process. It produces a useful artifact to support the INTASC core standard on becoming a reflective teacher.

Task Guidelines 1. Describe the steps you take in developing lessons.
2. What are the most important issues you think about?
3. What planning habits of your cooperating teacher or peers have you adopted?
4. What areas of planning and organization do you need to work on?

SEEK NATIONAL BOARD CERTIFICATION®

Background

The National Board for Professional Teaching Standards® (NBPTS) was created in 1987 to acknowledge professional teachers. Although the National Board was developed by a wide range of educators, the program enjoys a strong buy-in, as teachers helped to develop the standards. Teachers are a majority of the members on the organization's board of directors. In addition, teachers assess teacher-submitted materials against the board's standards. The program is voluntary. Teachers make a conscious decision to find the time and commitment to develop the performance-demonstrating materials required for board review. Teachers also receive certification in their specialty, such as early adolescence mathematics. (See www.nbpts.org for an updated list.) No matter what certificate a teacher applies for, all of the certifications are based on five core principles.

These principles state that all teachers should be advocates for their students, know their content areas, and know how to teach these subjects. Teachers are also responsible for student learning, and they systematically think about their classroom practice and learn from experience. Finally, teachers are not alone but are members of a learning community.

Several of the INTASC principles can be connected to one or more of the NBPTS core principles. For example, the second NBPTS core principle,

"Teachers know the subjects they teach and they know how to teach their subjects," connects with INTASC Principle 1, which we have labeled as *pedagogical content knowledge*. INTASC Principle 7, "Teachers know subject matters, students, the community, and curriculum goals," which we labeled as *pre-unit thinking*, supports the second NBPTS core principle. For new teachers, a teacher education program may adhere in some way to the INTASC standards and connect to the principles for National Board Certification®.

Another key point from the core principles worth highlighting is Principle 4, namely, that "teachers systematically think about their classroom practice and learn from experience." This core principle provides an important foundation for this text. We advocate that instructional design helps teachers become better teachers through systematic development, teaching, and reflection.

Certifications

Numerous different NBPTS certificates exist, and each is structured by the developmental level and age range of the students and the subject taught. A teacher may choose to complete either a "generalist" or a subject-specific certificate for a specific age group.

The different teacher specializations include the generalist category, art, career and technical education, English as a new language, English language arts, exceptional needs, library media, mathematics, music, physical education, school counseling, science, social studies–history, and world languages other than English.

Each certificate includes its own set of standards. To prepare for the assessment process, it is helpful to become familiar with the standards for one's chosen specialization and age level and begin putting them into action in one's classroom.

Procedures

The National Board Certification® program requires that certain eligibility requirements must be met. Consult the program's website for up-to-date requirements. The NBPTS assesses a significant fee, and a nonrefundable payment of this fee is submitted to begin candidacy. The balance of the fee is due prior to a portfolio's review. Despite the high fees, some states and/or counties may provide incentives or rewards for those teachers achieving National Board Certification®. In addition, NBPTS may offer scholarships on a first-come, first-served basis.

The program works around a specific calendar, so the program's website should be consulted. After submitting the down payment of the candidate fee, you receive your portfolio materials. It is important to pay attention to whatever deadlines and assessment windows you have applied for. Once you are given a portfolio deadline, this date cannot be extended.

Portfolio materials

Candidates for National Board Certification® submit their materials in a portfolio. New teachers may be accustomed to this practice from their teacher education program. A teacher education portfolio may have been structured around the ten INTASC standards. Evidence of teacher performance in the National Board Portfolio® is described as "entries." Entries generally consist of samples from one's teaching combined with written commentaries. The three types of evidence for all certification areas include samples of student work, videotapes of classroom practice, and documentation of accomplishments outside the classroom. Specific requirements, however, may differ across certificates for each of these three entries.

The following Design Activity prompts you to think about seeking National Board Certification® and what steps you can take now to prepare for this step. You should consult the organization's website for the most up-to-date information, as well as the standards for the category in which you are interested in becoming certified.

Choose a National Board Certification® Area

Task Rationale Decide on a possible certification area for National Board Certification®.

Task Guidelines
1. **Professional development goal.** Do you ultimately want to be National Board certified?
2. **Certificate area.** What certificate would you be working toward? Consult the organization's website: www.nbpts.org
3. **Certificate portfolio.** Obtain the portfolio requirements and the standards for your desired certificate and record here how you will develop this competence in your teaching.

Specific Area Standards	How Will I Develop These?

Reflectivity Consider forming a peer working group for supporting each other during the certification process.

IMPROVE YOUR TECHNOLOGY SKILLS

Improving technology skills involves two areas: (1) hardware and software tool use and (2) curriculum integration experience. Both are necessary to become instructional technology (IT) literate.

Improve Your Technology Skills

Task Rationale Developing IT literacy requires first recording on paper what you want to improve.

Task Guidelines Use the chart to record what areas you would like to develop and learn more about.

Curriculum Integration Skill Improvement	Technology Tool Use Improvement
What would you like to have to learn about using media and technology in your teaching?	What media and technology tools do you want to learn how to use?
What technology integration skills would you like to develop?	What tools would you like to know and why?

RECAPPING SECTION V: DESIGN IS LIFE

This book was designed to help you understand how instructional design can help you become a better teacher and how designed instruction can help students learn. Here we list the attributes for design as an activity worthy of teachers' professional development.

- Design is a pragmatic (and enjoyable) activity.
- Design processes aid in reaching a solution through a better understanding of the problem.
- Design processes invite human involvement.
- Design processes are teachable.
- Teachers are designers.

Much of life is teaching, whether as a parent, a teacher, or a mentor. "The big design problem," according to Richard Saul Wurman, an information designer, "is designing your life" (2001, p. 285). "Think of everything you do as driven by and connected to your real interests, and it will affect everything you do. So, I really measure my life by what I want to do each day, which is a design problem that we have some control over" (p. 286). Taking charge of your instructional development contributes to your development as a teacher.

What do you want to do with your life, and how does teaching contribute to your view of life? As a teacher or in whatever educational setting you may find yourself, you will be spending many hours developing and revising instruction.

An Idea Worth Thinking About	"To carry off the concept of self-directed professional development, we, as teachers, must begin to think of ourselves as designers. We must design ourselves, and continue to revise, redesign and learn from experience." *(Clark, 1995, p. 125)*

DEVELOP A PROFESSIONAL DEVELOPMENT PLAN

Our wish for you is to have a good life, one filled with good teaching and good decisions. Now, it is time to make some . . .

DESIGN ACTIVITY

40 Develop a Professional Development Plan

Task Rationale This final Design Activity records your decisions on growing as a teacher.

Task Guidelines How will you become competent in the INTASC core standards (Council of Chief State School Officers, 1992)?

Label	INTASC Core Standards	Your Goals?
1. Pedagogical content knowledge	**Principle 1:** The teacher understands the central concepts, tools of inquiry, and structures of the discipline(s) he or she teaches and can create learning experiences that make these aspects of subject matter meaningful for students.	
2. Developmentally appropriate teaching	**Principle 2:** The teacher understands how children learn and develop, and can provide learning opportunities that support their intellectual, social, and personal development.	
3. Learner differences	**Principle 3:** The teacher understands how students differ in their approaches to learning and creates instructional opportunities that are adapted to diverse learners.	
4. Teaching repertoire	**Principle 4:** The teacher understands and uses a variety of instructional strategies to encourage students' development of critical thinking, problem solving, and performance skills.	
5. Learning environments	**Principle 5:** The teacher uses an understanding of individual and group motivation and behavior to create a learning environment that encourages positive social interaction, active engagement in learning, and self-motivation.	
6. Communication	**Principle 6:** The teacher uses knowledge of effective verbal, nonverbal, and media communication techniques to foster active inquiry, collaboration, and supportive instruction in the classroom.	

(continued)

Label	INTASC Core Standards	Your Goals?
7. Pre-unit thinking	**Principle 7:** The teacher plans instruction based upon knowledge of subject matter, students, the community, and curriculum goals.	
8. Assessment	**Principle 8:** The teacher understands and uses formal and informal assessment strategies to evaluate and ensure the continuous intellectual, social, and physical development of the learner.	
9. Reflective professional	**Principle 9:** The teacher is a reflective practitioner who continually evaluates the effects of his/her choices and actions on others and who actively seeks out opportunities to grow professionally.	
10. Relationship building	**Principle 10:** The teacher fosters relationships with school colleagues, parents, and agencies in the larger community to support students' learning and well-being.	

INTASC Core Standards reprinted with permission of the Council of Chief State School Officers.

We end this chapter by recalling what Herbert Simon said about design:

An Idea Worth Thinking About

"The act of envisioning new possibilities and elaborating on them is itself a pleasurable and valuable experience....Designing is a kind of mental window shopping. Purchases do not have to be made to get pleasure from it....Design like science is a tool for understanding as well as for acting."

(Simon, 1996, p. 164)

Over the years in which we have taught instructional design, we have come to better understand the pressing needs of teachers. We see instructional design as a tool for helping teachers think about the complexities and challenges inherent to teaching, make responsive teacher decisions, and ultimately become a better teacher.

Reflective Teaching

"Be Proud! You're a TEACHER!"

It may be your first or your twentieth year as a teacher. You may feel like you have no idea what you are doing, or you may feel like you can do your job well with your eyes closed. You may feel bogged down by classroom management issues or addressing the state standards, or you may feel energized by the new challenges in these areas. Whoever you are and whatever you're feeling, take comfort in the fact that you are not alone. You are one of many who call themselves *teacher* and are proud to have chosen a career in the field of teaching.

Teaching is a unique profession because it truly offers the chance for continual growth and learning. Even if you stay in the same classroom and teach the same grade for twenty years, you know that each year will be different from the one before. Your teaching can evolve and grow with each new group of students.

The National Board Certification® process was created as a means to acknowledge teachers for the hard work and dedication that they put into their careers. Veteran teachers have an advantage when applying for National Board Certification®. A wealth of classroom experience provides much expertise to draw from when thinking about the type of artifacts to include in the portfolio. However, beginning teachers have been educated in compiling a professional portfolio and documenting anything and everything that showcases growth in teaching as well as student growth in learning. It is often helpful for candidates for National Board Certification® to seek out help from other teachers around them in order to benefit from the expertise and advice that other teachers have to offer.

The National Board Certification® process forces teacher applicants to become reflective teachers. If you have always been a reflective teacher, this will not be a huge adjustment for you to make. You are likely to have collected the types of portfolio entries required by the candidacy process. Being a reflective teacher is crucial to the art that is teaching. By being reflective, you can document and see your growth as a teacher as well as the growth of your students. Being reflective gives you the opportunity to vent your frustrations and tweak new ideas on paper that you're not quite ready to try or to verbalize. By being reflective, you can always be aware of where you are as a teacher—and where you want to go as a teacher.

Best wishes if you are beginning a career as a teacher. *Be proud* and let your teaching reflect pride back upon this rewarding profession!

Teacher Inquiry

- By now, you can begin to see that teaching can be studied in more detail. However, time is at a premium, and even expert teachers have difficulty in making time for teacher research.

- Similar to instructional technology, teacher inquiry is meant to improve teaching and thus improve student learning. One benefit from joint teacher inquiry is finding those disciplined enough and eager enough to study together. For those of you who are ready to take the risks, teacher inquiry can be a rewarding form of learning alongside your students.

REFERENCES

Bransford, J. D., Brown, A. L., & Cocking, R. R. (2000). *How people learn: Brain, mind, experience, and school* (expanded ed.). Washington, DC: National Academy Press.

Clark, C. M. (1995). *Thoughtful teaching*. New York: Teachers' College Press.

Council of Chief State School Officers. (1992). *Model standards for beginning teacher licensing, assessment and development: A resource for state dialogue*. Washington, DC: Author. Available at www.ccsso.org/content/pdfs/corestrd.pdf

National Board for Professional Teaching Standards. *Guide to NBPTS national board certification*. Retrieved March 19, 2005, from www.nbpts.org/candidates/guide.

Simon, H. A. (1996). *The sciences of the artificial* (3rd ed.). Cambridge, MA: MIT Press.

Wurman, R. S. (2001). *Information anxiety 2*. Indianapolis, IN: Que.

RESOURCES

Print Resources

Gunter, M. A., Estes, T. H., & Schwab, J. (2003). *Instruction: A models approach* (4th ed.). Boston: Allyn and Bacon.

A practical survey of different teaching strategies, including variations, steps in their use, and a scenario for each. The book is prefaced with a discussion of goals and objectives and of organizing lessons and units. A set of unit case studies are provided for kindergarten, middle school, and high school.

Hubbard, R. S., & Power, B. M. (2003). *The art of classroom inquiry: A handbook for teacher-researchers* (rev. ed.). Portsmouth, NH: Heinemann.

For experienced teachers who want more out of their teaching and yearn for colleagues to study teaching.

Joyce, B., Weil, M., & Calhoun, E. (2004). *Models of teaching* (7th ed.). Boston: Allyn and Bacon.

Another resource in building a teaching repertoire. Teaching models are organized around different types of "families" of teaching.

Samaras, A. S. (2002). *Self-study for teacher educators: Crafting a pedagogy for educational change*. New York: Peter Lang.

An example of a teacher studying her own teaching by using Vygotskian principles.

Taggart, G. L., & Wilson, A. P. (1998). *Promoting reflective thinking in teachers: 44 action strategies*. Thousand Oaks, CA: Corwin Press.

Makes a case for three types of reflective thinking: technical, contextual, and dialectical. Describes activities to introduce reflective thinking to teachers. Describes observations, journals, teaching evaluation rubrics, narrative, mental models, and action research as tools to develop reflectivity.

Valli, L. (Ed.) (1992). *Reflective teacher education: Cases and critiques*. Albany: State University of New York Press.

Different ways that reflection is used in teacher education programs. The individual critiques examine the value of reflection in these programs but also for the learning teacher.

Web-Based Resources

NTASC Core Standards
http://www.ccsso.org

International Society for Technology in Education (ISTE)
www.iste.org

This professional organization focuses on technology use in pre-K–12 settings and has released standards for student and teacher use.

http://cnets.iste.org/

ISTE's NETS standards for use of technology, aligned with most of the states' departments of education standards; NETS standards exist for students, teachers, and administrators.

My Portfolio
http://teacherline.pbs.org/teacherline/myportfolio/myportfolio.cfm

A portfolio-support link from the PBS Teacher-Link site, including a private, online journal where you can set goals on your professional development, and save bookmarks of your favorite websites. Registration is required but a free.

National Board Professional Teaching Standards
www.nbpts.org

Home page for the National Board Certification® program. Teachers interested in pursuing this professional development opportunity should begin here and check frequently for updated standards and application procedures and deadlines.

Glossary

Affective taxonomy: a hierarchical relationship involving attitudes and values, ranging from a general awareness of an issue to developing an attitude that consistently guides one's behavior.

Assessment: From the Latin word, *assidere*, meaning "to sit beside someone." Assessment serves multiple purposes, providing teachers with a judgment on how students have performed, are performing, or are likely to perform. Includes a family of methods to provide information on students, including placement, diagnostic, formative, and summative information (Linn & Gronlund, 2000) (see Chapter 5).

Assistive technology: any technological device used to help students access the curriculum.

Behavioral psychology: a view that people and objects in the environment influence a person's behavior.

Classroom management: Plan for organizing a classroom in terms of materials, physical environment, and behavior in that environment. The behavioral component includes general and specific rules, procedures, and routines.

Cognitive psychology: a study of how people think, including remembering, learning, and problem solving, focusing on a person's internal, mental events.

Cognitive styles: differences in how an individual perceives, organizes, and acts on information.

Cognitive taxonomy: a hierarchical relationship between levels of thinking, ranging from recall of facts to intellectual problem solving.

Communication: Principle 6 of the INTASC core standards for new and experienced teachers, involving the development of strategies to foster activity learning and teaching in the classroom.

Communities of learners: a learning environment where everyone involved in the educational enterprise is learning, including students, teachers, peers, and colleagues.

Conditions of learning: factors that relate teaching strategies to student learning. Internal conditions include students' skills, thinking strategies, knowledge, attitudes, values, and beliefs. External conditions include any form of teaching. Thus, external conditions (teaching) influence students' internal conditions (learning).

Constructed-response assessments: assessment tools in which students must provide a response, such as writing an essay.

Constructivism: in education, a view that people make sense of or construct their own understandings of new knowledge. Many sources have influenced this view of learning, ranging from totally individual constructions, a *radical constructivist* view (von Glaserfeld), to primarily individual with a social influence, or a *cognitive* *constructivist* view (Piaget), to a blend of individual and social influence, a *social constructivist* view (Vygotsky).

Content knowledge: Knowledge of a subject content area. Could refer to a content expert or a teacher.

Conventional level: a second level of moral development, as viewed by Kohlberg, where a child's judgment is based on the approval of others.

Curriculum: a documented set of decisions on what is to be taught and learned. Curriculum design is the organization of these decisions, while instructional design addresses not only what is to be taught but how it is to be taught assessed, and overall evaluated for success.

Decay rate: a length of time when a learned skill or knowledge is not performed adequately or is forgotten.

Developmentally appropriate teaching: Adapting teaching decisions to the developmental needs of students, including physical, cognitive, and social needs.

Diagnostic: one purpose for assessment, which provides teachers with information on what areas students are having difficulty with.

Evaluation: making judgments on student learning for the purpose of assigning grades and promoting students to a higher grade level. Commonly used interchangeably with assessment.

Facets of understanding: different ways to characterize and assess student learning, as advocated by Wiggins and McTighe (1998) (see Chapter 4 and 7), including explanations, interpretations, applications, perspective, empathy, and self-knowledge.

Formative assessment: one purpose for assessment, which provides teachers with information on students' learning progress.

Hidden curriculum: expectations for student performance not openly addressed but suggested as important based on actions of teachers and administrators.

Inclusion: a policy in which all students are educated together in a general education classroom.

Individualized educational plans (IEPs): a learning plan that is developed and periodically reviewed by a group of educators responsible for determining the appropriate education of a student.

Instructional analysis: a means to determine how a task should be taught, based on a task analysis.

Instructional events: a list of nine aspects of most teaching, as conceptualized by Gagné, ranging from gaining students' attention to enhancing retention of learning.

Instructional media: any medium that carries messages of instructional intent. Common examples include chalk and blackboards, construction paper, physical manipulatives, maps, books, and audio-visual materials.

Instructional technology: any form of technology that is used to support teaching. Instructional technology can be characterized as low level (e.g., overhead transparency) to high level (e.g., video conferencing).

Instructional technology literacy: ability to use technological tools and the knowledge of how to use technological tools to support student learning.

INTASC standards: a list of ten standards that characterize effective teachers, as determined by the Interstate New Teacher Assessment and Support Consortium.

Learner characteristics: categories to describe a learner, such as age, gender, educational level, achievement level, socioeconomic background, learning preferences, styles, experiences, and attitudes.

Learner differences: A broad category characterizing the range of differences across students such as age, gender, developmental, cultural, family, personal history, learning preferences, and current understanding, skills, and motivation.

Learning dimensions: a means to categorize forms of learning not covered by the learning taxonomies but that educators may value. In this text, we identified possible human dimensions to include literacy, arts, design, creativity, social learning, moral development, and diversity.

Learning disabilities: a category of special needs involving problems with language, thinking, or mathematical abilities.

Learning focus: at the lesson level, a learning focus briefly describes the learning purpose of a lesson, rather than labeling the lesson as an activity, which may not convey the activity's purpose for student learning.

Learning goals: broad directions for student learning, appropriate for the school, grade level, and classroom use. Learning goals are appropriate for use in units, whereas learning objectives provide specific learning outcomes in lessons.

Learning objectives: specific learning outcomes, usually at the lesson level, that specify what students will know, appreciate, understand, or do, and at what level of proficiency. Learning objectives can be connected to state standards, content-area standards, or one or more learning taxonomies.

Learning outcomes: a broad term encompassing decisions on what students will learn. Learning outcomes can include goals and objectives.

Learning preferences: a broad term, usually referred to as learning styles, that describes ways in which students tend to learn. These preferences can include different approaches to note taking, reading patterns, drawing pictures, or task-management habits.

Learning principle: a research-based statement on how people learn.

Learning styles: a broad term that characterizes a student's general approach to learning and studying. One example is deep-processing, where students learn for the sake of learning and see teaching activities as a means to increase their understanding. A surface-processing style characterizes students who are motivated by grades and external evaluation.

Learning taxonomies: a hierarchical means to characterize learning. Taxonomies can be separate or combined, as in Gagné's learned capabilities taxonomy, which integrated the cognitive, affective, and psychomotor taxonomies.

Least restrictive environment: the physical environment determined to be the most appropriate for a student's learning success.

Literacy: ability to read, write, speak, listen, and communicate visually.

Literate environment: homes where reading and writing and other forms of literacy take place and are modeled by teachers and parents.

Logical-mathematical knowledge: according to Piaget, the mental invention of patterns or understanding of numbers acquired through the handling of objects.

Metacognition: a human capacity to think about one's thinking.

Null curriculum: what students learn in schools but what is not directly taught.

Pedagogical content knowledge: Knowledge of how to teach content.

Performance assessments: assessment tools in which student learning is determined through an actual performance, such as projects or portfolios.

Performance objectives: specifying what learners should be able to know, appreciate, or do.

Physical knowledge: knowledge about objects in the world.

Placement: one purpose for assessment, which helps to identify prerequisite knowledge and skills, mastery of content, or some evidence that demonstrates where a student should be placed in an instructional setting.

Portfolio: a form of performance assessment in which student performance can be documented either in progress (developmental portfolio) or mastery (showcase portfolio).

Postconventional level: a third and culminating level of moral development, as viewed by Kohlberg, where an individual's judgment is based on one's decisions on what is right.

Preconventional level: a first level of moral development, as viewed by Kohlberg, in which a child's judgment is based on personal needs.

Pre-lesson thinking: A term given in this book to conducting an analysis of the classroom prior to developing lessons by examining content to be learned, the students, and the context of the school and classroom setting.

Preparedness: One capability of effective teachers, supported by adequate thinking about content, students, and context and making teaching decisions about learning outcomes, assessment, teaching, and technology.

Prerequisites: a general term denoting what students should know or be able to do before moving on to new learning. An essential prerequisite is one, students must have; a supporting prerequisite is learning that students may have or would be helpful to have.

Pre-unit thinking: an instructional design strategy to help teachers learn more about their school and classroom in preparation for developing a new unit; organized by content, students, and school/classroom context.

Procedures: teacher decisions about how activities and tasks are done.

Professional development school: usually a public school, that has joined with a university-based teacher education program to provide professional development opportunities for teacher candidates, public school teachers, and university teachers.

Project-based learning (PBL): a public school form of problem-based learning, where an overarching goal drives student activity and where student learning is assessed in actual performance in problem solving and presentation of findings. Serves to cover a large number of state standards or content area standards.

Psychomotor taxonomy: a hierarchical relationship in the learning of physical skills, ranging from simple skills to more complex skills or physical coordination.

Reflective professional: A view of the teacher as one who constantly appraises one's teaching and makes adjustments.

Reteaching: a general teaching strategy used in public schools to repeat instruction using different strategies or examples so as to ensure that students learn what was originally intended.

Routines: teacher decisions on how activities and tasks are done on a regular basis without supervision.

Rubric: an assessment tool used to make judgments on complex student work such as writing and creative performance. A rubric includes a matrix of categories that comprise the overall learning against different levels of performance for each category.

Rules: teacher decisions on how students should behave.

School curriculum: the official body of decisions on what is to be taught and learned in school.

Scope and sequence: a commonly used term to characterize what a unit will cover and what order teaching will take place.

Scope–learning focus–sequence: an organizing framework that helps a teacher make initial decisions about units, including content, student learning, and sequence.

Selected-response assessments: assessment tools in which students must make choose one or more options, such as multiple choice, matching, and true-false tests.

Sequencing: an instructional design term used to identify the rationale behind what

is taught and in what order. The rationale could be conceptual or a simple-to-complex skill.

Social knowledge: knowledge of people in the world gained through action with people.

Summative assessment: one purpose for assessment, to determine student grades.

Task analysis: a means to break apart a complex task into its component parts, so as to understand the nature and complexity of the task.

Taught curriculum: a translation of the official school curriculum into what is actually taught.

Teaching and assessment overview: an instructional design strategy used to identify different teaching and assessment strategies used in either a lesson or a unit. Serves to communicate to other teachers the specific strategies featured in the lesson or unit, that these choices support each other, and that teaching and assessment strategies may be identical.

Teaching model: a framework for teaching that tends to be useful across most content areas and educational levels (i.e., cooperative learning, discussion) and backed up by research.

Teaching repertoire: A range of teaching skills, including use of strategies and teaching models to support learning outcomes.

Teaching strategy: a general term for any set of teaching decisions designed to achieve student learning. Frequently, a teaching strategy can be general (i.e., brainstorming) or specific to a content area (reader's theater).

Think-aloud: a technique in which an individual talks about how one is performing a task while actually doing the task.

Transfer: a desired goal of educators to enhance student learning across different settings or problem types or to promote using school learning in the world.

Unit: a set of related lessons connected by an overall learning focus, organized by a theme (e.g., "neighborhood profile") or a conceptual topic (e.g., "ecological succession"), and scheduled across a time period (e.g., weekly).

Unit evaluation: a set of teacher decisions that specifies how a unit will be judged to be "successful."

Universal design for learning (UDL): a view that curriculum can be designed to support a range of students' physical and mental capacities.

Index